OVERKILL

Mass Murder and
Serial Killing Exposed

OVERKILL

Mass Murder and
Serial Killing Exposed

James Alan Fox
and
Jack Levin

Plenum Press • New York and London

Library of Congress Cataloging-in-Publication Data

Fox, James Alan.
    Overkill : mass murder and serial killing exposed / James Alan
  Fox, Jack Levin.
        p.   cm.
    Includes bibliographical references and index.
    ISBN 0-306-44771-1
    1. Mass murder--United States. 2. Mass murder--United States-
  -Case studies. 3. Criminal psychology--Case studies. 4. Mass
  murder--United States--Investigation.   I. Levin, Jack, 1941-
  II. Title.
  HV6529.F69   1994
  364.1'523'0973--dc20   94-28520
                                                                CIP

10 9 8 7 6 5 4 3 2

ISBN 0-306-44771-1

© 1994 James Alan Fox and Jack Levin
Plenum Press is a Division of Plenum Publishing Corporation
233 Spring Street, New York, N.Y. 10013-1578

Printed in the United States of America

To our families:

Sue Ann, David, Jennifer, and Alexander
Flea, Michael, Bonnie, and Andrea

Preface

Previous decades hold memories that many would like to forget. The 1960s had the Vietnam war and a number of shocking political assassinations, the 1970s Watergate and the Iranian hostage takeover. But since 1980, the tragedies etched into our national consciousness have been of a different kind.

What would be in a time capsule to record the most painful events since 1980? We fought a war in the Persian Gulf, but it lasted only a few weeks—extremely brief by any standard of warfare. The invasion of Grenada was even shorter, measured in days and hours, not even weeks. America suffered through two recessions in which millions of workers lost their jobs, but in each case, the economy rebounded with unanticipated strength. Fortunately, there was no Great Depression. Hurricanes Hugo and Andrew, the floods through the Midwest, and the major earthquakes in San Francisco and Los Angeles killed dozens of Americans, but these catastrophes were overshadowed in their devastation by much more powerful *unnatural* disasters—those of human origin.

In 1982, for example, seven innocent people were poisoned to death by cyanide-laced Extra-Strength Tylenol capsules, the first of many product tamperings. The Tylenol tragedy permanently changed our confidence in mass-produced consumer products, not to mention packaging strategies. In 1984, McDonald's, a symbol of modern America, was stained with the blood of 21 children, massacred at the hands of an enraged gunman. This single event significantly altered our sense of security in public places. In 1988, snipers declared open season on schoolchildren around the country. As a result, not only did school officials begin barricading their classrooms from intruders, but several cities passed ordinances prohibiting the sale of assault rifles. The gruesome discovery in 1991 of Jeffrey Dahmer's cannibalistic killings—his apartment cluttered with human body parts—pushed our level of cynicism to a new limit. Among those who have paid close attention to the darker side of human nature, many will remember the years since 1980 as the age of mass murder and serial killing—the age of overkill.

A decade ago, when we published *Mass Murder: America's Growing Menace*, we could not have anticipated the full extent to which multiple murder would invade our lives. We expected that mass and serial killing would be a "growing menace," but not that these hideous and frightening crimes would become part of our popular culture as well as of our everyday concerns for safety.

The purpose of this book is to describe and explain the most infamous and deadly murders of our time. We are not, however, just chronicaling new cases. It should be clear throughout the book that we have revised and refined our thinking and knowledge about the sadistic acts of serial killers and the vengeful minds of mass murderers. Not only do we explain the specific motives and rationale for dozens of cases of multiple homicide, but we also discuss the reasons underlying the growth of these hideous crimes.

In researching this book, we benefited from the help of police investigators, attorneys, reporters, victim's families, even multiple murderers and their families. So many people were involved in this process that we could not possibly name them all and will not attempt to identify some for fear of slighting others. We would, however, like to thank specifically those of our Northeastern University students who assisted us through their kindness and interest in our work: Chris Baker, Julie Bonsteel, Panagiota Diles, Kevin Donahue, Jen Klein, Mark McHugh, Julie Mulholland, and Jeff Ruck. We also thank our wives and families, who complained only once in a while when we had to write or travel. We apologize to them for all the time away, but then at least they didn't have to listen to us talk about this gruesome topic.

JAMES ALAN FOX
JACK LEVIN

Contents

I

Gory without Glory

Christina Powell's parents had grown increasingly upset about their inability to reach their 17-year-old daughter at school. At first, they assumed that she was probably out partying. After all, this was August 1990, during orientation week for freshmen at the University of Florida, and she more than likely was out making new friends and buying things for her new apartment before hitting the books. But after a few more days without a word from Christina, the Powells became frantic. As a last resort, they called the Gainesville Police Department to ask them to meet at their daughter's apartment in the Williamsburg complex. Suspecting that something was wrong, a Gainesville police officer entered the apartment by breaking down the door on the second floor. He was sickened by what he discovered.

Immediately he saw the bloodied and ravaged body of Sonja Larson, Christina's 18-year-old roommate. She had suffered multiple stab wounds to her arm and right breast, and a large gash to her leg. From the pattern of blood marks on the sheets, she appeared to have been dragged across the bed; her legs dangled over the edge in a hideous pose.

Moving cautiously down the stairs to the bottom floor, the officer then encountered the corpse of Christina Powell. Revealing evidence of ritualistic murder, the young victim lay spread-eagled on the living room floor, a bottle of detergent and a towel placed between her legs. The nipples of both her breasts had been removed with surgical skill, leaving almost perfect circles (nearly 3 inches in diameter) where her nipples had been.

As shocking as these murders were, they appeared to be an isolated case. The police expected that they would soon find the culprit, perhaps a disgruntled boyfriend who had been rejected and went berserk. But that theory soon dissolved in the face of new and equally chilling events.

Just two days after the homicides at Williamsburg, 18-year-old Christa Hoyt, a part-time file clerk for the Alachua County sheriff's office, uncharacteristically failed to report for work. A deputy sheriff was dispatched to her apartment on 24th Avenue to check on her. After getting no response at the front door, he walked around the rear of the apartment and peered through the sliding glass door leading into her bedroom.

Hoyt's lifeless, decapitated body was slumped over on the waterbed, naked except for her pink-trimmed athletic socks and tennis sneakers. Her nipples had been cut off, and her torso sliced open from the chest straight down to the pubic bone. Hoyt's severed head had been trimmed neatly at the neck and carefully placed on a bookshelf for all to see. The tranquil expression on her face masked the horror of her last moments of life.

Similarities between the Powell/Larson murders and the Hoyt killing suggested to the police that they probably had a serial killer on the loose in Gainesville. Any hope that these killings were linked only by coincidence evaporated with the discovery of two more victims the very next day.

Gatorwood was a popular off-campus apartment complex that had experienced a series of break-ins over the past year, but no one had gotten hurt. Tracy Paules and Manny Taboada were not so lucky. Long-term friends from American High School in Miami, they had moved into Gatorwood just prior to the fall semester at the University of Florida. Disturbed by Tracy's absence from class, a friend of hers contacted the maintenance man at Gatorwood, who used a master key to enter the apartment that Tracy and Manny shared.

Because of the recent slayings, the maintenance man was understandably apprehensive about what horror he might find inside. Still, he was stunned when he opened the door. Paules's nude body was displayed in the hallway. A trail of blood leading from her bedroom indicated that she had been stabbed in bed and then dragged into the hallway for effect. Manny Taboada was also dead, although it was clear from the defensive wounds on the inside of his arms and the blood sprayed on the wall behind the headboard that he had put up a frantic struggle.

News of the five murders spread quickly throughout the college community, igniting widespread anxiety—if not hysteria—on the campus. In a massive evacuation, thousands of frightened students left town. All the flights out of Gainesville's community airport were booked solid, and long lines of cars and buses led students away from the campus.

But the traffic into town was just as heavy. Journalists and camera crews from around the country, and as far away as Italy, rushed to Gainesville, transforming the usually peaceful college town into a three-ring circus. Newspapers across the state competed fiercely to be the first to uncover and publish the gruesome details of the case. Even talk-show host Phil Donahue did a live telecast from the center of town, despite the efforts of some residents to sabotage the broadcast. Citizens of Gainesville were outraged by the invasion of their privacy and by what they perceived to be an undeserved stigma against their hometown. To the chagrin of University of Florida officials, students nicknamed the school "Murder U."

Given how grotesque and hideous the Gainesville slaughters were, it is not surprising that Americans were repulsed by the gory details. At the same time, however, many found themselves drawn to learning precisely what the killer did to the victims. Others demanded to know how the investigation was being handled. Eventually everyone wanted to understand what motivated the Gainesville culprit not only to kill, but to do so in such a gruesome, savage way.

The pervasive curiosity many people have about multiple murders, from Gainesville to Puget Sound, is evident to anyone who walks into a popular bookstore anywhere in the country. The true-crime genre (a fairly recent creation) is actually in response to Americans' insatiable interest in people like Ted Bundy. More than a half-dozen books about Bundy have surfaced—as many as written about Jimmy Carter, who was president when that serial killer was caught. Other infamous multiple murderers (John Wayne Gacy, David Berkowitz, and Kenneth Bianchi) have had numerous books written about them as well. Ten years ago, the few true-crime accounts that were published were interspersed among biographies of Hollywood and Washington celebrities. But in the 1990s there are so many entries into this market that the true-crime section has swollen into one of the largest in the bookstore. And it's not just the Bundys and Gacys whose exploits have attracted the reading public; even paperbacks on the most obscure killers line the shelves of America's favorite booksellers.

The Gainesville murder case is just the kind of horrible, vicious crime that typically becomes the focus of true-crime books. Some books in this genre do little more than describe the lurid details, whereas others attempt to analyze the traumatic events in the criminal's past. Whether written by journalists, psychologists, or criminologists, virtually all true-crime books—including this one—tend not to spare the reader the most upsetting and graphic details.

Is it gratuitous to report all the gory details of these heinous crimes? Does true-crime reporting merely fuel the reader's morbid fascination, or does it serve a meaningful and important purpose? Writers could, of course, sanitize their portrayals of murders as many of the better newspapers do for their general audiences. But if true-crime authors softened the details of these murderers' misdeeds, readers would carry away the false and misleading impression that the likes of Ted Bundy was just as advertised: "the boy next door," the man with the charming smile and charismatic personality, the brilliant law student who defended himself in court, the promising young Republican who worked to elect the governor of Washington, the concerned humanitarian who worked on a suicide hotline in Seattle, or even the teary-eyed, "remorseful" death row inmate who warned the parents of America about the evils of pornography. What a guy! He just happened to go wrong somewhere.

What true-crime readers need to know is that Bundy was more than a cunning criminal, more than a clever escape artist who twice extricated himself from custody, more than a man who outwitted law enforcement authorities in several states. They also need to be reminded, in no uncertain terms, of the enormity and virulence of his crimes. He suffocated a child to death by holding her face in the mud. He mutilated many of his victims, dismembering their bodies and having anal sex with their corpses. He even masturbated into the mouth of a victim's severed head. What a guy—indeed, what a monster!

If the brutal and vicious details were censored, the reader would be left with the inaccurate image of multiple murderers as master criminals, or perhaps rebels or even antiheroes, rather than the ghouls or fiends that they really are. Thus it is not at all gratuitous to reveal the sickening side of multiple murder. Indeed, by *not* doing so, it becomes far too easy to romanticize the culprits and even to view these monsters as heroes.

Hero worship has always been an integral part of popular culture. We celebrate those members of society who have reached the pinnacle of success in their fields by honoring them in movies, TV documentaries, magazine profiles, and other media. Recently, though, we have extended our celebration to what some consider our new antiheroes, those who have distinguished themselves in the worst possible ways.

In 1985, the *National Lampoon* spoofed America's glorification of criminals by publishing a series of mass-murderer trading cards, complete with photos, autographs, and statistics. As a parody, the *Lampoon* had placed despicable killers in a context generally reserved for superstars. But in 1991, a California trading card company published its own series of mass- and serial-killer cards, spotlighting such infamous criminals as Jeffrey Dahmer, Theodore Bundy, and Charles Manson. Selling for 10 dollars per pack (without bubble gum), it was no joke. Several other card makers soon followed suit, hoping to cash in on the celebrity of multiple murderers.

Even comic books have been used as a vehicle for celebrating the exploits of vicious killers like Jeffrey Dahmer, rather than traditional superheroes. By giving him a starring role once held by the likes of Batman and Superman, the killer is unnecessarily glorified; as in Marshall McLuhan's famous adage, "the medium is the message." Moreover, the victims' memory is trivialized by placing them in a comic book format.

In a more respectable context, the coveted cover of *People* magazine has become a spotlight for infamous criminals ranging from David Koresh to Mike Tyson. It was bad enough that Milwaukee's confessed cannibal Jeffrey Dahmer was on the cover of *People,* an honor usually reserved for Hollywood stars and Washington politicians. But this magazine also chose Dahmer as one of its "25 Most Intriguing People of 1991," placing him on the list between actresses Anjelica Huston and Elizabeth Taylor. If cancer were cured tomorrow, would the medical researcher making the discovery get such royal treatment as Dahmer?

Television has also helped to turn our criminals into celebrities. Docudramas—the "Sunday night true-crime of the week"—are often biographies of vicious criminals, many of whom are played by leading actors and actresses (Mark Harmon as Theodore Bundy, Brian Dennehy as John Wayne Gacy, and Jean Smart as Aileen Wuornos). Having glamorous actors cast in the roles of vicious killers unfortunately infuses these killers with the stars' glamour.

Besides the undeserving focus on the criminal as the "star" in these programs, television docudramas are sanitized by virtue of the restrictions that are placed on network television. Ironically, though, theatrical films such as *Silence of the Lambs* or *Sea of Love* are able to depict all the horrible details of purely fictional crimes without fear of censorship. A rare true-crime film that does not glorify a serial murderer is *Henry: Portrait of a Serial Killer.* In this low-budget and hard-to-find motion picture, serial murderer Henry Lee Lucas and his partner Ottis Toole are shown for what they are—cruel and inhumane men without any redeeming social value. They weren't portrayed as smart, friendly, handsome, or charming, and they weren't played by any actor most people would recognize as a star. Most important, the film refused to soft-pedal the monstrous acts of this killing team, showing their unmitigated cruelty without compromise.

The glorification of mass murderers has created a market for almost anything that they say or do. For example, the artwork of John Wayne Gacy became much in demand, but only after he was convicted of killing 33 young men and boys in Des Plaines, Illinois. His very ordinary paintings of clowns have been displayed in art galleries and have become collector's items. These paintings have special significance because he had been known to dress as a clown to entertain children at neighborhood birthday parties. Similarly, the paintings of deceased mass murderer Richard Speck, who slaughtered eight nurses in Chicago in 1966, now sell for up to $2,000. Though this kind of price tag may seem relatively inexpensive for original art, his paintings would hardly be worth the canvas they were painted on were it not for his notoriety.

A song written by Charles Manson became a cult classic when recorded by the heavy-metal rock group Guns 'N' Roses in their 1993 album *The Spaghetti Incident.* To publicize their newest release, lead singer Axl Rose wore a Charles Manson T-shirt in live performances. Patti Tate, a sister of Hollywood actress Sharon Tate (who was murdered in 1969 by Manson followers), said in response that the record company "is putting Manson up on a pedestal for young people who don't know who he is to worship like an idol."[1] Drifter Danny Rolling, convicted in the Gainesville student slayings, performed his own musical compositions. Rolling sang love songs to his sweetheart, both in court and, with guitar accompaniment, on the national television program "A Current Affair."

Not only is the value of mass-killer artwork and music inflated, but their statements to the press, both spoken and written, are treated as words of wisdom. Suddenly they become instant experts in everything from psychology to criminal justice. Their opinion is often solicited by the media about how victims might protect themselves from serial murder, what motivates other serial killers, and the role of pornography in the development of a sexual sadist. In fact, Ted Bundy's "expert testimony" on the eve of his execution concerning the dangers of erotic materials became ammunition for ultraconservative groups lobbying for federal anti-pornography legislation (widely called the "Bundy Bill").

Thirty-eight-year-old serial killer Leslie Allen Williams, after his 1992 arrest as a suspect in the slayings of four women, exploited the Detroit-area media to the hilt. Rather than giving an interview to every media outlet that wanted one, Williams created a contest—the outcome of which he alone would decide—to grant one local television station an exclusive interview with the alleged serial killer. In addition, one daily paper, the *Detroit News*, was chosen for the "privilege" of printing his 24-page open letter to the public, which expounded on his presumably valuable theories and philosophy. Anyone who would question whether this was a privilege for the *Detroit News* should consider what it did to boost street sales over its competitor.

Donald Harvey, who confessed to killing scores of patients while working as an orderly in Cincinnati-area hospitals, agreed to a face-to-face interview with popular talk show host Oprah Winfrey as part of a show on "nurses who kill." During the taped segment Harvey showed visible enjoyment in recounting the details of how he killed his victims. He described with glee how he had injected some with poisons and had suffocated others. Realizing that Harvey was having the time of his life talking about murdering patients, the show's producers wisely decided that it would be insensitive—if not unethical—to air the program, and they cancelled it. By doing so, they deprived Harvey of a chance for stardom on a national stage. The producers correctly recognized the fine but critical line that divides informed analysis from unhealthy glorification.

In this book, we also appreciate the important distinction between analyzing the gory details of a crime and glorifying the image of the criminal. At times, we describe the sickening circumstances of a multiple murder, but always with a purpose: to shed light—*not* a spotlight—on the motivation and character of these vicious killers.

Imagine trying to understand the Nazi holocaust without knowing the particulars of the sadistic medical experiments, the concentration camp ovens and gas chambers, and the piles of decaying and emaciated human corpses. In a sense, removing the gore from the movie *Schlinder's List* would make it seem like *Hogan's Heroes*. For the same reason, we must be nothing less than candid about what atrocities modern-day serial and mass killers have committed. Leaving out the gruesome details might reduce the reader's discomfort, but it would inadvertently minimize the horror of the murders and maximize the potential sympathy for the perpetrators.

Because of their celebrity status, multiple murderers attract the extreme adoration and sympathy of a surprising number of so-called groupies. Several convicted serial killers, such as Hillside Stranglers Kenneth Bianchi and Angelo Buono, were pursued and married while serving life sentences. Other serial killers have married from death row, giving the vow "Til' death do us part" an ironic twist.

Why would someone in her right mind correspond, visit, and even fall in love with a man who has raped, tortured, and mutilated innocent victims? Why would hundreds of women attempt to visit Los Angeles Night Stalker Richard Ramirez, who was convicted of stealthfully entering over a dozen homes in the dark of night and killing the occupants? Why would a woman like Veronica Crompton be so attracted to Sunset Strip killer Douglas Clark that she would break off her relationship with Kenneth Bianchi? (That's a new one for the talk shows: Women who dump one serial killer for another.)

Actually, there are several reasons why serial killers are pursued by adoring women. Some groupies may be attracted to their idol's controlling, manipulative personalities. A Freudian might attempt to trace this attraction to a woman's need to resurrect her relationship with a cruel, domineering father figure. At least a few killer groupies strive to prove that their lover is a victim of injustice. These women's fight for "right" gives their otherwise unfulfilling lives a strong sense of purpose. Others wish to break through the killer's vicious facade: "The whole world sees Johnny as a monster. Only I see the kindness in him; he shares that with only me. . . . I feel so special." Still other devotees are just comfortable in always knowing where their man is at 2 o'clock in the morning—even if it's on death row.

Underlying all of these motivations, however, is the glamour and celebrity status that groupies find exciting. One young teenager from Milwaukee appeared on a national TV talk show to say that she would give "anything" to get an autograph from serial killer Jeffrey Dahmer; it is likely that she also collects the autographs of rock stars. In general, serial killers are more accessible than other celebrities. If a fan wants to get close to a rock idol such as Bruce Springsteen, she generally doesn't have a chance. But with someone like Richard Ramirez, all she would have to do is write a few gushy love letters and she might get to meet him, and perhaps even marry him!

Is the glorification of multiple murder—through trading cards, art exhibits, song recordings, and killer groupies—nothing more than harmless media hype? Certainly the families of murder victims don't think so. From their point of view, the sanitized, romanticized, and glamorized image of a sadistic destroyer of human life only adds insult to injury. But the harm extends well beyond the victims and their loved ones. Worshipping a killer whose actions are so hideous that he or she ought to be soundly condemned debases our entire society.

2

An Anatomy of Serial Murder

Andrei Chikatilo of Russia, serial killer extraordinaire, was arguably more power hungry and control minded than Ted Bundy and John Wayne Gacy put together. Between 1978 and 1990, Chikatilo killed, dismembered, and occasionally devoured 21 boys, 14 girls, and 18 women in and around Rostov while he worked as an office clerk and part-time teacher. The 54-year-old father of two didn't particularly care about the age or gender of his prey, as long as they were naive and willing to follow him from a bus or rail station, café, or other public meeting place. Some of his victims were too young to know better, and others were mentally retarded or homeless drifters, but many of those whom Chikatilo destroyed were bright youngsters from middle-class families.

What all his victims shared in common was a trusting nature; any twinge of caution that they may have felt easily dissolved because of the killer's kind and assuring manner, what Chikatilo himself termed his "magnetic personality." Once he had them alone, however, his demeanor would change instantly and dramatically. "I was like a crazed wolf," explained the predator. "I just turned into a beast, a wild animal."[1] Sometimes he tore out and ate their hearts, lips, or tongues; sometimes he cut off their fingers, eyes, or genitals—whatever suited his passion at the moment.

Chikatilo's sexual problems dated back years before his first murder. Chronically impotent (although he did manage to father two children), he found some degree of pleasure and comfort from molesting young boys and girls. This was nothing, however, like the arousal he discovered when he first committed murder (after abducting a 9-year-old girl). He soon learned what pleased him, what atrocities made him feel whole. "When I used my knife," he explained, "it brought psychological relief."[2]

In recent years, Americans have been fascinated but at the same time shocked by serial killers operating here and abroad. While they occasionally surface in other countries, including Russia, these killers are much more common in the United States. Destroying some 200 Americans per year in total, serial murderers kill repeatedly over a period of weeks, months, or even years, generally not stopping until they are caught.

With each new discovery of another serial killer, the level of brutality and gore seems to sink even deeper into the abyss of inhumanity. In the 1970s we became acquainted with the term *serial murder* in the context of the hideous rapes and murders committed by Ted Bundy. In the 1980s we were introduced to new and even more grotesque atrocities—a Philadelphia man who kept sex slaves shackled to a post in his basement, and a gruesome twosome who operated a torture chamber at their Northern California hideout. The 1990s produced even more chilling abominations, such as the crimes of Milwaukee's Jeffrey Dahmer, who cannibalized and engaged in postmortem sex with at least 17 young men.

Perhaps because they do not fit the popular stereotype of a crazed lunatic, serial killers who seem like "the boy next door" have become household names. It certainly would be comforting if real-life serial killers acted like those in classic horror movies. If they looked like Jason from the *Friday the 13th* film series, we would beware whenever they approached. If they were introverted loners like Norman Bates from Alfred Hitchcock's classic film *Psycho*, they could not charm victims so easily into their deadly clutches. But the frightening truth is that serial killers like Ted Bundy and Jeffrey Dahmer are incredibly credible and, therefore, so very dangerous. Underneath the trustworthy and smooth veneer often glorified by the media lies the heart of a monster whose supreme passion is stalking his prey.

Even when it is known that a serial killer is on the loose, the precautions that worried citizens take may be inadequate. Many serial killers are clever and inventive. Some will pose as police officers or as stranded motorists in need of assistance. Others will answer classified newspaper ads in order to get into the homes of unsuspecting victims eager to sell a television set. Still others simply grab victims off the street by force. If they really want to get someone, they will likely find a way.

This does not mean that all or even most serial killers are handsome and smooth geniuses. Many people consider Ted Bundy a prototype serial killer in large part because of his attractiveness, charm, and intelligence. While these qualities are important in understanding his keen ability to lure his victims and elude the police, Bundy is more the exception than the rule. At the other end of the spectrum are some serial killers who are high school dropouts and some who might even be called ugly. Most, however, are fairly average, at least to the casual observer. But there is one trait that tends to separate serial killers from the norm: they are exceptionally skillful in presenting themselves so that they appear beyond suspicion. This is part of why they are so difficult to apprehend.

In the modern mythology of serial murder, the killer is characterized also as a nomad whose compulsion to kill carries him hundreds of thousands of miles a year as he drifts from state to state and region to region, leaving scores of victims in his wake. This may be true of some well-known and well-traveled killers like Ted Bundy and Henry Lee Lucas, but not for the majority. John Wayne Gacy, for example, killed all of his 33 young male victims at his Des Plaines, Illinois home, conveniently burying most of them there as well. Gacy, like Milwaukee's Jeffrey Dahmer, Kansas City's Robert Berdella, and Long Island's Joel Rifkin, operated within driving distance of home. Moreover, most serial killers are not the recluses that movies often portray them to be. They typically have jobs and families, go to church on Sunday, and kill part-time—indeed, whenever they have some free time to kill.

A more specific profile of the typical serial killer is that of a white male in his late 20s or 30s who targets strangers at or near his place of residence or work. According to criminologist Eric Hickey, who has assembled the most extensive database on the demography of serial murder, 88% of the serial killers were male, 85% were Caucasian, and the average age when they claimed their first victim was 28.5. In terms of victim selection, 62% of the killers targeted strangers exclusively, and another 22% killed at least one stranger. Finally, 71% of the killers operated in a specific location or area, rather than traveling wide distances to commit their crimes.

In terms of motivation, most serial murderers kill not for love, money, or revenge, but for the fun of it. Like Andrei Chikatilo, they enjoy the thrill, the sexual satisfaction, or the dominance that they achieve over the lives of their victims. Not only do they savor the act of murder itself, but they rejoice as their victims scream and beg for mercy. Like Leonard Lake and Charles Ng, the buddies who killed dozens of people in Calaveras County, California, some serial killers record on video or audiotape their victims' worst moments of terror for the purpose of later entertainment.

The thrill-oriented killer hardly ever uses a firearm. A gun would only rob him of his greatest pleasure: exalting in his victim's suffering and misery. He enjoys the whole experience of murder—of squeezing from his victim's body the last breath of life. California serial killer Douglas Clark's greatest fantasy was to kill a woman as he was having intercourse with her; his wish was to feel her death spasms in the heat of passion.

For some thrill killers, the need for dominance is not expressed through sexual sadism. A growing number of murders have been committed by hospital caretakers who seek to "play God," exploiting their patients in order to feel the exhilaration of making life-and-death decisions. In 1987, registered nurse Richard Angelo was arrested and later convicted for poisoning a number of patients in a hospital in West Islip, Long Island. Because of a burning desire to be recognized as a hero, he purposely poisoned his patients and attempted to "save" their lives. Sometimes he succeeded, but not always.

Though not in an official caretaker role, a few serial killers find satisfaction by making healthy human beings into totally dependent pets or sex toys. Milwaukee's Jeffrey Dahmer, for example, expressed his need to control others by attempting literally to lobotomize his victims into submission. He was not interested in inflicting pain and suffering; he actually sedated his victims before performing surgery on them.

As another expression of their need for power and quest for attention, thrill-motivated serial killers often crave the publicity given to their crimes. It is not just the celebrity status that they enjoy; more importantly, they are able to control the lives of thousands of area residents, who are held in their grip of terror. These killers do not specifically turn to homicide as an attention-getting move, but the media hype is a powerful fringe benefit. Some might even exaggerate the scope of their crimes to attract the television cameras and front-page coverage.

Murder for profit, jealousy, or revenge, although unjustifiable, makes sense to most people at some level. By contrast, anyone who kills for fun, pleasure, or power would appear to be insane; after all, it would not seem to make logical sense that taking another person's life could be in any respect entertaining. Contrary to the popular view, however, most serial killers are not insane in either a legal or medical sense. They know right from wrong, know exactly what they are doing, and can control their desire to kill, but they choose not to do so. They are more cruel than crazy.

Psychologically the thrill-motivated serial killer tends to be a sociopath (or antisocial personality), someone with a disorder of character rather than of the mind. He lacks a conscience, feels no remorse, and cares exclusively for his own pleasures in life. Other people are seen merely as tools to fulfill his own needs and desires, no matter how perverse or reprehensible.

It has been estimated that 3% of all males in our society could be considered sociopathic. Most sociopaths are not violent: They may lie, cheat, or steal, but rape and murder are not necessarily appealing to them. The other critical ingredient to the profile of the serial killer is an overpowering need for control. Most thrill killers, for the sake of sexual gratification, tie up their victims in order to watch them squirm and torture their victims to hear them scream. Others find personal fulfillment and control by taking the life out of their victims—by "mercifully" killing a hospital patient or drugging a captive to make him or her an obedient zombie.

The overwhelming majority of serial killers pursue their victims for the thrill; they seek to satisfy their cravings for sexual or psychological dominance through murder. Some serial murderers, however, are motivated instead by a strong urge to further a social, political, or religious cause. This second kind of killer is on a mission to rid the world of filth and evil. This kind of moral crusade sometimes motivates killers to target marginal groups, such as prostitutes, gays, or homeless people, who are seen as destroying the moral fiber of the community or country. In a profoundly warped sense of good and evil, the criminals view their killing spree as "self-defense."

From 1981 to 1987, for example, at least a half-dozen members of a Miami-based cult known as the Temple of Love conspired to kill "white devils" in retaliation for the oppression of blacks. Their black-separatist leader, Yahweh Ben Yahweh (translated from Hebrew as "God, Son of God") preached that all whites were "demons and serpents." The temple's "entry fee" required that new members murder a white man and then produce his severed ear as proof. In the name of racial justice, temple members savagely murdered eight homeless vagrants, who probably had no idea that they were chosen for slaughter strictly because of the color of their skin.

As a result of severe mental illness, other mission killers actually see their victims as devils. In their delusions, they believe that they must extinguish the lives of their victims for the good of the world. Their inspiration to kill is not religious or political fanaticism, but psychosis. They hear the voice of the devil or God instructing them to kill. Driven by these delusions, they tend to be psychotic, confused, and disorganized.

In 1972 and 1973, for example, Herbert Mullin of Santa Cruz, California, killed 13 people over a span of 4 months in order to avert an earthquake—at least according to what his voices told him. Mullin was raised in an oppressively religious home, and his crimes had decidedly religious overtones. He believed that he was obeying God's "commandment" to make human sacrifices for the greater good of humanity.

Mullin's severe psychological problems began in late adolescence, a point in life when schizophrenia characteristically surfaces. He was institutionalized on several occasions, diagnosed as a paranoid schizophrenic. The same voices that told him to kill had previously commanded him to shave his head and to burn his penis with a cigarette— orders that he also dutifully obeyed. While hospitalized, Mullin wrote dozens of letters to strangers, signing them, "A human sacrifice, Herb Mullin."

There are very few serial killers whose motivation, like those of Mullin, arises out of a psychotic illness. Though many more mentally ill individuals may repeatedly have thoughts that compel them to commit murder, most lack the clearheaded state of mind needed to carry it out. For example, 26-year-old Cleo Green of Louisville, Kentucky, had the ambition, but not the wherewithal, to become a serial killer. During the summer of 1984, he assaulted four elderly women by inflicting multiple stab wounds to their necks and throats. Each attack gave him temporary relief from the "red demon" that he felt inhabited his body and unmercifully tortured his soul. In one case Green was able to succeed in taking a life, but only after stabbing his victim 200 times and decapitating her. On other occasions, he was simply too out of touch to complete the act of murder.[3]

The distinction between fanaticism and severe mental illness is significant, but not always obvious. Both zealots and lunatics are motivated by a righteous mission—to eliminate what they see as evil. The fanatic believer responds in a seemingly logical, though depraved, manner to an actual person (a charismatic leader) or a genuine social problem (for example, racism or prostitution), whereas the psychotic responds to hallucinations, delusions, and voices.

In 1969, members of the Charles Manson "family" slaughtered seven wealthy residents of Beverly Hills in two separate incidents; they may have been responsible for other murders as well. Their motivation was symbolized by the hideous graffiti, such as "Death to Pigs," that the killers scrawled using the blood of their victims. The murders and their excessive brutality were a critical part of Manson's grand scheme. According to his plan, the savage murders of affluent suburbanites would, at a time of racial unrest, inflame racial tensions and be blamed on radical blacks. This would help to precipitate an all-out race war, which ultimately would be won by the blacks. In the meantime, Manson had moved his commune out to the desert, where they would be sheltered from the impending conflict. Manson reasoned that the victors would be ineffective in leading the new world and would be forced to call him from his hideout to take over the reigns of authority.

Manson's mission sounds as crazy today as it did in 1969. But it was grounded in a certain reality of the times: the flower children, the generation gap, the antiestablishment spirit, the antiwar movement, civil rights demonstrations, and the rise of radical groups such as the Black Panthers and Students for a Democratic Society. Even given this social and political context, Manson's response was absurdly extreme and fanatical, but not psychotic. Like thousands of small-time political rebels around the world who have unsuccessfully attempted to overthrow their governments, Manson responded to social discontent in the streets rather than to imaginary voices in his head.

The third kind of serial murderer kills for the sake of expediency or profit. In 1992, for example, a series of murder/robberies occurred in "Mom and Pop" convenience stores through the Midwest. After taking the money from the cash register, the robbers would attempt to cover up their identity by executing their victims. The important distinction between the thrill killer and the profit-motivated killer can be seen in the style of murder: Whereas the thrill killer eliminates his victim in the most brutal manner possible, the profit-oriented serial killer almost always uses a gun. The former enjoys the killing, whereas the latter just feels that it is necessary.

In 1989 and 1990, 35-year-old prostitute Aileen Wuornos perpetrated a 13-month serial-killing spree along Florida's highways. Her motive was greed. Typically she would be picked up by a stranger, have sex with him, ask for payment, shoot him several times, take his money, and then dump his body. After being found guilty of first-degree murder, Wuornos whispered in the direction of the jurors as they filed out of the courtroom, "I am innocent; I was raped." In her view, it was absolutely necessary to kill each and every one of her seven victims—men whom she felt had threatened her—in order for her to stay in business. Given the constant danger under which she operated as a highway hooker, Wuornos saw killing a few violent johns as self-defense. Of course, most people would get out of the business rather than shoot seven customers in "self-defense," and Wuornos's failure to do so is why the jury found her guilty.

Although her premise was reprehensible, Wuornos's way of thinking was not unlike that of a liquor store proprietor in a crime-ridden neighborhood who decides to keep a gun at his side. Rather than closing the store, he reasons that he might have to shoot some intruders. The key difference between the proprietor and Wuornos is, of course, that the liquor store business is legitimate, but highway prostitution is not.

Aileen Wuornos was not the first female serial killer, as the press often made her out to be. For example, Beverly Allitt murdered four children and attempted to kill nine others under her care at the Grantham Hospital in Lincolnshire, England. The 24-year-old nurse suffocated some of her young victims and injected others with fatal doses of insulin or potassium. Over an 18-month period, teenager Christine Falling of Perry, Florida, killed six children for whom she baby-sat. The deaths were initially diagnosed to be the result of sudden infant death syndrome (SIDS), but when the death toll reached alarming proportions, authorities took a closer look at the 19-year-old high school dropout. Falling later described her method of killing as "smotheration."[4] In 1985 Betty Lou Beets was sentenced to death for murdering her fifth husband, a Dallas firefighter, in order to collect his $100,000 insurance benefits. Suspected of foul play in the mysterious deaths of her former spouses, she was charged with murder when the body of her "missing" fourth husband was discovered buried in the back yard.

Although Wuornos is far from alone in the annals of female serial killers, she is unique nonetheless. Unlike other women who killed repeatedly, she targeted perfect strangers rather than family members or acquaintances. Also unusual was the fact that her victims were exclusively middle-aged males. While almost anyone is at some risk of victimization, serial killers tend to prey on the most vulnerable targets—prostitutes, drug users, skid-row alcoholics, homeless vagrants, hitchhikers, runaways, children, and elderly hospital patients. Part of the vulnerability concerns the ease with which these classes of victims can be abducted or overtaken. Because of physical stature or disability, many children and elders are not able to defend themselves against a sudden attack by a 200-pound killer. Hitchhikers and prostitutes become vulnerable as soon as they step into the killer's car or van; hospital and nursing home patients are vulnerable because of their total dependency on their caretakers.

The vulnerability of the elderly is shown dramatically in the case of 64-year-old Sacramento landlady Dorothea Montalvo Puente. Her victims, because of their advanced age and relative poverty, had nowhere else to go and no one else to take care of them. And take care of them she did: In 1988 Puente was arrested and charged with killing nine of her boarders and then stealing their government checks.

Looking more like a grandmother than a grand larcenist, the white-haired diminutive landlady argued in her defense that her tenants had died of natural causes or suicide. She admitted having taken the boarders' money after they died, and to having buried most of their bodies in the yard of her ramshackle Victorian home. But she had nothing to do with their deaths, she insisted.

Puente even had an excuse for failing to report the deaths to the authorities. She was on parole following a 1982 conviction for drugging and robbing two elderly tenants. As a condition for her parole, she was prohibited from taking in any boarders. Informing the police of the deaths would have jeopardized her freedom; she was only protecting herself through her silence.

In 1988 the silence was broken. A social worker became suspicious upon discovering that her client, Alvaro Montoya, had been missing for 3 months, yet his social security checks were being cashed. Based on this lead, the Sacramento police went to Puente's F Street boardinghouse and were immediately alarmed by a nauseating stench emanating from the back yard. As the police starting digging for evidence, Puente skipped town, only to be arrested several days later in a hotel on Los Angeles's skid row.

The prosecution argued that Puente had deliberately poisoned her elderly roomers in order to cash in their social security checks and then buried the bodies to conceal the crime. Over a 3-year period, Puente collected $75,000 from her scam. This was more than a crime of opportunity, claimed the prosecution; Puente had aggressively recruited her victims. On parole following a 1982 robbery conviction, she was able to convince a social worker that she was equipped to care for 19 senior citizens living on fixed incomes. Puente counted on the inefficiency of social agencies, and she was right. The lack of coordination among agencies that dealt with indigent elders enabled her to kill such a large number of people without being detected for years.

Puente's first victim was initially thought to have committed suicide by an overdose of codeine; her body was found in Puente's boarding house. The body of the second victim, an old boyfriend of Puente, was discovered floating in a wooden box down river. Seven bodies, in varying stages of decomposition, were found buried in Puente's yard. Deliberating a record 24 days, the jury returned a conviction on three of the nine counts of murder. Because of the length of time that many of the victims had been buried, physical evidence was sparse. Although traces of a sedative were found in all of the bodies, the cause of death—drug overdose—could only be established in one case. Regardless, the three convictions were sufficient to earn Puente a life sentence.

Prostitutes (with the exception of Wuornos, of course) are also quite vulnerable because of the accessibility required by their trade, which explains their extremely high rate of victimization by serial killers. A sexual sadist can cruise a red-light district, shopping around for the woman who best conforms to his deadly sexual fantasies. When he finds her, she willingly complies with his wishes—until it is too late.

Because of these risk factors, prostitute slayings have occurred in Rochester, New York; Seattle, Washington; New Bedford, Massachusetts; San Diego, California; Detroit, Michigan; and dozens of other locales across the country. Even when it is widely known that a killer is prowling the streets, far too many prostitutes place profit over protection, hoping or assuming that they can avoid death. Some see no other life for themselves, particularly if they have expensive drug habits to support.

The vulnerability of one additional class of victims—young boys and girls—stems both from their naïveté and their small size. For decades, pedophiles (adults who desire sexual relations with children) have capitalized on the ease with which many children can be deceived by a contrived story or ruse. Even the most streetwise child will not necessarily think twice about going with someone impersonating a police officer. Still other children can be easily grabbed, so that their attempts to scream or flee are futile.

By the time he was 27, Westley Allan Dodd had logged years of experience in molesting and raping young boys. As a teenager, Dodd started out by exposing himself. But as he grew into adulthood, that simply wasn't enough to gratify him. His sexual desire for young boys continued to escalate. "[Exposing myself] wasn't fun anymore," recalled Dodd. "I needed more physical contact. I started tricking kids into touching me. Then that wasn't fun anymore, so I started molesting kids."[5]

At first, Dodd's passion was purely sexual; he never felt compelled to murder any of his victims. Because many of his young victims reported him, Dodd had had numerous brushes with the law, and he served 4 months of a 10-year sentence in an Idaho prison. Upon his release from custody, he was determined to stay out of jail. He had no intention to "go straight," however—only to avoid apprehension.

"In Seattle, June 13, 1987, I tried to kidnap a boy," said Dodd. "My intentions, at this point, were to kidnap him, rape him, and kill him so that he couldn't report me."[6] He realized at that point that murder would be a necessary evil to enable him to continue his career of rape and molestation. The boy he accosted in Seattle screamed his way to freedom, however, sending Dodd back to prison for another short stay. Dodd had to prepare himself mentally—to psych himself up—to cross the line into homicide. "I wasn't sure that I could kill, so in my mind I had to fantasize about it. To be able to kill, I had to make that thought exciting," Dodd explained. "And in a matter of just a couple of weeks . . . I was ready to kill."[7]

After his release, Dodd was prepared to try again, and this time he was determined not to fail. His first murder occurred during Labor Day weekend of 1989. Dodd jumped 11-year-old Cole Neer and his 10-year-old brother Billy as they rode their bikes through a park in Vancouver, Washington. Dodd stabbed both children to death after molesting the older boy. One month later, he abducted 4-year-old Lee Iseli from a playground, molested him, and then hanged him by a rope in the bedroom closet. Dodd had clearly developed a taste for murder; he was totally hooked. In his own words, "I became obsessed with [killing]. That's all I thought about 24 hours a day. I was dreaming about it at night, constantly all day at work—all I thought about was killing kids."[8]

Fortunately, Dodd had neither the skill nor the luck of more prolific serial killers. Two weeks after the Iseli murder, Dodd was again on the prowl. He attempted to abduct a boy from a movie theater bathroom, but his victim started screaming frantically. Dodd managed to wrestle the boy into his car. The vehicle was in poor mechanical shape, however, and not equipped for a quick getaway. Unable to accelerate, Dodd was captured only two blocks from the theater. On January 15, 1993, following months of intense publicity surrounding his unusual choice of mode of execution, Dodd was hanged at Walla Walla prison in eastern Washington state.

The vulnerability of certain groups of victims rests not so much in their naïveté, accessibility, or small stature, but in the sense that serial killers can feast upon them with relative impunity. Specifically, when extinguishing the lives of elderly nursing home residents, a caretaker can capitalize on the normalcy of death in such an environment. A thrill killer, when trolling for prostitutes along a red-light strip, can be reasonably assured that because of their typically transient lifestyle, the disappearances of his victims will not be immediately deemed foul play. Moreover, society devalues women and men who sell their bodies. The capture of their killer therefore often takes low priority, and the killer knows it. Some serial killers select other marginal groups—minorities, immigrants, or gays—to assure themselves that the public and police response will be muted. If nothing else, serial murderers are opportunists, and they seek out conditions that will allow them to kill repeatedly without detection or apprehension.

A long-standing myth consistently runs through popular television shows and mystery novels that serial killers, at least at some level, wish to get caught. According to this view, serial killers—even the most sociopathic—actually do have a conscience strong enough to affect their behavior. Therefore they subconsciously leave clues in order to get punished for their sins. This notion dates back at least to the 1946 case of William Heirens, the "lipstick killer" who scrawled a message for the Chicago police on the apartment wall of one of his victims: "For heaven's sake, catch me before I kill more. I cannot control myself."

Unlike Heirens, most serial killers do everything they can to avoid getting caught. They are clever and careful; when it comes to murder, they are brilliantly resourceful. They methodically stalk their victims for the best opportunity to strike and not be seen, and they smartly dump the bodies far away so as not to leave any clues. The cool and calculating manner in which many sociopaths cover their tracks arises out of the fearlessness that typifies this personality type. They respond unemotionally and without panic to the prospect of capture, undeterred by the risk of appre-hension. A self-selection process operates to separate the coolheaded men from the hot-tempered boys: If killers like Chikatilo and Dahmer weren't so good at killing and cover-ing their trail, they would never have remained on the streets long enough to qualify as serial killers.

Murders committed by methodical serial killers are typ-ically difficult to solve because of the lack of either a motive or useful evidence. Unlike the usual homicide, which involves an offender and victim who know one another, sexually motivated serial murders are almost exclusively committed by strangers. Thus the usual police strategy of identifying suspects (boyfriends, neighbors, or coworkers) by examining their possible motives—whether jealousy, revenge, or greed—generally helps very little. With no such clear-cut motive, there are no immediate suspects.

In Gainesville, Florida, for example, a large task force investigating the murders of five college students in August 1990 had a wealth of crime-scene evidence for the lab to analyze, including pubic hairs and semen. For months the task force operated in a "pubes and tubes" strategy, collect-ing hundreds of hair and blood samples from just about anyone who possibly could have had a connection to the crime. But because the police were seeking a stranger who had no prior relationship to the victims, this hunt was like searching for a needle in a haystack. The high-profile char-acter of the Gainesville murders, furthermore, enlarged the pile of suspects as well-intentioned citizens from around the country phoned in the names of people they thought might be involved.

Although the Gainesville investigation team was for-tunate to have plenty of clues (perhaps more than they needed), other serial murder investigations have very little evidence of a tangible nature to go on. The more successful serial killers transport their victims from the scene of the murder to a remote site or makeshift grave. The police may never locate the body and thus never determine that a homicide has occurred. Even if the bodies of the victims do eventually turn up at a dump site, most of the potentially revealing forensic evidence remains in the killer's house or car, where the victim was slain—but without a suspect, the police cannot find these places to search. Moreover, any trace evidence (such as semen within the vagina and skin beneath the fingernails) left on the discarded body tends to erode as the corpse is exposed to rain, wind, heat, and snow.

In 1988, for example, the police in New Bedford, Massachusetts, were stymied by a profound lack of physical evidence in their hunt for a killer of at least nine prostitutes and drug users. The unidentified predator had abducted his victims from the sleazy Weld Square area of town and discarded their remains along highways in southeastern Massachusetts. By the time the decomposed bodies were finally discovered, the police had enough trouble identifying the skeletal remains, much less the killer. This case remains unsolved, perhaps permanently so.

Serial killers do not always travel great distances to remote mountains and densely wooded areas in order to dispose of the evidence. John Wayne Gacy buried his victims in the crawl space under his suburban home. Jeffrey Dahmer tried to dissolve his dead companions in a barrel of acid that he kept in his Milwaukee apartment. In Detroit and neighboring Highland Park, Michigan, a homeless drug addict confessed to killing 11 women, whose bodies he dumped in abandoned buildings. In one particularly chilling discovery, the police had found three corpses in the shower stalls of three different rooms of a boarded-up motel.

In addition to the traditional forensic approaches, a relatively new strategy for serial murder investigations is to search the crime scene for psychological clues. Although occasionally used earlier by forensic psychiatrists, the psychological profiling technique has been enhanced since the early 1980s by behavioral scientists at the FBI. Based on a behavioral assessment of crime-scene photos, autopsy records, and police incident reports, FBI profilers compose a portrait that speculates on the killer's age, race, sex, marital and employment status, sexual maturity, possible criminal record, relationship to the victim, and likelihood of committing future crimes.

The profiling team distinguishes between organized and disorganized killers based on general personality types—the former being methodical or careful, and the latter being haphazard or frenzied. The organized and disorganized types are distinguished by clusters of personal and social characteristics. The organized killer typically is intelligent, socially and sexually competent, of high birth order (first- or second-born child), and a skilled worker. He lives with a partner, is mobile, drives a relatively new car, and follows his crime in the media. In contrast, the disorganized killer generally is unintelligent, socially and sexually inadequate, of low birth order, and an unskilled worker. He lives alone, is nonmobile, drives an old car or no car at all, and has minimal interest in the news reports of his crimes.[9]

According to the FBI analysis, the personality of the killer is reflected in his behavior at the crime scene. Specifically, the organized killer uses restraints on his victims, hides or transports the body, removes weapons from the scene, sexually molests the victims prior to death, and is methodical in the style of killing. The disorganized killer tends not to use restraints, leaves the body in full view, leaves a weapon at the scene, sexually molests the victim after death, and is spontaneous in his manner of killing. The task of profiling therefore involves drawing inferences from the crime scene to the behavioral characteristics of the killer.

Psychological profiles are designed as an investigative tool to identify a range of suspects, rather than to point precisely to a particular suspect. Even in meeting this limited objective, however, the profiles are not completely successful. Psychological profiles may be perfectly on target in novels like *The Silence of the Lambs,* but they are more or less a rough indicator in real life, even when constructed by the most skillful profilers. Simply put, a psychological profile cannot identify a suspect for investigation, nor can it eliminate a suspect who doesn't "fit the mold." Rather, a profile can assist in evaluating suspects whose names surface through more usual investigative strategies (e.g., interviews of witnesses, canvassing of neighborhoods, and "tip" phone lines).

One of the problems confronting the investigators in the 1988 New Bedford case was that the task force was not launched until months after the murders had begun. It was not until the fourth victim's body was discovered that the police determined that a serial killer was on the loose.

This time delay is not unusual. Even before trying to solve a case, police are not always certain that a serial killer is operating in their area. Serial killers do not always leave unmistakable and unique signatures at their crime scenes. A particular murderer may target a redhead on one occasion and a blonde on another, whomever is available. He may also vary his style or mode of killing, using a knife on one occasion and a club on another. His varying modus operandi may not be so much an attempt to confuse the police as it is a wish to experiment with different kinds of victims and different styles of killing. As a result, the police may not recognize multiple homicides as the work of the same perpetrator.

Moreover, some serial killings, even if consistent in modus operandi, cross jurisdictional boundaries. A killer might abduct a woman in Wyoming and duplicate the crime with another victim two states away. Criminologist Stephen Egger calls this obstacle to detection "linkage blindness." To aid in the detection of serial murder cases that involve multiple jurisdictions, the FBI has created a computerized database for linking unsolved and bizarre homicides. The Violent Criminal Apprehension Program (VICAP) is designed to flag similarities that might otherwise go unnoticed in unsolved homicides around the country.

While an excellent concept, VICAP has encountered numerous practical limitations in constructing a national clearinghouse of unsolved murder cases. One problem is that the questionnaires that local police use to provide information for VICAP are long and complicated; consequently, cooperation from local law enforcement agencies in reporting cases has been less than satisfactory. VICAP cannot link cases that are not reported to it. Even with full participation by police agencies around the country, however, recognizing a pattern to unsolved murders in different states is not as easy as some people might believe, no matter how powerful the computer or how sophisticated the software.

Though forensic investigation, psychological profiling, and VICAP can all play integral roles in trying to apprehend serial killers, there is no substitute for old-fashioned detective work and a healthy dose of luck. In some cases the killer slips up. He may begin to feel after awhile that he is invincible and that the cops cannot match his skill or cunning. Becoming complacent, he starts to cut corners and take chances, which leads to his ultimate demise.

In June 1993, the police of Mineola, Long Island, simply got lucky. Stopping a gray pickup truck in the middle of the night because of a missing license plate, state troopers discovered a woman's body in the back of the truck. The driver, 34-year-old Joe Rifkin, was en route to dump the body of his 17th victim.

London's Colin Ireland also failed to work out every important detail. During several months in 1993, the 39-year-old Briton stalked and killed members of London's gay community without leaving so much as a clue. All of his five victims were men who engaged in sadomasochistic sex, and they allowed Ireland to bind and gag them at will. Hence they were completely at his mercy.

Ireland was methodical. Before each murder, he emptied his pockets so that nothing would fall out and implicate him. Afterward he spent hours wiping away the evidence, even destroying the clothes he wore at the scene of the crime. Despite his preparation and planning, however, Ireland made a fatal blunder. A security camera captured his presence as he walked behind his fifth and last victim at a subway station just prior to the murder. Seeing his photo reprinted in the newspaper, Ireland panicked and came forward to confess.

Police have utilized a variety of behavioral, investigative, and scientific techniques designed to help identify and capture serial killers. On occasion, however, authorities have lucked out through inadvertent means. On December 12, 1983, Sheriff Pat Thomas of Sarpy County, Nebraska, was interviewed by the press concerning the murder and mutilation of two local boys, 13-year-old Danny Joe Eberle and 12-year-old Chris Walden. Talking with reporters about the murder investigation, Thomas referred to the unidentified killer as a "sick, spineless . . . coward" who didn't have the guts to pick on someone his own size.[10]

Little did Sheriff Thomas realize that the killer was closely following the progress of the investigation. Insulted by the sheriff's remark, 19-year-old John Joubert decided to prove that "he didn't just pick up little boys."[11] He reacted by selecting an adult—a preschool teacher—as his next victim. Unlike the two murdered children, she was able to break away from her assailant; she also had the presence of mind to memorize the license number of his car. She then called the police, and Joubert was apprehended and later convicted. As luck would have it, Joubert's vanity got the better of him.

3

Murder without Guilt

The gruesome discovery in June 1985 of the vicious crimes of 39-year-old Leonard Lake and 24-year-old Charles Ng left residents of Northern California shaking their heads. For the San Francisco police, it began routinely enough on the afternoon of June 2. They were called by the owner of South City Lumber when he observed Ng stealing a vise from the store. Arriving at the scene, the police witnessed the young thief depositing goods in the trunk of his buddy's car. But before they could reach him, Ng ran off, leaving Lake holding the bag. In Lake's trunk, alongside the stolen vise, the police found an illegal .22-caliber automatic pistol equipped with a silencer.

Leonard Lake was arrested and brought to the police station for questioning. During the interrogation, he asked for some water with which to take an aspirin. Almost immediately, he slumped over, appearing to have suffered a heart attack. Instead, it was the lethal effects of a cyanide pill that Lake had ingested. The investigation of this bizarre suicide led the San Francisco police to Leonard Lake's small ranch near Wisleyville, about 150 miles northeast of the Bay

Area in Calaveras County. *Calaveras* is Spanish for skull; but the police found much more than skulls when they arrived at Lake's two-bedroom bungalow on Blue Mountain Road.

It did not take investigators long to realize that the ranch was not so much a rural retreat as it was a torture chamber. They found hooks and chains, and photographs on the walls of women in various poses of submission. The backgrounds indicated that the photos had been taken from inside the ranch itself. The police also found a library of homemade "snuff" films in which real-life murder victims were captured on tape. Viewing the movies on the living room television, the police replayed gut-wrenching scenes of victims being raped, tortured, and murdered by the directors—Leonard Lake and Charles Ng. One chained-up woman had been filmed as she pleaded on behalf of her child, who was being tortured in front of her eyes. Another woman, while tied naked to the bed, was shown being told by Lake, "You'll wash for us, clean for us, fuck for us."[1] Outside the house, the police found the killers' refuse: large garbage bags filled with the bones of between two and four dozen people.

Unlike most other serial killers, who prefer certain kinds of victims, Lake and Ng showed no favorites. They killed acquaintances and strangers, men and women, children and adults, and people of all races. They abducted their captives in equally diverse ways. One man was kidnapped from his home when Lake and Ng answered a classified ad for a camcorder he was selling (the same one they later used to produce their torture films). In another instance, they snatched two young lovers who were camping in the woods.

In part, Lake and Ng were motivated by a ghoulish desire for sexual sadism. The torture tapes revealed the vicious rapes that the gruesome pair perpetrated against their defenseless victims. The murders were also part of a power game in which the two set loose some of their victims into the woods, only to hunt them down as if they were wild animals. The police found at the hideout an inscription bearing the killers' creed: "If you love something, set it free. It if doesn't come back, hunt it down and kill it."[2]

Lake and Ng were also inspired by their survivalist theory that a nuclear war would soon destroy the world. At their ranch, they built a concrete bunker to shelter them from the impending apocalypse, and they planned to stock it with sex slaves who would keep them entertained and later bear the children of the new world.

The crimes committed by Lake and Ng surely were horrific. Still they reflect, in an obviously extreme form, a disturbing general trend in which more and more people feel unconstrained by either conscience or social norms from offending other human beings. Most of this unscrupulous behavior is relatively innocuous. More people today are willing to cheat their neighbor, lie in a job interview, or steal "souvenirs" from their hotel room.

During the 1960s and 1970s, America fought two major wars. The war in Vietnam claimed thousands of lives and occupied the attention of a whole generation of baby boomers. On the domestic front, though, Americans also fought a war against guilt. For years they were encouraged not to feel guilty: do your own thing, love the one you're with, and be assertive.

Blended with the message of individualism that Americans received during the 1960s was a more altruistic theme encouraging social responsibility and equality of opportunity. It was this positive focus that led the baby-boom generation to join the civil rights movement and push for women's rights. When double-digit inflation and repeated energy crises enveloped the American psyche during the 1970s, however, altruism quickly dissipated, leaving only selfish individualism in its wake. Economic exigency forced Americans of all ages to abandon the humanitarian impulse.

We continue to be veterans of the war against guilt. The slogan of the day used to be "I'm OK, you're OK"; now for many people it is "I'm OK, you're dead." At a societal level, the decline in moral responsibility has been so profound that some observers have called us a "sociopathic society." In his recent book *Money, Murder and the American Dream: Wilding from Wall Street to Main Street,* sociologist Charles Derber suggests that the collective conscience of America has been seriously debilitated. He sees a declining sense of morality in everything from business decisions to interpersonal relationships. Thus Americans may still know the right thing to do, but to an increasing extent they don't feel morally compelled to do it. Behavior is determined more by what is convenient and practical than by what is ethical; morality has taken a back seat to expediency.

As a result of this trend, there have been repeated scandals at the uppermost levels of society: Chappaquiddick, Watergate, Abscam, Irangate, the S & L collapses, Packwood, Milken, and Helmsley, to mention but a few. Youngsters are now more inclined than ever to resort to violence over seemingly trivial issues—over a pair of Nikes, a leather jacket, or a challenging glance, or for no reason at all. In California, for example, two teenaged girls recently murdered their best friend because they were jealous of her beautiful auburn hair. In Florida, a teenage boy killed a homeless man when the beggar stole an extra slice of pizza. Beyond these white-collar criminals and youthful desperadoes, our culture may be creating more serial killers at the extreme moral margins of society. Unrestrained by conscience, they feel free to satisfy their goals, regardless of whom they hurt in the process.

Of course, it takes much more than motive to become a serial killer. Many people seek thrills in their lives, but are able to satisfy this craving in legitimate if not entirely safe ways, such as skydiving or driving at excessive speeds. Other people may have an inordinate need for power and control, but they also are able to find socially acceptable modes of fulfillment. For example, certain business executives derive a sadistic pleasure by "eating alive" their competition; they wheel and deal not just for the profit but also for the feeling of power.

There may be tens of thousands of people who are motivated in such a way that they could find serial murder to be psychologically rewarding. Most have other outlets; a few may experiment with violence but find it distasteful, repulsive, or even more difficult than they had imagined. Remaining a serial killer at large requires some level of criminal savoir faire. Some potential serial killers lack the ability to avoid detection long enough to accumulate large numbers of victims. They may leave physical evidence at crime scenes, abduct their victims in the presence of eyewitnesses, or select a victim who is resourceful enough to escape. Even if they successfully avoid detection and find murder enjoyable, feelings of guilt and remorse may deter some would-be serial killers after one or two attacks. For example, the Zodiac Shooter repeatedly terrorized the city of New York during the summer of 1990—until one of his victims died. Apparently upset over having taken a human life, the attacker abruptly stopped.

For several possible reasons, guilt does not seem to control the behavior of those men and women who make a career—or at least a hobby—out of killing. Unencumbered by guilt, they murder with moral impunity. The common wisdom among experts is that serial killers can typically be described as sociopaths (who, as noted earlier, possess a disorder of character rather than of the mind). A sociopath lacks a conscience, feels no remorse, is incapable of feeling empathy and warmth for others, and cares exclusively for his own pleasures in life. He uses other people to fulfill his own needs and desires, no matter how perverse or reprehensible. The sociopath is bad, not mad; his crimes are sickening, but his mind is far from sick.

For example, criminologists have described Danny Harold Rolling, who brutally slayed and mutilated five college students in Gainesville, Florida, in August 1990 as a sociopath. He had a long history of criminal activity prior to the student murders, including theft, robbery, and assaultive behavior. Not only did he butcher five innocent strangers, but he attempted to kill his own father. Rolling may also have committed a grisly triple murder in a family that lived only a few blocks from his home in Shreveport, Louisiana. Anyone who got in his way or who could satisfy his sadistic desires—family, neighbors, or strangers—was totally expendable.

Henry Lee Lucas was similarly devoid of any feelings or concern for his victims. Lucas has talked, without emotion, of killing someone just because they were around and he decided that it might be fun. "Killing someone is just like walking outdoors," explained Lucas. "If I wanted a victim, I'd just go get one."[3] When an absolute stranger for whatever reason struck his fancy, he would stalk his prey until the time and place were right to move in for the kill. At one time he boasted of killing several hundred people, although this claim was likely an exaggeration.

One of Lucas's earliest victims was his 74-year-old mother, Viola. He stabbed her to death after she struck him with a broom and nagged him incessantly. The murder was a payback for years of cruelty and mistreatment when he was a child. In his first year of grade school, Viola would dress Henry as a girl and curl his hair in ringlets. She beat him repeatedly, and she forced him to watch as she performed sexual acts for money.

Another one of his victims was a 14-year-old girl whom he claimed to have loved. Frieda "Becky" Lorraine Powell was Lucas's traveling companion until she acted out of place and slapped him across the face. Without hesitation Lucas stabbed Becky to death, raped her, cut her body into pieces, and stuffed them into pillow cases. Asked why he would commit such an atrocity against someone he purportedly loved, Lucas said, "It was the only thing I could think of."[4]

The commonly accepted conception of the sociopathic serial killer may fit the moral immaturity found in violent offenders like Henry Lee Lucas. We question, however, whether sociopathy is present (at least in such an extreme form) in most other serial killers. That is, many probably do have a conscience—some weaker than others, perhaps—and should not be considered pure sociopaths. According to Ansevics and Doweiko, many serial killers appear to suffer from a related character abnormality called borderline personality disorder (BPD), which is marked by a pattern of instability in their mood, relationships, and self-image. In response to a stressful situation, the borderline-type individual may become nearly psychotic for a short period of time. The behavior of persons with BPD often includes impulsivity, intense anger, and chronic feelings of boredom. They often feel a profound sense of abandonment and rejection, and they may be extremely manipulative with other people.[5] Unlike the antisocial personality, however, the borderline personality type is capable of feeling remorse and empathy when he or she hurts other people.

Disorganized killers who are not genuinely psychotic but have BPD may be confused and angry, but have the capacity for empathy and compassion when they are not killing. BPD may possibly help to explain impulsive attacks of killers who repeatedly murder in a state of frenzy without making much of an effort to cover their tracks. Because of their confusion and impulsivity, they are generally discovered and apprehended before amassing a large victim count.

Despite the merits of their argument, though, Ansevics and Doweiko appear to overstate the role of BPD among serial killers. Given the care and planning with which they kill, most serial killers are organized in the way they both approach and leave the crime scene, and they do not possess the pattern of unstable mood and impulsivity that characterizes borderline personality disorder. Even so, many serial killers are not classic sociopaths. Many possess powerful psychological facilitators for overcoming or neutralizing whatever pangs of guilt might otherwise plague them. They are able to compartmentalize their attitudes by conceiving of at least two categories of human beings—those whom they care about and treat with decency, and those with whom they have no relationship and therefore can victimize with total disregard for their feelings.

For example, Hillside Strangler Kenneth Bianchi clearly divided the world into two camps. The group toward whom he had no feelings included the 12 young women that he brutally tortured and murdered. Ken's inner circle consisted of his mother, his wife, and his son, as well as his cousin

Angelo Buono, with whom he teamed up for the killings. "The Ken I knew couldn't ever have hurt anybody or killed anybody," recalled Kelli Boyd, his common-law wife and the mother of his child. "He wasn't the kind of person who could have killed somebody."[6]

According to psychiatrist Robert Jay Lifton, the Nazi physicians who performed ghoulish experiments at Auschwitz and other concentration camps similarly compartmentalized their activities, attitudes, and emotions.[7] Through what he calls "doubling," Lifton suggests that any possible feelings of guilt were minimized because the camp doctors developed one distinct self for doing the dirty work of experimenting with and exterminating inmates, and another for living the rest of their lives outside of the camp. In this way, no matter how sadistic they were on the job, they were still able to see themselves as gentle husbands, caring fathers, and honorable physicians.

The compartmentalization that allows for killing without guilt is an extension of a phenomenon used by many normal people in their everyday roles. An executive might be a heartless "son of a bitch" to all his employees at work, but a loving and devoted family man at home. Similarly, many serial killers have jobs, families, do volunteer work, and kill part-time with a great deal of selectivity. The process of compartmentalization is especially pronounced in the case of a serial murderer who kills for profit—that is, who robs and then executes in order to silence the eyewitnesses to his crimes. Like a hit man for the mob, he kills for a living, yet otherwise leads an ordinary family life. Even a sexual sadist, who may be unmercifully brutal to a hitchhiker or a stranger he meets at a bar, might not dream of hurting family members, friends, or neighbors.

Serial killer John Wayne Gacy of suburban Chicago, for

example, was "not all bad," as those closest to him would attest. Despite his conviction on 33 counts of murder, Lillian Grexa, his former neighbor, still wrote to Gacy on death row. "I know they say he killed 33," explains Grexa, "but I only knew him as a good neighbor . . . the best I ever had." Gacy was voted the Jaycee "man of the year," was a respected member of the local Democratic party, and was photographed in the late 1970s with First Lady Rosalynn Carter. He played a clown at children's parties, and held theme bashes for the neighbors. On weekends when his wife was away, however, Gacy had private parties for special guests—young attractive males—that featured beer, drugs, sex, and torture. Then he would literally cover up the truth about his deadly passions by burying 29 of his victims in the crawl space under his house. Four others had to be buried elsewhere for lack of space.

It is difficult, if not impossible, to determine for certain if a particular serial killer mentally separates his friends from the rest of humanity or whether he is just a clever sociopath who successfully plays the role of a loving friend and family member. Although sociopaths lack the capacity for human kindness and compassion, they know the right thing to do. In fact, they are often very skillful at maintaining a caring and sympathetic facade, especially when it is in their self-interest to do so. Could John Wayne Gacy have fooled his wife, his child, and his neighbors? Or do they know more about his character than those who analyze his criminal behavior?

Returning to the extreme atrocities committed by the Nazi doctors, we can learn about dehumanization, another psychological process that effectively permits killing without guilt. Not only did the Auschwitz physicians compartmentalize their roles by constructing separate selves, but they were able to convince themselves that their victims were less than human. The Jews were seen as a disease or plague who had to be stamped out as vermin in semihuman form and had to be exterminated for the health of the country. Likewise, Jewish research subjects were viewed as guinea pigs who could be sacrificed for the sake of medical knowledge. Thus, by a process of dehumanization, concentration camp doctors made decisions as to who would live and who would die, and conducted twin studies in which inmates were forced to experience excruciating pain and suffering, all in the name of scientific inquiry.

Through the same process of dehumanization, many serial killers have slaughtered scores of innocent people by viewing them as worthless and, therefore, expendable. Prostitutes are seen as mere sex machines, gays as AIDS carriers, nursing home patients as vegetables, and homeless alcoholics as nothing more than trash. By regarding their victims as subhuman elements of society, the killers can actually delude themselves into believing that they are doing something positive rather than negative. They are, in their minds, ridding the world of filth and evil.

Dehumanization can occur not only for the purpose of selecting deserving victims, but also for the sake of justifying excessive cruelty to those who have already been chosen. For example, Kansas City's Robert Berdella, who tortured and sodomized his male captives, didn't necessarily hold a dehumanized view of his victims until he transformed them into sex toys. At that point, they lost their humanity in his eyes. He could then do anything he wanted to his "blow-up dolls." Similarly, Milwaukee's Jeffrey Dahmer, who confessed to killing seventeen young men, actually attempted to lobotomize his captives in an effort to change them into walking zombies with whom he could have sex. Both Berdella and Dahmer could avoid feeling guilty about performing ghastly sexual atrocities on their dehumanized playthings. In Dahmer's case, his ability to degrade his victims was aided by their minority status (most were gay and/or black or Asian).

The behavior of a serial killer after his capture provides some insight into his level of conscience. Genuine sociopaths almost never confess after being apprehended; instead they continue to maintain their innocence, always hoping to get off on a technicality, to be granted a new trial, or to appeal their case to a higher level. To this day, Lawrence Sigmund Bittaker, who was convicted of five murders in Southern California, maintains that his partner Roy Norris actually did all the killing. Confronted with an audiotape of a torture session containing his voice, Bittaker has a ready excuse: "You didn't fall for that act, did you? It was all a script. We were playing around. I'd slap my hand, and she would scream. It was all a fake."[8]

A few sociopathic serial killers have confessed to their crimes not because they were remorseful, but because they considered it in their best interest to do so. For example, Clifford Olson, suspected of killing 11 children in Vancouver, British Columbia, decided that the police had the goods on him. Thinking that he might as well turn his defeat into an advantage, Olson confessed and led the police to the bodies of his victims in exchange for a $100,000 "ransom." He had struck a deal by which his wife and son would receive $10,000 in trust for each dead child he helped locate; he graciously threw the last victim in for free. Olson was later asked to reveal information about other missing children, not for a fee but for the sake of the worried parents. In true sociopathic style, he responded, "If I gave a shit about the parents, I wouldn't have killed the kid."[9]

Thus, when sociopaths confess, it is not out of a need to expiate feelings of guilt, but instead for a self-serving reason. The benefit is not always as tangible as Olson's. For example, serial killer Danny Rolling continued to proclaim his innocence in the Gainesville murder case for years after his indictment, despite compelling physical evidence against him. On February 15, 1994, the opening day of what was to be a lengthy and closely watched trial, however, he shocked everyone with his confession. "Your honor, I have been running from first one thing, then another all of my life—whether from problems at home, or with the law, or from myself," Rolling told Judge Stan Morris. "But there are some things that you just can't run from, and this is one of them."[10] In a press conference, Rolling's attorney explained that the accused wished to spare the families of his victims the agony of a trial. But the prosecuting attorney argued more persuasively that Rolling's confession was more calculated than caring—a last-ditch effort designed to play on the sympathy of the court. Because he was already serving a life sentence for other crimes, Rolling's decision to plead guilty to the murders was a strategic move to try to escape the electric chair.

In a similar way, Henry Lee Lucas was able to delay his execution by the state of Texas by promising to help police solve their open murder cases. At one time, he boasted of having killed 600 people. Shortly after Jeffrey Dahmer made the cover of *People,* Donald Evans falsely confessed to more than 60 murders around the country, perhaps attempting to become famous in his own right. Clifford Olson boasted from his prison cell about his celebrity: "Henry Lee Lucas was small potatoes. I'm like Hannibal Lecter."[11]

Unlike true sociopaths, who are incapable of feeling remorse, serial killers who must dehumanize their victims frequently confess after being caught. Joel Rifkin of Long Island, for example, freely confessed on the day after his capture to killing 17 prostitutes and provided all the evidence that could be used against him in a court of law. Although caught red-handed with only one victim, he willingly implicated himself in a killing spree that would likely put him behind bars for life.

Cannibalistic serial killer Jeffrey Dahmer similarly confessed to his crimes. After his conviction, when it was no longer self-serving to do so, he then apologized both in court and on the national television program "Inside Edition." His statement to the judge asked for no mercy:

> I just want to say that I hope God has forgiven me. I know society will never be able to forgive me. I know the families of the victims will never be able to forgive me for what I have done. I promise I will pray each day to ask for their forgiveness when the hurt goes away, if ever. I have seen their tears and if I could give my life right now to bring their loved ones back, I would do it. I am so very sorry.
>
> Your honor, I know that you are about to sentence me. I ask for no consideration. I know my time in prison will be terrible. But I deserve whatever I get because of what I have done. Thank you, your honor, and I am prepared for your sentence, which I know will be the maximum. I ask for no consideration.[12]

So long as they are alone with their fantasies and private thoughts, serial killers like Rifkin and Dahmer are able to maintain the myth that their victims deserved to die. After being caught, however, they are forced to confront the disturbing reality that they had killed human beings, not animals or objects. At this point, their victims are rehumanized in their eyes. As a result, these serial killers may be overcome with guilt for all the horrible crimes they committed and may freely confess.

Some serial killers, the true sociopaths, are beyond redemption. They failed to develop early in life the capacity for empathy and affection. As a result, they are totally lacking in the internal mechanisms that usually inhibit selfish and hurtful behavior. Unlike psychotics, sociopaths understand the wrongfulness of their assaultive behavior. Unlike normal people, however, they only understand it at an intellectual level; the emotional component is absent. Consequently, sociopathic serial killers cannot be rehabilitated. They missed the boat on developing a conscience when they were young, and the boat never returns.

Other serial killers are driven by strong urges—sexual sadism, dominance, and pedophilia—that overpower whatever conscience they possess. Treatment strategies do exist for managing or controlling some of these motivating forces, but they have met with limited success. Though some serial killers could potentially be treated for their behavior, the gravity of their crimes makes rehabilitation a moot issue. Public opinion is clear in this regard: Serial killers should never be released from custody, cured or not.

4

Stay with Me

"Hi, I'm Jeff. I like the way you dance." Jeffrey Dahmer's icebreaker may not have been a clever come-on, but it was effective enough for his purposes. Dahmer, a 31-year-old chocolate factory worker, spent his spare time trolling gay bars in Milwaukee's decaying Walker's Point, seeking out pretty young men he could make his own. Sometimes he offered money, other times just a drink. But all of his victims got more than they bargained for.

Tracy Edwards was luckier than the rest. He lived to tell what went on inside of apartment 213 at 924 North 25th Street. Edwards looked much younger than his 32 years, primarily on account of his diminutive frame. Dahmer liked them young or small, especially with dark skin, and he surely liked Tracy Edwards.

The night of July 22, 1991, was typically warm and humid in the city known for its beer and social tolerance. Edwards was out for the evening with some friends when he met Jeffrey Dahmer, who invited them all over to his place for a few beers. Dahmer suggested that he and Edwards go buy some six-packs and then meet up with the others at his apartment. Wanting to get his new friend alone, Dahmer purposely gave Edwards's companions the wrong address.

Arriving at the second-floor flat in the dilapidated Oxford Apartments, Edwards first noticed the photos of nude males hanging from the living room walls. He was repulsed by a sickening stench, and he thought about how he could make a graceful yet quick exit. But before Edwards could plan his escape, his host returned from the kitchen with drinks. As Edwards guzzled down his beer, Dahmer kept asking, oddly, "Are you high yet?"[1]

Things soon went from strange to worse. Dahmer suddenly pulled out a knife and pressed the blade against Edwards's chest, warning him, "You die if you don't do what I say." Dahmer then maneuvered his latest captive into the bedroom to watch his favorite film, *The Exorcist*, on the VCR. As Dahmer was readying the tape, Edwards glanced at the photos on the bedroom walls—photos more outrageous than those he had seen earlier in the living room. These pictures—hanging on the walls of the "dying room"—portrayed nude men whose bodies had been mutilated as though eaten up by acid. Edwards also noticed in the corner of the room a large barrel that gave off a putrid odor. He was not aware that Dahmer had used the drum to dispose of his earlier guests.

As the soundtrack from *The Exorcist* blared on in the background, Dahmer made his move. At knifepoint, he grabbed Edwards from behind and attempted to handcuff him to the bedpost. "I'm going to cut your heart out and eat it," Dahmer warned. But before Dahmer could secure his victim, Edwards fought back. Trained in the martial arts, he belted Dahmer across the face and kicked him in the groin.

As Dahmer struggled to recover, Edwards bolted from the apartment, the handcuffs still dangling from his left wrist.

Flagging down a passing police cruiser, Edwards excitedly told of his escape and convinced the officers, Rolf Mueller and Robert Rath, to return with him to Dahmer's apartment. Once inside, the police found Polaroid photographs of butchered corpses. They were shocked to realize that the backdrop for the pictures was the very room in which they were standing. Continuing to search the premises, Mueller peered inside the refrigerator and found a human head on the bottom shelf. He also discovered a chilled human heart, which Dahmer later explained he had kept as a leftover in the event that he wanted a light snack. The police had more than enough evidence—fingerprints, and the fingers to which they belonged—for probable cause to make an arrest. A more thorough search later that evening turned up more sinister evidence of Dahmer's sickening preoccupation with death and destruction, including hearts, heads, skulls, scalps, and other body parts. Inside the drum in the bedroom, the police found the remains of three bodies, all apparently dismembered with an electric saw.

The more atrocious a crime is, the greater the tendency is to point fingers in an effort to place the blame. As one of the most hideous serial killings of all time, the Dahmer case triggered extreme accusations and condemnations, some legitimate and some not. Dahmer's family was first to be put on trial in the court of public opinion. Neighbors from his hometown of Bath, Ohio, stepped forward (and onto national television) to recall all their favorite "weird Jeff" stories, as well as evidence that his parents were negligent, if not abusive. His mother and father, they charged, should have known and done something about his excessive drinking and about his fascination with dead things. Dahmer's family life gave "Monday morning psychologists" plenty of material to analyze in the worst possible light. Dahmer felt abandoned by his mother and was allegedly abused as a child. Even his stepmother was implicated in his abnormal upbringing; the fact that she didn't even meet her stepson until he was 18 years old didn't prevent her from being scapegoated as well.

The accusations weren't limited to just Dahmer's family. Dahmer's probation officer, who was entrusted with supervising him following a conviction for sexually molesting a 13-year-old boy, failed to make home visits. Even one visit to Dahmer's den of destruction might have revealed his evil hobby (assuming, that is, that the probation officer lived to file a report). And shouldn't the residents of the Oxford Apartments have recognized the fetid odor that filled the hallway outside of Dahmer's unit? How could they possibly have believed him when he explained that the meat inside his broken freezer had spoiled in the heat? And why did the police ignore the phone call from one concerned resident who complained about Dahmer's strange activities?

What about the victims themselves? Weren't they pretty stupid not to have detected the odor of death once they entered Dahmer's place? And what about the ones who were lucky enough to survive? Why did four would-be victims who escaped from Dahmer only tell their friends about their bizarre encounter and not go to the authorities? And what about the 14-year-old Laotian boy who fled from Dahmer's captivity, only to be brought back by the police? How could three cops have been so irresponsible in returning a minor back to Dahmer's custody, despite reports that the boy was naked, bleeding from the rectum, and intoxicated?

Critics in Milwaukee charged that much of the blame could be ascribed to racism. Were the victims middle-class whites, they argued, the police would have been more aggressive, and Dahmer would not have gone unnoticed for so long. Clearly, this argument would seem to have at least some degree of accuracy. There is a disgraceful tendency for public officials around the country to discount the complaints and grievances of marginal groups, including immigrants, gays, and people of color. To the police officers who negligently returned Dahmer's Laotian captive, the boy would have appeared to be all three.

Notwithstanding the questionable police response, how could so many neighborhood residents have let the bizarre circumstances involving Jeffrey Dahmer continue for years without intervening? Very easily, given the variety of social norms, customs, and rules telling us to mind our own business, to keep our nose out of other people's affairs, and that somebody else will do something if there is a problem. Even if one is inclined to intervene, the very last thing one imagines in smelling a horrible odor from a nearby apartment is that someone is cutting up bodies and eating human organs. When the occupant attributes the stench to a malfunctioning freezer, neighbors naturally accept his plausible explanation. Psychologists may call this denial; if so, it is not a negative form of denial. It would be unfortunate indeed if people were so jaded that they automatically imagined only the worst of one another: "There's that smell again; Jeff must be cooking bodies."

Of all the people who might be blamed for the hideous crimes in Milwaukee, the one who clearly is most responsible is Dahmer himself. Although legitimate questions remain surrounding the ineffectual actions of the Milwaukee police and of Dahmer's probation officer, the killer himself refused to deflect blame and instead assumed total responsibility for the crimes. Speaking in court prior to sentencing, Dahmer testified as follows:

> I take all the blame for what I did. I hurt many people. The judge in my earlier case tried to help me and I refused his help and he got hurt by what I did. I hurt those policemen in the Konerak matter [the Laotian boy] and shall forever regret causing them to lose their jobs. And I hope and pray that they can get their jobs back because I know they did their best and I just plain fooled them.
>
> For that I am so sorry. I know I hurt my probation officer, who was really trying to help me. I am so sorry for that and sorry for everyone else that I have hurt. I have hurt my mother and father and stepmother. I loved them all so very much.[2]

Notwithstanding his courtroom remorse after-the-fact, what was Dahmer's motive for killing? Why would an ordinary-looking, even handsome man who didn't hear voices or see things that weren't there, held a steady job, and came from a substantial family background desire to have sex with dead bodies and to eat their organs? According to British author Brian Masters, Dahmer felt so rejected and was so devoid of satisfying human relationships that he killed for companionship. He was almost a carbon copy of Dennis Andrew Nilson, the case study for Master's true-crime classic, *Killing for Company*. From December 1978 to February 1983, Nilson, a 37-year-old British government worker, killed and mutilated 15 young men in his north London flat. Typically soliciting his victims from a nearby pub, Nilson invited them home for a nightcap. In a ritualized manner, he waited for them to pass out from drinking and then strangled them. He then dunked their heads in a pail of water to ensure that they had stopped breathing.

Afterward he scrubbed their bodies in the bathtub, then carried them to his bed for lovemaking.

But sex wasn't Nilson's only motive. Being lonely and needing companionship, he realized that dead men don't leave. He dined with his dead friends, watched television with them, and even carried on one-sided conversations. Nilson saved his favorite corpses by temporarily storing them under the floorboards in the living room. The cool temperature under the floor, however, could only preserve his partners for so long. Once his silent partners were too decomposed to be either desirable or satisfying, Nilson carefully dismembered the bodies, boiled the remains, and either burned them or flushed them down the toilet.

Jeffrey Dahmer, in a similar way, wanted to keep his victims around for a while. He, too, was lonely and forlorn. Ever since his youth, Dahmer had trouble making friends and spent much of his time alone. Not wanting to be rejected anymore, Dahmer attempted to find lasting friendship with his victims. He sedated them, strangled them to death, and then had sex with their lifeless bodies. Unlike his English counterpart, however, Dahmer also sought (unsuccessfully) to keep some of his captives alive by drugging them into unconsciousness and performing a crude lobotomy. In this way, he hoped that they would permanently become zombielike sex toys, capable of fulfilling his every desire.

Surgery wasn't Dahmer's only strategy for keeping his victims around. As disgusting though it may seem, Dahmer's practice of eating his victims was as much an expression of love or affection as of hate. In order to maintain the presence of his lovers, he actually consumed their body parts. Through what anthropologists have called "affectionate cannibalism,"[3] Dahmer's young captives literally became a part of him.

Both the affectionate and aggressive motivations for cannibalism can be found in the psychological and symbolic meaning of some of the language that we use everyday. For example, a parent will say lovingly to his or her child, "I could just eat you up," and complimentary remarks are known as "buttering someone up." Conversely, "grilling someone" indicates a hostile interrogation, and harsh criticism is known as "chewing someone out."

From a Freudian point of view, separation from a loved one through death gives rise to mixed feelings of sadness and anger. Feeling abandoned, grieving children confronted with the premature death of a parent, for example, often express feelings of hostility toward the deceased. Not understanding illness or death, they blame the parent for "choosing" to leave them. Already suffering from a profound sense of rejection, Dahmer similarly resented the death of his victims, even though he was the one who caused it.

The desire for total control of another human being can be seen most clearly in the case of 36-year-old Robert Andrew Berdella, owner of Bob's Bizarre Bazaar in Kansas City, Missouri. Berdella's curio shop was nowhere nearly as bizarre, however, as his three-story home on Charlotte Street, inside of which he murdered six young men between 1984 and 1987. Berdella may have killed seven—and possibly more—had not 22-year-old Christopher Bryson been lucky enough to escape his 3-day captivity. Pretending to be Berdella's obedient sex slave, Bryson waited for an opportunity to make his break for freedom. Jumping from a second-floor window, he ran down the street wearing nothing but a dog collar. The deep ligature marks on the escapee's wrists and ankles and his badly swollen eyes gave the police an ominous preview of what they would find in Berdella's house of horrors.

In Christopher Bryson, Berdella thought he had succeeded in achieving his dream of owning a doll-like sex object that he could play with in whatever way he chose. His plan, which had failed with his earlier captives, involved breaking the will and spirit of strong young men until they would comply with his every desire.

Berdella sedated his victims with animal anesthetics and tranquilizers that he had obtained from a local veterinary supply house. In order to render his captives unconscious, he placed drugs into their food or gave them potent sedatives in place of vitamins, aspirin, or recreational drugs. Once they had passed out, he restrained them with ropes, gags, and a dog collar around the neck. In the days that followed, Berdella progressively dehumanized his captives, depriving them of all sensations except those that he inflicted. He blinded his victims with chemicals and probed his finger down into their eyes, poured drain cleaner down their throats, squirted bathtub caulking into their ears, and restricted their intake of food and water.

At the same time, Berdella used instruments of torture on his victims, including an electrical transformer and metal spatulas to apply electric shocks to their bodies. He beat them on the head with a rubber mallet, stuck them with needles, and pounded their limbs with boards, sticks, and a heavy metal pipe. In some cases, Berdella sodomized his victims with his arm and a variety of vegetables.

The circumstances surrounding the deaths of Berdella's sex slaves varied in many respects, but apparently none of them was killed for the sake of pleasure or excitement. Two of the victims were suffocated with plastic bags when Berdella feared he would be discovered. Others died from medical complications, (e.g., drug overdoses, infection, and head injuries) arising from their maltreatment. In order to hide evidence of his dark passion, Berdella dismembered each corpse by cutting it at the joints, then wrapped the body parts in plastic bags that he set out for the garbage collector. None of these bodies was ever recovered, although police did find two heads that Berdella had kept—one hidden in a closet, and the other buried in the back yard.

Berdella confessed to experiencing an exhilarating sense of power by holding his victims captive. He wanted his victims "reduced to the level of, say, a blow-up doll or clay figure you would make as a kid: moving [them] around, having complete control [of them]."[4] This explanation is quite revealing. Like Dahmer and Nilson, he sought not so much to kill his victims as to dominate their existence. This notion of power is very different from the kind of control sought by purely sexually sadistic killers like Theodore Bundy and Kenneth Bianchi. Typically, these serial killers celebrate suffering, the more their victims scream and beg for mercy, the more stimulated they become. A killer like Bundy (or Bianchi) would never have sedated his victim before raping (or strangling) her. That would have taken all the fun out of it.

5

Fantasy Island

Randy Kraft was considered by neighbors, friends, and business associates as a decent and intelligent man whose casual lifestyle seemed to fit the California scene. A thirty-something homeowner, computer consultant, and college graduate, Kraft was meticulous in his personal appearance and caring in his demeanor. His short walrus-style mustache and sandy blond hair were always trimmed and neat, and his frequent visits to the beach left him looking tanned and healthy.

Carefully concealed behind the facade of civility and kindness, however, there was another side to Randy Kraft. When he wasn't busy tinkering with his computers or visiting relatives, he was off butchering young men. Over a period of at least 12 years, he sodomized and mutilated as many as 67 victims in California, Oregon, and Michigan. And until May 14, 1983, nobody suspected.

It was one o'clock on a warm spring night, about 50 miles south of Los Angeles on Interstate 5. Randy had been drinking heavily. He tried to control his brown 1979 Toyota Celica, but it weaved back and forth across the shoulder of the highway— so much so that Kraft attracted the attention of Orange County highway patrol officers. They had been following his Toyota in the right-hand lane for several minutes, and they finally pulled him over to see if he was under the influence.

The two officers discovered more than a few bottles of beer. Slumped in the passenger seat was the body of a 200-pound, 25-year-old Marine who had been strangled with a belt. His penis and testicles were exposed through the open fly in his jeans. There were fresh ligature marks deeply imbedded into both of his wrists, and his shoes had been removed and placed beneath the front seat.

A search of Kraft's car uncovered evidence of much greater carnage. First, even though the dead Marine had not suffered open wounds, the passenger's seat was soaked with blood. Under the driver's side floor mat was an envelope containing 47 color photographs of young men. Some were nude; others were clothed. Some looked unconscious or asleep; many looked dead. In the trunk, investigators found a briefcase that contained a two-column list of 61 printed notations, all in code. The list turned out to be a record of Kraft's murder victims.

Randy Kraft never admitted to the killings, and to this day his family believes him to be innocent. But in a 13-month trial, prosecutors presented enough physical evidence—fibers from Randy's carpet, stolen property in his home, his sofa shown in one of the photographs—to convict the defendant. They also showed that Kraft had the opportunity: Between June 1980 and January 1983, he had worked for a California company that required him to make visits to its offices in Oregon and Michigan at precisely the period of time when the unsolved murders in these states occurred.

It wasn't only the large number of killings that shocked

the members of the jury; it was also the grotesque and brutal quality of the crimes. Kraft was incredibly cruel and vicious, torturing his victims by burning their scrota, nipples, lips, and eyes with an automobile cigarette lighter, slicing deeply into their arms and legs with a knife, jamming sharp instruments into their penises, hacking off their testicles, cramming leaves into their rectums, and stuffing dirt down their bronchial tubes until they gagged to death. On May 12, 1989, after 11 days of deliberation, the jury found Kraft guilty of committing 16 murders. During the penalty phase of the trial, however, the prosecution brought up the details of 21 more brutal killings in order to support its request for the death penalty. Sickened by the evidence, the jury gave the prosecution the sentence it sought.

Like a ballplayer who keeps the baseball from his first major league hit, Randy Kraft saved the memory of his crimes in gruesome photographs and maintained an up-to-date scorecard of his exploits. Actually, many serial killers collect memorabilia and souvenirs—diaries, clothing, photos, or even body parts—to remind them of their most cherished moments with their victims. For example, Danny Rolling removed and kept the nipples of some of his female victims. Joel Rifkin kept his victims' underwear, shoes, sweaters, cosmetics, and jewelry in his bedroom. Jeffrey Dahmer proudly displayed pictures of the dead on the walls of his apartment. New Jersey serial killer Richard Cottingham collected the clothes and jewelry of his victims at his home in a special room that he kept locked away from his unsuspecting wife and children.

When police searched the apartment of child slayer Westley Allan Dodd, they found plenty of incriminating evidence. Dodd had maintained a neatly labeled photo album of his victims, including grotesque pictures of one boy hanging by the neck. Dodd had also kept a diary of his crimes that included an itemized list of whom he had killed and a chart of murder techniques classified by the speed with which they would cause death. Kansas City killer Robert Berdella had a particularly rich collection of souvenirs, including two human skulls, a pouchful of teeth, and more than 200 photographs of his victims in degrading poses during various stages of captivity and after death. He also chronicled his accomplishments in a detailed log of his tortures. Methodically recording the time and date of each physical attack, each sexual assault, each injection of sedative, and each physiological response of the victim, his hand-scrawled notebooks resembled a hospital's medical chart more than they did the ravings of a madman.

Even though it was ultimately used as condemning evidence against him, Berdella's prized collection of macabre mementos served several important purposes. First, for a man who had otherwise led an unremarkable life, his treasures made him feel proud. They represented the one and only way in which he had ever distinguished himself. It may have been fiendish, but it was a power trip that few others had ever attempted, let alone achieved. More important, the souvenirs became tangible reminders of the "good times" Berdella had spent with his playmates. With the aid of his photographs, he could still get pleasure—even between captives—from reminiscing, fantasizing, and masturbating.

Not all fantasy life is pathological. In fact, ordinary, healthy human beings often dream about their hopes and pleasures, even those that are beyond their reach. Some of the fantasies may include such deviant and bizarre sexual practices as fetishes, pedophilia, bondage, and rape. These people might lust in their hearts and their heads, but not in their habits. Because of their strong sense of conscience or concern over their public image, they resist translating the desire for sexual violence into action.

Lack of self-control is not the only characteristic separating the serial killer from those who do not act on their aggressive fantasies. The serial killer tends to have incredibly rich, detailed, and elaborate fantasies inspiring him to disregard both law and convention. Through murder and mayhem, the serial killer literally chases his dreams. With each successive victim, he attempts to fine-tune the act, striving to make his real-life experiences as perfect as his fantasy.

As his crimes become more vicious with time, though, the serial killer's mental script becomes more demanding. Not only is his behavior inspired by fantasy, but the fantasy is nourished by the offenses that he has committed. As a result, the killer's crimes grow increasingly brutal and grotesque as he pursues his dreams in a never-ending spiral of image and action.

Because of the important role of thought and fantasy, serial killers often have remarkably vivid and detailed memories of their killings. Using his "torture diary" as a guide, Robert Berdella recounted to authorities the specific events of crimes dating back several years as though they had just occurred. In a matter-of-fact fashion, Berdella described how his victims were captured and subdued, how they responded to his "experiments," and how they died.

Many other serial killers keep only a mental diary, yet they are no less precise in their recollections. For example, in his lengthy confession, Joel Rifkin amazed the New York state police by reciting the specifics of each of his 17 prostitute murders. Rifkin recalled the criteria for choosing his victims, the color of their hair, the clothing they wore, his method of strangling them after performing sex in his truck, and his strategy for disposing of the bodies. With chilling precision, he told how he dismembered some of the murdered women and stored others in his garage. During the entire 8-hour confession, Rifkin was nothing less than calm, cool, and dispassionate. In between lurid revelations of murder and mayhem, he munched on hamburgers and sipped tea.

How could Rifkin have kept straight in his mind so many details of the slayings? How could he remember exactly what he did to whom, and when he did it? The answer has less to do with intelligence and memory skills than with motivation. Like a boy who remembers every detail of a major league ballgame he attends but not his assigned vocabulary words, Rifkin easily kept track of what was really important to him. Killing was his passion, and these were his most precious memories. Not only could he experience the thrill of killing, but he could relive them over and over again in his fantasies.

When the police search the home of a suspected serial killer, they sometimes uncover not just clothing and jewelry (as in Rifkin's residence) but extensive libraries of films and tapes that depict acts of rape and murder. Sometimes the movies are homemade. Leonard Lake and Charles Ng, as we have noted, used a camcorder that they had stolen from one of their victims in order to record their torture sessions. In other cases, pornographic materials are commercially produced. John Wayne Gacy, for example, had a prized collection of pornographic videotapes that would be the envy of most any serial killer.

According to FBI research on sexual homicide, serial killers typically collect hard-core pornography, especially materials containing themes of violence, dominance, and bondage.[1] Undoubtedly the preoccupation with violent pornography plays a role in the fantasy life of a serial killer. Films showing rape and torture may provide examples to enrich his own imagination. The critical question, however, is whether pornography operates as a drive mechanism for murder—that is, does an interest in violent sexual films and photos cause or merely reflect the serial killer's fascination with murder?

The problems of distinguishing cause from effect have long plagued researchers eager to understand the development of violent impulses. Not surprisingly, people who are predisposed to violence (for whatever reason) will be drawn to violent pornography. This does not necessarily mean that the pornography created their predisposition toward violence, although it may reinforce or exacerbate it. It may also tend to desensitize the viewer to the pain and suffering of real-life victims of sexual violence.

In the same way, it is commonplace to learn that serial killers, when captured, are found to possess extensive libraries of violent pornographic materials. This, too, is not surprising, nor does it implicate violent pornography as a fundamental cause of serial murder. Rather, it reflects a general preoccupation with sexual violence that pervades every aspect of their leisure time. When they are not killing, serial murderers can at least fantasize about killing with the aid of photographs and videotapes.

In other areas of life, we find a correspondence between what people do for work or a hobby and what they choose to read or watch in their leisure time. A successful business executive may read the *Wall Street Journal* on a regular basis, but we would hardly claim that his or her interest in business resulted from the choice of reading material. Similarly, an avid hunter may subscribe to *Field and Stream* to entertain himself when he's not out hunting.

Thirty-nine year-old Leslie Allen Williams, who in 1992 confessed to killing four women and raping several others in suburban Detroit, diagnosed the impact of sex in the media. In a detailed 24-page letter to the *Detroit News* about his crimes, he wrote the following:

> Females are fortunate in that they are pretty much given one message from the very beginning: "no, no, no" . . . Save it for love and marriage. Meanwhile, males are given messages of "go, go, go" . . . Get it when and if you can to be a man.
>
> Along with and on top of that, males are subjected to a barrage of stimulators . . . everything from advertisers and TV shows, books and tabloids, to entertainers and role-models.
>
> Everywhere they turn, they are told it is OK to be sexually active and aggressive.[2]

Some multiple murderers may pattern their behavior—their modus operandi—after real or fictional accounts of similar crimes. But the larger problem is, as Williams suggests, found in our popular culture. Some isolated individuals may learn how to kill from the media, but countless others get the message that violence is acceptable.

The belief that media portrayals (particularly visual images of fictional events aimed at a younger audience) may normalize the expression of violence has existed for decades. To concerned parents of the 1960s, motion pictures were responsible for teaching America's children the dangerous lesson that the consequences of violence are temporary and trivial. Cinematic characters who were shot, slashed, or punched in the mouth rarely ever bled. Their injuries or death were typically presented in a sanitized or cleaned-up manner.

If one were to judge only by the body counts, movies of today are no more violent than their counterparts of 25 years ago. But their portrayal of murder and mayhem no longer leaves anything to the imagination. In fact, the consequences of violence are now routinely depicted as graphically as possible, without regard for how they may affect impressionable young viewers. Violence is not just central to the plot; it is central to the purpose. Displaying the various ways of bringing about a gory death become the main object of the movie.

In one motion picture after another, children are treated to disgusting scenes of decapitation and dismemberment. Victims are shown with their brains literally blown apart, their heads missing, their fingers sliced off, and their intestines exposed. The *Faces of Death* video film series strings together footage of death scenes—from people jumping from high-rise buildings to ritualistic cannibalism. Because of the videocassette, moreover, children can now replay their favorite gory scenes over and over, never leaving the privacy of their own homes.

Parents who used to be worried about teaching their children that violence has consequences now have a much more difficult problem: how to keep them from becoming totally desensitized to human misery, mayhem, and murder. An even worse dilemma is how to keep them from lusting for scenes in new movies showing more novel ways of inflicting pain and torture on a victim. The fun once achieved in a "spook house"—anxiously anticipating the next horror to scare you personally—has been replaced by the sadistic kick in seeing someone else tortured. Because of the steady diet of gory films to which they are exposed, from

Terminator II to *Exorcist III,* children of the 1990s are slowly but surely growing more tolerant of the effects of violence. They are no longer repulsed by stories of extreme brutality, even when they are real.

The change in mass culture involves more than just how graphic a portrayal of violence we will accept or desire. Virtually all forms of media violence, whether in movies, TV commercials, or rock videos, have become sexualized. Not only does the combination of sex and violence suggest that violence is pleasurable, but it also identifies certain kinds of people (and women in particular) as appropriate victims. In these forms of entertainment, women are depicted as objects. They are dehumanized, cast in the role of "sex machines" whose only purpose in life—and in death—is to give men pleasure. By dehumanizing certain groups of people ("fast" women, prostitutes, and gays), we are told not only that violence is OK, but which victims are OK.

So-called slasher films routinely fuse sex with violence to seduce a youthful market. In *The Toolbox Murders,* promiscuous girls are punished for their passions by a moralistic maniac with power tools. In one particularly powerful scene, an attractive young woman is nailed to the wall after she masturbates in a bubble bath; all the while, a romantic country ballad plays gently in the background. In *I Spit on Your Grave,* a young woman is stalked and tormented by four men in a remote wooded area. They gang-rape and humiliate her for nearly a half hour in a spirit of fun and friendship. For many youths, whose first exposure to sex is a rape scene in a movie, the lesson is that violence is sexually arousing.

The possible effects of such pornography (whether R, X, or NC-17 rated) have not gone unnoticed. For example, a 1986 task force assembled by U.S. Attorney General Edwin

Meese strongly denounced this form of entertainment as being harmful to young Americans. Spearheading the movement to ban pornographic films, Focus on the Family, a Colorado-based nonprofit group, publishes eight magazines and broadcasts six radio programs, one of which is carried by nearly 2,000 radio stations in North America. Its outspoken leader, Dr. James Dobson, interviewed Ted Bundy just prior to his execution by the state of Florida. According to the condemned man's eleventh-hour confession, pornography is responsible for the rise of serial murder during recent years:

> People need to recognize that those of us who have been so much influenced by violence in the media—in particular pornographic violence—aren't some kind of inherent monsters. We are your sons, and we are your husbands. We grew up in regular families.
>
> Pornography can reach out and snatch a kid out of any house today. It snatched me out of my home 30 years ago. And as diligent as my parents were, and they were diligent in protecting their children, as good a Christian home as we had—and we had a wonderful Christian home—there is no protection against the kinds of influences that are loose in society.[3]

Ted Bundy's condemnation of pornography as an excuse for his own violent impulses was not so much a fabrication as it was a misunderstanding of the role of pornography in our culture. Violent pornography may not directly cause or inspire its consumers to develop into serial murderers, but it unquestionably provides a cultural context in which sexual homicide is encouraged. In this respect, violent pornography hurts all of us.

6

Crazy Like a Fox

In June 1987, 40-year-old Arthur Shawcross was granted his freedom—freedom to kill. He had been convicted in 1972 of murdering two young children in upstate New York. His first victim was 10-year-old Jack Blake, who was kidnapped while on his way to a friend's house to play. Shawcross confessed to raping and butchering the boy, then devouring his genitals. Shawcross's other victim was 8-year-old Karen Ann Hill, whom he raped and murdered. Shawcross served the minimum of a 15- to 25-year sentence before being paroled.

Despite his hideous past, Shawcross blended well into the Rochester community where he settled after his release from custody. It didn't take him long to pick up where he left off, only this time victimizing prostitutes rather than children. The middle-aged killer appeared to the hustlers he targeted as just another john. Overweight and balding, he hardly seemed threatening to the women he picked up, even after they had been alerted that a serial killer was on the loose and preying on streetwalkers.

By March 1988, the police in Rochester had discovered

the partially nude bodies of two prostitutes floating in the Genese River gorge. One woman had been asphyxiated, and the other shot. The police saw no clear-cut link between these homicides other than the victims' occupation, and it was hardly unusual for prostitutes to get killed, given the sleazy clientele with whom they did business. Six months later, however, the police had found the skeletal remains of two more victims in the river gorge. By this point the police were forced to confront the frightening probability that a serial killer was on the prowl and targeting women of the night.

By Thanksgiving 1988, the tenth body, that of 29-year-old June Stott, was discovered. This case, however, was strikingly different from the other nine. Not only was the murder particularly grotesque (the woman's body had been eviscerated from the neck down to her pubic bone), but Stott was the first victim who was not a prostitute. It is common-place for serial killers to increase the level of brutality as they get bored with less vicious behavior and as they grow more comfortable with murder. It is also not unusual for them to branch out to more respectable victims as they become convinced that they are smarter than the police and will never be apprehended.

Shawcross was no different in this regard; his care-lessness and sense of invincibility ultimately led to his de-mise. Long after dumping the body of his twelfth victim, June Cicero, in Simon Creek, Shawcross returned to mutilate her corpse. Surveying the area by helicopter, the Rochester police spied Shawcross getting into his car, which was parked on a bridge some 15 feet above Cicero's body.

After being picked up for suspicion of murder, Shaw-cross's mug shot was placed into a photo lineup. (Detectives often compile a sheet of photographs, mixing a suspect's picture with those of several others, in order to approximate an actual station-house lineup for field use.) The police showed the photo lineup to local prostitute Joanne Van Nostrand. She immediately picked out Shawcross as the perverted john who needed her to "play dead" in order for him to get sexually aroused.

"He was real nervous," recalled Van Nostrand about her encounter with Shawcross. "That made me nervous, and I carry a knife to protect myself. . . . So I just let him know point-blank that I had a weapon and that I was nervous that there was a serial killer. The only time he was really abusive to me is when I asked him why was it taking so long—I had been there, like, 40 minutes. That's when he really said, 'Well, if you just play dead, bitch, we'll get this over in a few minutes.' Little things kept clicking, and the hairs on the back of my neck started standing up and I said [to myself], 'This is the guy. I just know this is the guy.' "[1]

After his arrest, Shawcross confessed and explained why he had killed 13 women. "I was taking care of business," he stated. Clearly, Shawcross's explanation for his crimes begged the question. Why did he kill these women, and why was he aroused by death and sexual mutilation? Several experts, including New York University psychiatrist Dr. Dorothy Otnow Lewis, who testified on Shawcross's behalf to support his insanity plea, traced the sources of his behavior back to his childhood, particularly to mistreatment at the hands of his sexually provocative mother.

The psychiatric case study of Arthur Shawcross runs true to form. Whenever the background of an infamous serial killer is examined, journalists and behavioral scientists tend to search for clues in his childhood that might explain his seemingly senseless murders. Many writers have emphasized Ted Bundy's concerns over being illegitimate. Biographers of Kenneth Bianchi, the Hillside Strangler of Los Angeles, capitalized on his having been adopted. When it was alleged that Jeffrey Dahmer was abused, some Americans felt satisfied that at last they had an answer to his puzzling crimes.

Ever since Sigmund Freud's psychoanalytic theory revolutionized thinking about childhood development, we have embraced the idea that the first few years largely determine the script by which we play out the rest of our lives. As a result, there is a strong tendency in our culture to blame parents—and particularly mothers—for almost everything that goes amiss later in a child's life, including violent behavior. Thus, when the allegations of sexual abuse in Dahmer's background surfaced in the press, some in the public uncritically accepted childhood trauma as the primary cause of his crime. Oprah Winfrey's television talk show went so far as to air a program on "future Jeffrey Dahmers," featuring mothers who were concerned that their incorrigible youngsters were destined to develop into cold-blooded criminals. Ironically, Winfrey herself had survived a troubled upbringing, involving severe child abuse, yet had become the most successful talk show host in television history rather than a killer.

Many experts have identified the role of childhood problems as the primary cause of serial killing. According to Dorothy Lewis, "In the serial killers I've seen, there's almost invariably a history of early and ongoing sexual abuse. The murder victims sometimes represent a symbolic revenge against the abuser, or sometimes the reverse—the killer is identifying with whoever tortured him, and is now the one in power."[2] Psychiatrist David Abrahamsen, author of *The Murdering Mind*, similarly speculated that serial killer Ted Bundy may have killed dozens of women as an indirect way to kill his mother: "The victim is not really the target. The victim is a substitute, and that is why these crimes seem so random and capricious."[3] Psychologist John Watkins, in probing the mind of Kenneth Bianchi, offered the same analysis: "Consumed by pent-up rage at his mother, Bianchi killed the women."[4] Defense psychiatrist Donald Lunde went one step further by suggesting that Bianchi would never satiate his compulsion to kill until he could murder his mother (which he never attempted to do).

This mother-hate theory suggests that serial killers get even for the real or perceived abusive treatment they received at the hands of their parents by displacing their aggression onto surrogate victims who resemble the offending parent (usually the mother), in terms of physical appearance or behavior. By this reasoning, a killer who targets prostitutes is acting out his hostile feeling for a mother he saw as a "slut." Alternatively, a killer who preys upon victims with reddish hair is conjectured to be avenging mistreatment by his redhaired mother.

There may be isolated examples of serial killers who, motivated by such hatred, seek out victims that ignite angry memories of their childhood. For example, serial killer Henry Lee Lucas included his mother among his many victims (as noted earlier, she had dressed him in girl's clothing and forced him to witness her sexual exploits). In most cases, however, victim selection reflects much more directly issues of opportunity, victim vulnerability, and the character of the killer's sexual fantasies. By selecting hookers as victims, Arthur Shawcross was able to drive to an area of town where he knew they congregated. He could shop for one that most closely fit his sexual urges and entice her into his car without making a scene. And he was assured that her disappearance would likely not be considered foul play.

What then is the role of childhood in understanding the nature or cause of Shawcross's serial killing? The early biography of most people includes an array of both positive and negative events. There is a tendency in our culture, however, to focus selectively on those incidents that are consistent with the outcome we are trying to explain. Thus, in searching for clues to explain how a serial killer has developed, a psychiatrist who subscribes to the troubled-childhood view would tend to emphasize the negative experiences. Some have even utilized hypnosis to aid in their search for abuse and trauma that might lie deeply hidden beneath the surface of consciousness.

Dr. Lewis, for example, testified that Arthur Shawcross suffered from posttraumatic stress disorder brought on in part by experiences of abuse during his childhood. Lewis based this conclusion on sessions of hypnosis in which she age-regressed Shawcross for early memories of mistreatment. At first he recalled having a normal upbringing and failed to reveal any abusive experiences. After lengthy and persistent probing under hypnosis, however, Shawcross finally "remembered" being sodomized by his mother with a broomstick and being forced to perform oral sex with her. Lewis explained the killer's recalcitrant memory as follows: "Most violent men I see would much rather be considered bad or evil than crazy. So they really don't want to talk about the voices they hear or times they have blacked out. And many of them . . . are still intent on protecting their families, even though their families hideously abused them."[5]

Did Lewis's discovery of suppressed and painful memories of abuse in Shawcross's background reflect an uncompromising effort to uncover the truth about deeply hidden secrets? Or did Shawcross finally give his examiner exactly what he figured she expected to hear? Either way, Shaw-cross's mother called her son a liar, and given his attempts to save himself through the insanity plea, he certainly had very good reason to fabricate or exaggerate bad childhood experiences. We cannot know for certain.

The therapeutic uses of hypnosis—from treating com-pulsive behavior to identifying the sources of emotional conflict—are well documented and widely accepted. The forensic applications of hypnosis, however, are much more controversial. Research on hypnosis indicates that the so-called hypnotic trance is little more than accepting the sug-gestions of a highly credible source. According to psycholo-gist Theodore X. Barber, author of *Hypnosis: A Scientific Approach*, almost every extraordinary act or recollection that a subject gives under hypnosis can be obtained without hypnosis. All that is needed is a respected and trusted au-thority figure to make commands (under hypnosis or not) such as "You will lose weight," "You will not smoke," or even "You will remember being abused as a child."

The other important finding uncovered by researchers is that hypnosis increases the level of confidence, but not of accuracy, in recalling events. For example, under hypnosis, witnesses to a crime involving a masked gunman have been asked mentally to remove the criminal's disguise and describe his face. Filling in the details on their own, these hypnotized subjects become convinced about the descrip-tion they give. It is a figment of their imagination, but one of which they are absolutely sure. In the same way, psy-chologists studying hypnosis have compared age regres-sion with age progression. After first taking their subjects back several years in life to recall events at that time, they then take them forward into the future and ask them to describe what they are doing. Subjects tend to recollect the future with as much detail and certainty as they recall the past.

The fact that hypnotized subjects can confidently recall, create, or alter their biographies casts doubt on the accuracy of memories. On the one hand, it is quite possible that a hypnotized subject will reveal painful yet accurate memories of childhood. On the other hand, subjects can fabricate events in their past if it suits the occasion, the context, or some ulterior motive.

In forensic work, the hypnotist deals with a subject who may have a stake in faking a hypnotic trance and divulging inaccurate information about himself and his past. According to Jack Tracktir, a psychologist who specializes in hypnosis, someone can be in a trance and still provide false information. The hypnotist can actually create the information through subtle and perhaps not-so-subtle suggestions to the subject. Thus it is possible for an individual who may indeed have felt intimidated as a child to recall under hypnosis experiences of abuse, particularly if the hypnotist solicits such recollections and the subject has a self-serving interest in providing them.

The case of Kenneth Bianchi provides another revealing example of how hypnosis has been exploited to find support for the child-abuse explanation for murderous impulses. In 1977 and 1978, Bianchi and his cousin Angelo Buono abducted, tortured, raped, and murdered 10 young women, whose bodies they dumped along roadsides in the Los Angeles area. Bianchi's defense was centered on the theory that he suffered from a multiple personality disorder. This psychiatric illness, characterized by the presence of two or more distinct and separate personalities that share the same body, is generally attributed to child abuse. In this view, an abused child escapes from cruel parental treatment by developing a fantasy world of pleasure and kindness. At the same time, the angry and hateful feelings toward the abusive parent are stored in a reservoir that the child suppresses. In later life, the two perspectives—the loving and the hateful—split into their own personalities which compete for control. The angry "person" takes turns with various alter egos for dominance over the body.

If Bianchi was in fact a multiple personality, this could easily explain and reconcile how someone as seemingly nice as Ken could also commit the heinous crimes with which he was charged. Through hypnosis, a second personality surfaced—that of "Steve," a hostile, crude, impatient, and sadistic character who proudly claimed responsibility for the slayings. "Killing a broad doesn't make any difference to me,"[6] bragged Steve. Everything now made sense to the psychiatrists.

Court-appointed experts on multiple personalities found ample support within Ken's extensive medical history for holding his adoptive mother, Frances Piccione, responsible. For example, Dr. A. W. Sullivan of the DePaul Clinic in Rochester, where Ken was seen at the age of 11 for chronic enuresis, suggested that Frances played a major role in her son's childhood problems: "She has dominated the boy and indulged him in terms of her own needs. Her anxious, protective, clinging control has made him ambivalent, but he represses the hostile aggression and is increasingly dependent upon her."[7]

Medical records from Ken's childhood characterized Frances as a neurotic and ineffective parent. But to account for the emergence of Ken's vicious personality, court-appointed psychiatric experts needed to find specific evidence of severe child abuse. Bianchi was advised by his hypnotist that his medical history failed to include the documentation of child abuse that would be needed to support his defense. Hypnotized once more, Bianchi then recalled a dream about "a woman putting his hands over a kitchen stove fire while he was young."[8] Finally, the psychiatrists had the evidence of abuse that was lacking.

When later asked about her son's dream, Frances was candid. She admitted having used the stove as a threat, but not with the intent to inflict pain or injury: "When Ken was 8 years old, I caught him stealing. He had taken some pieces of coral from a greenhouse we had just visited. We had a small kitchen, six or seven feet wide, with a doorway at one end and the stove at the other. Ken was standing at the door with his father. 'See this fire,' I said. 'If I catch you stealing once more, I'll hold your hand over this stove.'"[9] Although harsh and threatening discipline of this sort can be interpreted as abuse, it is usually not considered to be at the level needed to create a dissociative personality state. Had Frances done anything more than threaten, surely the many doctors whom Ken had seen for his medical problems would have reported burns or scars on his hands. Had she been a "severely abusive mother," as some labeled her, there would have been many more stories of brutal treatment.

A number of psychiatrists hold that the roots of "homicidal proneness" reside not only in maternal brutality but also in sexual seduction, which can be played out in anything from incest between mother and child to inappropriate or excessive conversation about sexual matters. The victim of maternal seduction grows up overly anxious about his sexuality. Fueled by this anxiety, the hostility toward his mother generalizes later in life to sexual violence against women.

Court-appointed psychiatrists also attempted to weave a picture of Bianchi's mother as a wantonly seductive woman. A physician at the DePaul Clinic in Rochester had years earlier scrawled some cryptic—barely legible—observations about Frances that became part of Ken's medical file. An unexplained reference to "sex magazines" was later interpreted by court-appointed psychiatrists to mean that she "showed him sex magazines." It could just as easily have meant that she had punished him for reading them, but this interpretation would not have fit the psychiatrists' point of view and so was never seriously considered.

Having failed to prove insanity and having been found guilty of murder, Ken Bianchi no longer had a self-serving motive for implicating his mother. "There has never been child abuse in my family," Ken later admitted. "I greatly exaggerated certain childhood incidents after they could not find an origin for the alleged multiple personality. I was told that multiples usually begin with child abuse. I lied. My lies were not supposed to have been released. Originally, they were mentioned in confidence. I am not proud of what I did."[10]

Whether or not Bianchi's criminal behavior could be traced to parental abuse and seduction, childhood trauma does generally play an important role in explaining the development of murderous impulses. Children who are abused, neglected, or abandoned tend to grow into needy adults. Lacking control over their own lives as children, many remain insecure as they mature, continuing to possess an intense need for control over their environment.

This overpowering need for control can be fulfilled, however, in many different ways—some bad and others good. For example, some victims of abuse become abusive parents themselves, whereas others are driven toward careers devoted to helping victims of abuse. Additionally, some former abuse victims who have excessive needs for power and control are able to satisfy their needs in un-scrupulous but nonviolent ways.

For example, some college professors achieve a thrill when flunking students; they gain pleasure by hurting their students' chances for a successful education and career, and enjoy it all the more when they beg for another chance at a make-up exam. Similarly, some business executives savor the experience of firing employees or destroying the career of a competitor. They profit from the experience not just financially, but in the sense of power they derive as they rule over the fate of others.

Thus there are important similarities indeed between the ruthless tycoon and the ruthless serial killer. Had Kenneth Bianchi grown up to be an insensitive business executive—unkind, but successful—rather than an infamous killer, his biographers would have pointed to the same childhood issues as critical turning points that ultimately strengthened his determination to succeed. Had Theodore Bundy been able to accomplish his goal of becoming an attorney, he might have done his "killing" in the courtroom to satisfy his need for power.

More than a few serial killers (including David Berkowitz and Joel Rifkin) were raised by adoptive parents. The apparent overrepresentation of adoption in the biographies of these killers has been exploited by people looking for simple explanations for heinous crimes, without their fully recognizing the mechanisms behind or the value of the link between adoption and criminal behavior.

The first possible triggering mechanism surrounds the effects of rejection by birth parents. As a consequence of such rejection, some adopted children may develop feelings of abandonment and intense anger that stay with them throughout life. For example, New York's "Son of Sam" killer, David Berkowitz, who shot and killed six strangers while they sat in parked cars, may have been reacting in part to feelings of rejection. After returning from military service in the Korean War, Berkowitz learned of his adoption and was able years later to locate his biological mother and sister in Long Beach, Long Island. He was shocked, however, when he discovered that they wanted nothing to do with him. Shortly thereafter, his killing spree began.

In addition, some adopted children may be deprived of warmth and affection during the first few months of life, either because of a delay in locating a suitable placement or because the adoptive parents hesitate in making a full emotional commitment until the legal process is finalized. As a result, some of these children may fail to bond emotionally and never develop a capacity for love and empathy.

In addition to these environmental contributors, certain biological deficiencies related to criminality (e.g., retardation and learning disabilities) may be more prevalent among the population of adopted children because of traits common to their biological parents. To whatever extent that criminal propensities are genetically linked, the high rate of prostitutes, drug users, and incarcerated women among mothers who give up their children for adoption will translate into a higher involvement of adoptees in criminal behavior. Also, the poor prenatal care of many of the groups from which adopted children are drawn can similarly predispose these children to the same biological deficiencies that correlate with criminal behavior.

If any or all of these linkages between adoption and crime are true, then is it fair to say that children of adoption are destined to kill? As a society, should we not intervene in the lives of these "children at risk" before it is too late? The methodological problems, however, in predicting violence are well known. For a category of violence as rare as serial murder, the consequent false positive dilemma is overwhelming. Simply put, there are millions of adopted Americans, many of whom may suffer from some form of insecurity as a result. But the vast majority of them will never kill anyone, let alone commit serial murder.

To illustrate further the absurdity of attempting to predict such rare characteristics as murder proneness, consider the link between gender and serial murder. Most serial killers are men, but clearly most men are not serial killers. The same reasoning prevents us from identifying future murderers on the basis of such childhood factors as abuse, seduction, or even cruelty to animals, all of which are often found in the backgrounds of serial killers.

Looking retrospectively at the childhood of serial killers, it comes as little surprise that many were long fascinated with death and dying. Some of them, as children, enjoyed torturing animals and experienced a thrill in determining the fate of small, defenseless creatures. This became a proving ground for later experimentation with human beings. For example, California serial killer Edmund Kemper, who was convicted in 1973 of killing six female college students before murdering his own mother, tortured and dismembered the family cat when he was 13. Other serial killers were fascinated with dead beings rather than with the act of murder itself. For example, as a child, Milwaukee's Jeffrey Dahmer collected road kill in the way that his classmates collected baseball cards.

Though practicing on animals, from insects to cats, may have been instructive for people like Kemper and Dahmer, such childhood experimentation hardly guarantees that a youngster will graduate to human subjects. Many children maintain a vigorous fascination with dead animals; some even enjoy dissecting frogs in high school biology class. Such children, however, are far more likely to grow up to become surgeons, pathologists, nurses, or even morticians than they are to be serial killers.

Caution regarding the vital difference between explanation and prediction applies equally to today's sensitivity to child abuse. The "cycle of violence" hypothesis rests on the finding that many abusive parents were themselves abused as children. Based on this linkage, many well-meaning therapists help child abuse victims deal more effectively with anger and frustration, in the hope that they themselves will not become abusive parents.

This strategy may indeed be a good thing, but for the wrong reason. It is appropriate to be concerned about the emotional well-being and quality of life of those who have been victimized by their parents. But to target them and thus stigmatize them for the hideous acts that they *may* commit sometime in the future (whether child abuse or serial murder) is to victimize them once again. By labeling them as the abusers of tomorrow, we may actually create the very outcome that we are trying to prevent.

The psychiatric evidence linking serial murder to a variety of childhood problems, including child abuse, is frequently disputed because of the questionable reliability of the source of the data—the killer himself. How can we rely on information from a known liar who has a reason to lie? In contrast, biological, physiological, and neurological approaches do not suffer the same reliability problems. It is harder to con an EEG, although the significance of the results may be as unclear as a killer's recollections of his childhood.

Some neurologists and a growing number of psychiatrists suggest that serial killers have incurred severe injury to the limbic region of the brain as a result of profound or repeated head trauma, generally during childhood. Psychiatrist Dorothy Lewis and neurologist Jonathan Pincus, for example, examined 15 murderers on Florida's death row and found that all showed signs of neurological irregularities. In addition, psychologist Joel Norris reported that excessive spinal fluid was found in the brain scan of serial killer Henry Lee Lucas; Norris argued that this abnormality reflected the possible damage caused by an earlier blow or a series of blows to Lucas's head.

It is incontrovertible that severe head trauma and resulting injuries to the brain can potentially have dire effects on behavior, including violent outbursts, learning disabilities, and epilepsy. It is noteworthy and suggestive that Henry Lee Lucas was reportedly beaten by his mother with pieces of lumber and broom handles, and that he later claimed to have experienced frequent dizzy spells and blackouts. Bobby Joe Long of Florida, who was convicted in 1986 and 1994 of a total of nine counts of first-degree murder, also appears to have received several severe head injuries. At the age of 5, Long was knocked unconscious when he fell off a swing. A year later, he suffered a serious concussion when he fell off his bicycle and crashed into a parked car headfirst. Several months later, Long hit his head again when he fell from a horse.

At the same time, it is critical that we place in some perspective the many case studies that have been used to link extreme violence to neurological impairment. Absent from the case-study approach is any indication of the prevalence of individuals who did not act violently despite a history of trauma. Indeed, if head trauma were as strong a contributor to serial murder as some would suggest, then we would have many times more serial killers than we actually do.

It is also important to recognize that neurological impairment must occur in combination with a host of environmental conditions to place an individual at risk for extreme acts of brutality. Dorothy Lewis cautions, for example, that "the neuropsychiatric problems alone don't make you violent. Probably the environmental factors in and of themselves don't make you a violent person. But when you put them together, you create a very dangerous character."[11] Similarly, Robert Ressler, a former FBI special agent, asserts that no single childhood problem indicates future criminality, saying that "there are a whole pot of conditions that have to be met" for violence to be predictable.[12] Head trauma and abuse therefore may be important risk factors, but they are neither necessary nor sufficient to make someone a serial killer. Rather, they are part of a very long list of circumstances—including adoption, shyness, disfigurement, speech impediments, learning and physical disabilities, abandonment, death of a parent, academic and athletic inadequacies—that may make a child feel frustrated and rejected enough to predispose (but not predestine) him or her toward extreme violence.

Thus we must approach with extreme caution and skepticism any attempt to use neurological assessments in a predictive way. The distinction between explanation and prediction is once again crucial. Let us say that some neurological, genetic, or environmental abnormality is more often found among serial killers than in the general population. This does not mean that we could or should screen children for violence proneness using physiological, psychological, or neurological examinations.

Joel Norris suggests that by the end of the decade, "most forms of episodic aggression—including serial murder—could be prevented through an organized program of testing and diagnosis and intervention."[13] There are several reasons why Norris is likely wrong. First, it is questionable that we will soon understand the causes of human behavior well enough to allow predictions to be made with reasonable accuracy. Most of our explanations are incomplete at best, involving a long list of possible contributors. They simply do not permit us to identify in advance who will and who will not turn out to be a serial killer.

But this has not stopped Norris from trying. He has published a list of biological warning signs that he suggests can be used as part of a pattern to identify future serial killers. Norris's list includes a variety of physical features, some general and others quite specific: for example, earlobes that adhere to the head, fine and unruly hair, abnormal teeth, a curved pinky finger, and a third toe that is equal to or longer than the second. Although many of these items may indeed be symptomatic of genetic damage, the connection between genetic abnormality and extreme criminality is tenuous. Even though researchers have found some association between biological makeup and violent behavior, the linkage is not nearly strong enough to allow for prudent predictions. Even if an individual is predisposed toward violence (whether for biological or environmental reasons), there is no guarantee that this propensity will ever be translated into assaultive behavior.

There is a final concern surrounding the overemphasis on environmental or biological determinism: the notion that family, developmental, or genetic abnormalities are always responsible for the propensity to kill. For example, FBI special agent John Douglas, an authority on serial murder, claims that "there are common denominators that you find with *each and every one* of these people. They come from generally broken homes. They are the product of some kind of abuse"[14] (emphasis added). For the serial killer who strives to deflect blame for his actions, the child-abuse syndrome, posttraumatic stress disorder, and an irregular EEG become the perfect excuse. "I'm not to blame," he insists, "I couldn't help myself. I'm a victim, too."

Unfortunately, clever and cunning serial killers who might exploit these syndromes to their own advantage frequently receive a sympathetic ear. Sociopathic serial killers are convincing and accomplished liars. As a professional trained to be supportive and empathetic, the psychiatrist of such a criminal may be easily conned. The case histories of malingerers like Kenneth Bianchi and Arthur Shawcross, both murderers who apparently fooled mental health professionals with fabricated tales of childhood trauma, remind us to be skeptical about the self-serving testimony of those eager to escape legal responsibility for their crimes.

7

Take Good Care of My Baby

On August 18, 1987, 35-year-old Donald Harvey admitted having committed an atrocity beyond the imagination of most normal people. He had killed 24 helpless, desperately ill hospital patients over a period of 4 years. To avoid Ohio's electric chair, the former nurse's aid plea-bargained with a Hamilton County prosecutor for a reduced sentence. In exchange for his confession, Harvey received three concurrent life terms, making him eligible for parole at the age of 95 if he should live that long.

The county prosecutor, Arthur Ney, claimed that his case against Harvey might not have led to a conviction at all without the killer's confession. There were no eyewitnesses to the crimes, or even any employees or patients who remembered Harvey acting improperly. And because the victims were long embalmed and buried, they failed to show any traces of the poisons that Harvey had administered to end their lives. Harvey actually had employed a wide variety of poisons (including arsenic, cyanide, and cleaning fluid), which he mixed into his patients' food or feeding tubes. In addition, he suffocated one hospital patient by placing a wet towel and then a plastic bag over his mouth to stop his breathing.

At first, Harvey confessed to only one murder. In March 1987, doctors performed an autopsy on a patient, John Powell, who had been hospitalized after a serious motorcycle accident. Finding traces of cyanide, the police attempted to administer a polygraph test to all hospital staffers who had been in contact with the victim. Harvey initially refused but later confessed, apparently believing that he had been discovered anyway. During a 9-hour confession in mid-April, Harvey described his poisoning as a "mercy killing." He claimed that he had only wished to put an end to John Powell's suffering and misery because the patient reminded him so much of his own father. Harvey also suggested that the cyanide he had used to poison Powell was originally meant for himself. When he began to feel sorry for his seriously ill patient, however, he decided to use it on Powell rather than to commit suicide.

Two months passed before an investigative report conducted by a Cincinnatti television news team ripped Harvey's suicide story to shreds. The team of reporters determined that another 23 hospital patients had died under mysterious circumstances during the time that Donald Harvey had been working in the hospital. Harvey eventually admitted being responsible for killing these 24 patients, as well as for murdering 30 others in southern Ohio and northern Kentucky beginning in the early 1970s, when he was a teenager.

People who had known Harvey for long periods of time were shocked; they characterized him as a sensitive and warm person who couldn't possibly be guilty of serial murder. But hospital workers held a different view, claiming that he had had a fascination with satanism. At his trial,

Harvey was anything but contrite: As the families of his many victims looked on with horror from their seats in the spectators' gallery, he appeared to be entirely at ease, laughing quietly and joking with his lawyer. Psychiatrist Emmanuel Tanay suggested that Harvey possessed an "inner need" that he satisfied by killing. According to Tanay, Harvey was very much in control of what he did. The prosecutor agreed, saying, "He talked about killing people so matter-of-factly you'd think he was talking about going to the drugstore or ordering a sandwich."[1]

Like serial killers who stalk their victims on the street, Harvey killed to satisfy his cravings for power and control. Unlike the stalkers who must seek out the opportunity to kill, however, Harvey had the opportunity right where he worked. The old and infirm are vulnerable to the misdeeds of "angels of death"—caretakers like Harvey, working in hospitals and nursing homes, who may have a particularly warped sense of mercy. Hospital homicides are particularly difficult to detect and solve. Death among elderly patients is not uncommon, and so suspicions are rarely aroused. Furthermore, should a curiously large volume of deaths occur within a short time span on a particular nurse's shift, hospital administrators are in a quandary. They are reluctant to bring scandal and perhaps lawsuits onto their own facility without sufficient proof, but most of the potentially incriminating evidence against a suspected employee is long buried.

Whereas most serial killers are men, it is not surprising that most "angels of death" (unlike Donald Harvey) are women. Traditionally, females have dominated the helping professions such as nursing. In addition, their need for power does not usually involve sexual sadism. Instead female serial killers derive satisfaction from "playing God"; as health practitioners, they hold life and death in their grasp. Whereas a woman might have difficulty subduing a healthy victim, she would have little trouble at all overpowering a defenseless patient who already is near death. Finally, men kill violently with brute force, but women choose less aggressive means, such as medicines, poisons, or even suffocation.

The slayings in the Alpine Manor Nursing Home near Grand Rapids, Michigan, involved not one but two female perpetrators. One of them was 26-year-old Catherine May Wood, who would do anything for her new lover, Gwendolyn Graham, a fellow nurse's aide. Catherine had already left her husband Kenneth and her 6-year-old daughter in order to be with Graham, a 25-year-old lesbian from Tyler, Texas. One evening in October 1987, Catherine came to Ken to reveal her dark secret. He was just getting used to the idea that his ex-wife and the mother of his child was gay; he wondered what other bombshell she was going to drop now. Was she sick? Had she lost her job? He never imagined that Cathy would confess that she and Gwen had killed several elderly patients in the nursing home where they worked.

Thinking that her story was nothing more than a wild tale, Ken figured that his ex-wife needed a vacation, so he took her to Las Vegas rather than to the police station. Over the next 14 months, however, it became increasingly difficult for Ken to deny that his ex-wife was a killer. Catherine described how she stood at the door as a lookout while her girlfriend Gwen forcefully smothered elderly patients with a washcloth over their nose and mouth. Their victims were chosen because of their frail state; each candidate for death was tested first by holding her nose to see if she resisted. After the first two victims (Marguerite Chambers and Edith Cook), the killing couple discussed the idea of spelling out the word *murder* with the initials of their victim's given names. Having difficulty finding a U—one candidate whose first name was Ursula was too strong to die—they abandoned their perverse anagram. They did it for fun—for emotional release. They also did it for love. According to Catherine, murder would be the special secret she shared with Gwen: a lover's pact to bind them together and seal their relationship forever.

When the news of the murders hit the newspapers, relatives of the victims were incredulous. They preferred to believe that their mothers had died peacefully in their sleep than violently through foul play. Linda Engman, whose 79-year-old mother had died of cardiac arrest according to the death certificate, gave a typical response. "There's no evidence," she insisted.[2]

Kenneth Wood and the relatives of the slain victims had their own reasons for choosing to deny that wrongdoing had occurred. But so did the killers. On a psychological level, Graham and Wood weren't killing human beings; they were killing "vegetables." They only targeted the weakest of the weak—those who were on the verge of death anyway. In one case, in fact, they even convinced themselves that they had mercifully ended the misery of a woman suffering from gangrene. In any event, killing the infirm had a practical advantage in that they were easier to overpower.

One of the most striking contrasts between male and female serial killers (aside from the far greater prevalence of male killers) involves the relationship or lack thereof between the killer and his or her victims. Overwhelmingly, male serial killers prey upon strangers whom they select on the basis of some sexual fantasy involving capture and control. By contrast, with the notable exception of Aileen Wuornos, female serial killers almost always kill victims with whom they have shared some kind of relationship, most often one in which the victim is dependent on them. Graham and Wood disposed of nursing home patients under their care. Marybeth Tinning of Schenectady, New York, killed several of her own children—not all at once in a murderous fit or rage, but one at a time in a cold, deliberate, and selfish attempt to win attention.

Tragedy first struck the Tinning household in 1972. Joe and Marybeth Tinning's third child, Jennifer, was born with hemorrhagic meningitis and died in the hospital after barely a week. Following Jennifer's death, Marybeth was understandably surrounded with friends and family who showered her with sympathy and compassion. The steady stream of support did much more than comfort Marybeth; she craved the attention, almost to the point of emotional addiction.

Just as the attention began to die off, tragedy again struck the Tinnings. Less than 3 weeks following Jennifer's death, 2-year-old Joey died; within 6 more weeks, 4-year-old Barbara died as well. Doctors attributed both deaths to Reye's syndrome. Now childless, Marybeth and her husband Joe tried to rebuild their family. But the couple's fourth child, born in late 1973, died just 3 weeks later. The cause of death was listed as sudden infant death syndrome (SIDS), also known as crib death.

A dreadful pattern was developing. Marybeth would give birth to yet another child, and soon thereafter the baby would die, usually from SIDS. Marybeth began theorizing—almost bragging—about a genetic defect that she was passing on to each of her babies. But as children numbers five, six, seven, and eight all died, sympathy for Marybeth was turning into suspicion. During one of her later pregnancies, a former coworker of Marybeth's quietly remarked to a mutual friend, "Marybeth's pregnant and she's going to kill another baby!"[3]

Following the death of the eighth child, Jonathan, in March 1980, the Tinning household remained childless for five years. Understandably, Marybeth was overjoyed with the birth of her ninth child, Tami Lynne, in August 1985. And as Tami Lynne's first Christmas approached, all seemed well indeed. The baby girl was growing beautifully and was full of health. But early in the morning of December 20, Marybeth went to check on her baby and found her lying on her stomach, motionless and breathless. Despite efforts to restore her breathing, Tami Lynne was pronounced dead. She, too, seemed to have fallen victim to SIDS.

Marybeth responded routinely following yet another loss. She called all her friends and relatives to announce the newest reduction in the Tinning family, expecting the usual round of pity and attention. Her death announcements had become as emotionally arousing for her as the birth announcements; both would make her the center of attention. As one relative would later say about Marybeth, "Every funeral was a party for her, with hardly a tear shed."[4] But her sister-in-law, unable to turn her head once again, called the police with her suspicions.

Out of concern for possible foul play, Tami Lynne was autopsied carefully and thoroughly. With improved methods for distinguishing SIDS from induced asphyxiation, it was determined that the baby had not died of natural causes, but instead had been suffocated. Despite the fact that implicating evidence from earlier deaths had long since been buried, there was enough direct and circumstantial evidence to convict Marybeth of murder. She had become so addicted to her role as grieving mother that she learned to create the tragedies on her own.

This bizarre pattern of behavior has been termed Munchausen syndrome by proxy, by which another person (typically a child) is used or even sacrificed for the sake of getting attention. The notion of proxy distinguishes it from the classic Munchausen syndrome, in which a patient will feign illness or self-inflict injuries in order to be pampered and noticed. The proxy form has been seen, for example, in child-abuse cases in which mothers induce illness in their children (by poison or other means) in order to place themselves in the role of concerned, distraught protector. For many of these mothers, the attention they earn from friends and family, as well as from being around a hospital and conferring with the medical staff, makes them feel important.

According to Dr. Herbert Schreier, chief of psychiatry at the Childrens' Hospital Medical Center in Oakland, California, and coauthor of *Hurting for Love*, Munchausen syndrome by proxy also has a more sadistic motivation. Dr. Schreier notes that women with this psychiatric disorder typically felt during childhood a profound sense of neglect and low self-esteem. As a result they later aspire to get even with their parents, but choose the doctors as parental surrogates. They induce illnesses in their youngsters and then parade them before bewildered medical specialists who unsuccessfully try to diagnose the mysterious symptoms. Not only do the Munchausen mothers attempt to outwit the doctors, but more importantly, they try to humiliate and embarrass them for the sake of vengeance—that is, to get even for the humiliation they had suffered as children. Schreier reports that these mothers often display a "sadistic glee at moments of crisis."[5] Their own children are little more than pawns to be manipulated in their sadistic game.

Munchausen by proxy, although often seen in emotionally needy mothers, is also implicated in certain angel-of-death cases. Typically a medical professional (for example, a nurse or nurse's aide) creates an emergency so that he or she can step forward in a seemingly valiant attempt to save the patient. Successful or not, the "angel of death" can expect to be showered with praise and adulation for the heroic effort.

Twenty-four-year-old nurse Beverly Allitt, for example, was convicted in Nottingham, England, on 13 counts of murder, attempted murder, and assault on children, many of them infants. Between 1987 and 1991, Allitt sought treatment dozens of times at Grantham Hospital's emergency ward for minor and apparently self-inflicted injuries to her hands, legs, back, and head. But it wasn't until a large number of young hospital patients under her care died or suddenly needed critical care that her activities were scrutinized. Autopsies on the children revealed that Allitt had been murdering the patients by suffocation or by injections of insulin or potassium.

When later examined by the court-appointed psychiatrist, Dr. James Higgings, Allitt confessed that she had been upset over not having been admitted to a nursing course and over having been chosen last for her nursing assignment. Allitt's scheme provided the validation that was otherwise missing in her life. By stealthfully killing a child, she could outsmart the brilliant doctors and play God. As she told the psychiatrist, "I had to prove I was better than what people thought."[6]

In an extraordinary case, licensed vocational nurse Genene Jones earned the nickname "Death Nurse" for her seeming affinity for death. In March 1982, Jones left her job at a San Antonio hospital under a cloud of suspicion. From

May to December 1981, 10 children in the intensive care unit had died suddenly and inexplicably, all while Jones was in attendance. An internal hospital inquiry was inconclusive: "The association of Nurse Jones with the deaths of ten children could be coincidental. However, negligence or wrongdoing cannot be excluded."[7] But despite the mysterious deaths, Jones was given a positive letter of recommendation from the hospital:

> To Whom it May Concern:
>
> Due to the recommendation of a recent pediatric Intensive Care Site Team Visit, the Pedi ICU Unit is being converted to an all RN Staff composition at Medical Center Hospital.
>
> Ms. Genene Jones, LVN, has been employed in the Pedi ICU since 1978. This move in no way reflects on her performance in the unit. She has gained valuable knowledge and experience in pediatric intensive care nursing. During the time of employment this employee has been loyal, dependable, and trustworthy.
>
> Ms. Genene Jones, LVN, has been an asset to the Bexar County Hospital District, and I would recommend continued employment.[8]

Shortly after leaving the hospital, Jones took a position at a small pediatric clinic in nearby Kerrville, Texas. One of the first patients in the clinic after her arrival was 15-month-old Chelsea Ann McClellan, whose mother had brought her in for an examination because of the sniffles. While the doctor discussed Chelsea's medical history with her mother, Jones took care of the baby in an examining room. Moments later, the nurse screamed out that the child had stopped breathing. She quickly took charge, performing so heroically in the ambulance on the way to the local hospital that little Chelsea pulled through. The McClellans were so relieved.

They told everyone they knew about the wonderful new nurse in town—a real lifesaver.

But lightning struck twice. A few weeks later, McClellan's mother was back at the clinic with Chelsea for a follow-up examination. Nurse Jones had just administered the girl with an injection when suddenly she stopped breathing, turned pink, and went into a seizure. Once again Jones went along on the ambulance ride to the hospital, but this time Chelsea was dead on arrival. Through their grief and disbelief, the McClellans placed an open-letter ad in the local paper, thanking everyone (especially Jones) for all that they had done:

> To All Our Friends in Kerrville:
> Often we live our lives without a tendency to acknowledge those friends around us. Then something will happen which causes us to become aware of others. Such was the case in the loss of our little Angel, Chelsea Ann McClellan. The response from the people of Kerrville, many of whom we only knew in passing, was both heartwarming and most helpful in our grief. The many beautiful flowers, cards and letters we received made us realize the city of Kerrville has a heart.
> A special thanks to Dr. Kathryn Holland and Genene Jones for extending Chelsea's stay longer by their caring in such a sensitive way. A care which extended beyond loss and helped us more than anyone could ever know.[9]

Chelsea's life-and-death emergency was just the first of many that occurred in children treated in the small clinic. In fact, during the first six weeks that Jones had worked there, six children had stopped breathing and were rushed to the hospital for resuscitation. The nurse was reportedly euphoric when she was able to administer CPR to help save their lives.

A pattern was emerging so clearly that officials at the local hospital launched an investigation. The critical question surrounded a missing bottle of Anectine, a powerful muscle relaxant that could debilitate a person's normal breathing response. Subsequent examination of Chelsea McClellan's body uncovered traces of Anectine, which had caused her respiratory system to stop. Nurse Jones, who apparently craved the fast pace and high drama of life-and-death situations, was convicted of murder in 1984.

Sociopathic serial killers and "angels of death" share more than just the fact that they have taken many innocent lives. Both types of killers are sadists: They inflict death, with or without suffering, for the sake of personal gratification. As noted earlier, this gratification can consist of sexual pleasure, as in the crimes of Arthur Shawcross or Andrei Chikatilo, or of psychological empowerment, as in the medical atrocities of Beverly Allitt or Marybeth Tinning.

When men manipulate and fabricate for the purpose of luring their victims and covering their tracks, they are called sociopathic killers. When women exploiting their role as caretakers are cunning and deceitful for the very same reason, they are labeled as victims of Munchausen syndrome by proxy. At the basis of both forms of serial murder, however, is the excessive need to overcome deep-rooted feelings of powerlessness and inferiority, the desire to control others, and the craving for attention.

8

The Devil Made Me Do It

Fighting back the nausea, Mexican police performed their unenviable task of digging for bodies. On April 12, 1989, they had unearthed a mass grave on an isolated ranch some 20 miles west of Matamoros, Mexico, just south of the Texas border. Among the 15 corpses buried in the makeshift grave was the body of Mark Kilroy, a blond-haired, 21-year-old University of Texas student who a month earlier had been literally grabbed off the street while he and three of his college buddies celebrated spring break.

Amid the stench of decaying human flesh, authorities uncovered the bizarre signs of ritualistic sacrifice. Several large cauldrons were filled with the remains of animals—a rooster, a turtle, a goat's head and feet—floating in a murky broth of human blood and boiled body parts. In a dilapidated shack nearby, searchers found a bloodstained altar surrounded by dozens of cigars, chili peppers, boxes of candles, and bottles of cheap Mexican tequila. Cameron County Sheriff Alex Perez described the grisly scene as "a human slaughterhouse."

Within 24 hours, police had arrested four young men

and sought several others—all members of a major drug ring—who allegedly were involved in the killings. In an unusual turn of events, the four suspects appeared before reporters at a crowded news conference and confessed to murder without the slightest hint of remorse. They laughed as they described their group's crimes, including the abduction of Mark Kilroy. Kilroy had been slashed to death with a machete when he attempted to flee his captors some 12 hours after he had been kidnapped. "We killed them for protection," claimed 22-year-old suspect Elio Hernandez Rivera of Matamoros, who gave police their first clue concerning the motive for what appeared to be random, senseless murders.

Rivera's idea of protection was physical and spiritual. His band of drug smugglers practiced Palo Mayombe. This black-magic derivative of Santeria ("the way of the saints"), a Caribbean voodoo belief, was blended with both satanism and Bruja, a form of witchcraft practiced by 16th-century Aztecs. Human and animal sacrifice was thought by the group to bring them immunity from bullets and criminal prosecution while they illegally transported 2,000 pounds of marijuana per week from Mexico into the United States. According to one member of the cult, Mark Kilroy was abducted because he resembled the group's spiritual leader. By removing his brain after death, they could feed off Kilroy's intelligence.

The police identified the ringleader of the cult as Adolfo de Jesus Constanzo, a 26-year-old native of Cuba. His loyal followers called their charismatic leader *el padrino*—the godfather. Because of his spellbinding influence over his devotees, Constanzo allegedly was able to convince them that their drug activities could never be touched by the law so long as they obeyed his command, among other things, to kill for survival.

The followers of Constanzo were hardly the crazed lunatics that many people associate with ritualistic slaughter and human sacrifice. Most of the cult members grew up in relatively affluent families and did not have histories of violence. The woman believed to be the high priestess or witch of the operation, 24-year-old Sara Maria Aldrete Villareal, was tall, thin, and attractive. An honor student at Texas Southmost College, Aldrete was listed in the college's "who's who" directory. According to professor Tony Zavaleta, "Sara was a model, respectful student. Little did we know that she was apparently leading a double life."[1]

How could apparently normal, intelligent people buy into a philosophy promising that human sacrifice would miraculously protect them from harm? As illogical and immoral as this belief may seem, many people could be made to accept it—even to the point of killing—given the right set of circumstances. Abnormal situations can make normal people do "crazy" things, especially if they perceive a strong self-serving purpose in doing so, such as profit, power, or protection. Adolf Hitler, as a charismatic leader, had transformed German citizens into brutal SS killers through constant marches, all-day group singing of the party's anthem, and required cheering. Hitler capitalized on the promise of turning around Germany's terrible economy to help convince his followers of the urgency of his grand plan. Constanzo similarly capitalized on a powerful economic incentive, as well as on group pressure in order to foster obedience to his command. Like Hitler's marches and chants, Constanzo involved his followers in elaborate and mysterious rituals—animal sacrifices and demonic incantations—in order to achieve in his flock selfless devotion to the cause.

Constanzo's final command was to perform a death ritual—this time involving his own death. Several of his followers obediently shot Constanzo as police authorities closed in on them in Mexico City. Apparently the practice of Palo Mayombe couldn't really protect Constanzo from bullets, nor could it immunize Aldrete and other cult members from prosecution for murder.

The Matamoros incident was widely publicized around America, but it was regarded by many as an isolated tragedy that could never happen in the United States. Skeptics suggested that the belief in the power of human sacrifice depended on ancient superstition that would surely be rejected by civilized Americans. Besides, the law enforcement authorities in the United States would have the operations of a dangerous cult under surveillance long before it could engage in mass homicide.

Such ideas may have been just wishful thinking. On April 17, 1989, barely five days after the Matamoros slaughterhouse was discovered, a cult killing did occur north of the border . . . far north in a sleepy Ohio town. The five members of the Dennis Avery family of Kirtland were sacrificed by a man who considered himself a prophet of God.

With the assistance of his loyal followers, 39-year-old Jeffrey Don Lundgren was determined to do God's work, or so he professed. Having broken away from the Reorganized Church of Jesus Christ of Latter-Day Saints, a branch of Mormonism, Lundgren was convinced that God sent messages to him directly. It was his sacred duty to carry out God's will, no matter how distasteful or violent. God's commandments transcended the law.

The forces of Satan would come, Lundgren had

preached, and he and his followers would have to live off the land until Christ returned. There would be no electricity nor shelter. They would have to protect the temple by whatever means possible. There would be much bloodshed. The Averys had given away all of their worldly possessions—worth more than $20,000—to join Lundgren's army. In exchange for their donation, Lundgren had moved them to Kirtland and promised to pay the rent on a small home for Dennis, his wife, and their three children. But even though Dennis had enlisted his entire family in Lundgren's prophecy, he remained somewhat skeptical of the cult leader's legitimacy and at times challenged his authority.

Less than an hour after Dennis Avery handed over his donation to the cause, Jeffrey Lundgren was in Kirtland buying weapons and supplies to prepare the members of his cult for Armageddon. At Veith Sports Supply he purchased a .45-caliber semiautomatic pistol. Then he drove over to Pistol Pete's Sporting Goods, where he bought a second .45-caliber semiautomatic and a .243-caliber Ruger rifle. A week later, Lundgren went into town again and purchased a Ruger .44-caliber magnum handgun. He also bought tents, camouflage clothing, canned food, camping supplies, and hundreds of rounds of ammunition.

Early in April, in one of many visions witnessed only by Lundgren, he was told that the enemy had already infiltrated his flock and must be eliminated. The prophet wasted little time carrying out the commandment. On the evening of April 17, he led the unsuspecting members of the Avery family, one by one, into the New England-style red barn behind his farmhouse. Lundgren and five of his men had already dug a deep pit in the barn's dirt floor. As each victim—Dennis, his wife Cheryl, and their three young daughters—was escorted from the farmhouse to the barn, their hands and legs were bound with duct tape. Then Lundgren repeatedly pumped his victims with hollow-point slugs from one of his .45 semiautomatics and kicked their lifeless bodies into the pit.

The murder of the Avery family may not have been shrouded in the intricate ritualism and symbolism of cult killings such as the Matamoros slayings. Like other instances of cult murder and the Nazi exterminations, however, Lundgren's massacre grew out of and reinforced the strong group bond that his members shared. And like the leaders in these other atrocities, Lundgren depended a great deal on maintaining obedience by convincing his followers that he was all-powerful, that he had the ability to lead them down the path of righteousness and to conquer all of their enemies.

Judgment Day came early for Jeffrey Lundgren—not at St. Peter's pearly gates, but in a crowded Ohio courtroom. On September 21, 1990, he was sentenced to die in the electric chair. After hearing the judge's decision, Lundgren told his attorneys that his death sentence was predetermined, and that everything was going according to God's plan for him. But, of course, Lundgren knew he would ultimately appeal to a much higher court.

Joining a cult like Lundgren's fulfills a lonely and frustrated person's need to feel good about himself and to be valued by others. Typically the would-be cultist is a failure in everyday life who feels unappreciated by his family and unaccepted by his peers. But even valedictorians, prom queens, doctors, and lawyers have been known to join cults. Even when successful by conventional standards, the recruit may resent the feeling that there are strings attached: In order to be loved and appreciated at home, in school, or on the job, he must compete successfully and behave in a respectful manner. In contrast, as Tufts University psychologist David Elkind has pointed out, the great appeal of cults is that when people join, "they are assured that support is *not* contingent on achievement."[2] Instead, the cultists, in order to be accepted, need only follow orders dutifully.

The cult welcomes the recruit into the "family" and provides him with a strong, charismatic father figure who structures his everyday life and goals. In turn, cults seek out those who are prime targets for mind control, cleverly screening those who are miserable—from an adolescent suffering an identity crisis to a mature adult experiencing a midlife crisis.

Slowly recruits may be initiated into cult activities, urged to reject traditional values, and praised for seeing "the truth." Participation in rituals further reinforces the bond between the newcomers and the cult. They may be instructed to decorate their bodies with symbols to show their loyalty, or to drink the blood of sacrificial animals for strength. They may even be asked to steal clothing to be used in rituals. As their ties to the cult grow deeper and deeper, they may finally be directed to participate in human sacrifice. As renowned psychologist Dr. Joyce Brothers has suggested, "When Papa says this is something you should do because the whole family will be safe, you do it."[3]

Because of the tremendous potency of cult leadership, there is a fine line between mass homicide and mass suicide. Out of loyalty to their spiritual mentor and to one another, cultists are especially vulnerable to commandments for self-destruction. Not only will cult members starve to death if instructed to do so, but they have been known to take poison, as hundreds did in Jonestown, Guyana, in November 1978.

More recently, Armageddon came for followers of 33-

year-old self-styled messiah David Koresh. On April 19, 1993, the world watched on television as more than 80 members of Koresh's Branch Davidian cult, including 24 children, perished in flames at their Waco, Texas compound. For weeks they knew that doomsday was near; they just didn't know how, when, or by whom their lives would be taken. In any event, they were prepared to follow Koresh to eternal salvation.

The prelude to the final conflagration started on the morning of February 28, 1993. More than a hundred agents from the U.S. Bureau of Alcohol, Tobacco and Firearms raided the remote Waco compound on the basis of evidence that Koresh was stockpiling illegal weapons. A 45-minute gun battle between the ATF agents and those inside the compound left as many as ten dead, including four federal officers. Over the next 51 days, cult members and federal agents competed for leverage in a bizarre standoff. While Attorney General Janet Reno went on television to defend her directives, David Koresh bargained for radio airtime to expound on his religious philosophy. As the weeks dragged on, more and more details emerged to explain the intense hold that Koresh exercised over his followers.

Born in 1959 as Vernon Howell, David Koresh grew up troubled. He was raised by a single mother, suffered from learning disabilities, and experienced problems in school, eventually dropping out of high school. Notwithstanding his many disadvantages, Koresh had one outstanding strength: He was able to recite passages of the Bible at length and to invoke biblical references to argue persuasively whatever position he held. Later, he was able to hold his followers spellbound with powerful lectures from the Bible that often lasted many hours.

It took more than his charisma and religious acumen,

however, to attract and hold devoted followers. Koresh skillfully manipulated their minds through ritual and punishment. He insisted that his Branch Davidians awaken before dawn and march in military fashion before they were permitted to eat or drink. He taught that all the women belonged to him, including girls as young as 12. He insisted that they have sex only with him and no one else, not even their spouses. Because he preferred his women lean, Koresh placed them on meager diets of popcorn and fruit. He also forced them to wear both their hair and their skirts long to conform with his image of womanhood. Koresh eventually "married" 19 of his followers and fathered at least ten children.

Koresh believed in strict discipline for all the youngsters in the compound. They were restricted from speaking—to be seen but not heard—and they were harshly punished for disobeying. Koresh often beat the children, some as young as eight months, until they were bruised and bloody. And he was equally fanatic about controlling disobedient adults. As if his rituals and regimes weren't enough to maintain order, Koresh carried a Glock 9-millimeter pistol for good measure.

Isolation from "infidels" of the outside world was a critical element in Koresh's ability to establish total control. The compound was situated in a remote prairie, miles from the city of Waco. The more isolated the residents became from their homes and families, the more focused on Koresh they were. He redefined their world, resocialized them, and replaced their belief systems with that of his own. In this way, Koresh came to own them.

The FBI tried to force out the Branch Davidians by isolating them further and harassing them. They cut off the utilities to the compound, controlled all lines of communica-

tion to the outside, and irritated the cult members with
noxious stimuli around the clock, including loud noise and
bright lights. Ironically, the strategies implemented by federal authorities served to intensify the bond between Koresh
and his followers in the compound, and may have made
them more intransigent. They were more than ready and
willing to follow their messiah anywhere, even to their
deaths.

The Waco cult included not only disenchanted youths
in the throes of identity confusion but also mature adults
who were alienated from the mainstream of society and
conventional religion. In today's world, millions of Americans feel powerless to determine their own fate. Instead,
they feel manipulated by big business, big government, and
the media and intimidated by the ubiquitous threat of nuclear war, natural disasters, and AIDS.

Cults can be organized around any theme. Some experts have suggested that satanic cult activity, in particular,
is expanding in the United States and that countless unsolved murders are actually the doing of the devil's disciples. These same experts have also claimed that even certain murders that authorities had attributed to a serial killer
acting alone may in fact be the work of a satanic cult.

David Berkowitz, the infamous "Son of Sam," confessed to killing six innocent people and wounding seven
others as they sat in cars parked on the streets of New York
City during 1976 and 1977. It was widely believed that Berkowitz killed in response to perceived demonic messages
relayed through the howling of dogs. Although many attempted to pass off the satanic elements as a product of
Berkowitz's diseased mind, investigative reporter Maury
Terry, author of *The Ultimate Evil*, contended instead that the
Son of Sam shootings, as well as many other murders

around the country (including the Manson family murders) were accomplished by an expansive network of satanic cults. "The evidence of a conspiracy is overwhelming, and this conspiracy is bound together by devil worship," said Terry. "This has been confirmed in Berkowitz's sworn depositions and in his statements and letters to me."[4] According to Terry's conspiracy theory, Berkowitz killed only two of his victims but served as a scout while his fellow cultists murdered the others.

To help understand Berkowitz's role in the murders, Terry looked for hidden messages in the killer's letters to *New York Daily News* columnist Jimmy Breslin. Consistent with what he saw as a common ploy used by satanists to encode their messages, Terry assumed that Berkowitz would have spelled words backward and used a system of word games:

> I looked at the first phrase, "keep em digging." Why, I wondered, would the ever-careful Son of Sam, so language-conscious throughout the letter, slip into "em" instead of "them"? Maybe it wasn't a slip: "em" backwards spelled "me." The word preceding it, "keep," then became "peek"—as in "look for" or "see." The last word, "digging," couldn't be reversed, but using the crossword or word association approach, it did become "home." In the United Kingdom, as the dictionaries pointed out, a "digging" is a home (often shortened to "digs"). The first phrase now read: LOOK FOR ME HOME.
>
> The next expression, "drive one," offered two possibilities. Reversing the word "on" resulted in "no."—the abbreviation for "north." If "drive" was left as it was, the phrase became: DRIVE NORTH. However, using word association, a "drive" was also a street, an avenue, a roadway or broadway. So the phrase could have said: NORTH AVENUE (street, roadway, etc.).[5]

Turning Berkowitz's seemingly nonsensical phrases into meaningful messages, Terry's interpretation of the Son of Sam letters is clearly intriguing. An important issue can be debated, however: Was Berkowitz really clever enough to have planted these hidden clues? Or, had Terry simply read too much into the ramblings of a semiliterate madman?

In a televised interview, Berkowitz concurred with the cult theory, self-servingly deflecting responsibility and appealing to a higher cause—the coming of Satan.

> In the Bible it talks about this person who is going to come one day in the future called The Beast. . . . In order to allow him to appear, his workers . . . those of us who dedicated our lives to his service, we had to create an atmosphere that would be conducive to his coming upon the world scene. . . . Our goal was to create havoc, lawlessness, create fear, to bring chaos to the city. We did succeed, tragically, in bringing the City of New York to its knees.[6]

More recently, Terry has proposed—based on the word of a "reliable" informant—that the 1990 Gainesville, Florida, student murders may have involved much more than just the passions of a single sexual sadist. Terry has hinted that the five killings were part of a larger scheme conceived by a satanic network involving a number of student slayings on various campuses around the state of Florida. However interesting Terry's hypothesis may be, it has never been substantiated by law enforcement authorities.

Larry Kahaner, author of *Cults That Kill*, has spent years studying the movement and practices of cults. He, like many of the experts, has seen a disturbing trend in satanic cult activity. Says Kahaner, "Crimes involving satanism, and murder in particular, are increasing."[7]

The principles embodied in satanism turn the teachings

of the Judeo-Christian ethic inside out. Rather than "love thine enemy," satanism preaches kindness only to fellow devil worshipers. Rather than "turn the other cheek," satanism preaches vengeance and getting even. Rather than self-denial, satanism preaches self-indulgence.

For those who are hate-filled and distrustful of others, satanism in particular, offers an identification with an omnipotent (though mythical) figure from whom they draw their own personal sense of strength and power. Kahaner has explained that "Satanism promises you that you will achieve power by performing rituals, including wearing robes, chanting, sacrificing animals or even humans, and burning special candles." For this reason, individuals who feel powerless and resentful may embrace some counter-cultural worldview, frequently a satanic one, even if they do not join an organized cult. Their actions then may be patterned, influenced, or justified by the directives of some external force, whether it is a cult leader or writings concerning the occult. Some satanists come together with like-minded cultists in Black Masses to worship and perform their rituals collectively. Others observe their faith more privately without joining an organized group: They chant incantations, burn religious candles, and draw such satanic symbols as inverted pentagrams (five-pointed stars inside circles) and the number 666.

Serial murderers have a particularly acute need for power, one that is far greater than that of the normal population. Thus the principles of satanism, when taken to their extreme, can provide these individuals with a convenient justification for satisfying their need for dominance through murder. According to Steve Daniels of the Wisconsin Department of Corrections, who has studied the connection between satanism and serial murder, "Satanic precepts seem to foster an 'if it feels good, do it' attitude. The twisted mind of the serial killer could certainly interpret this as a license to kill."[8]

During the summer of 1985, "Night Stalker" Richard Ramirez wreaked havoc on the Los Angeles area by entering homes at random and brutally attacking their occupants while they slept. Before fleeing his victims' homes, Ramirez offered his tribute to the "Great Satan." He inscribed satanic messages on the walls and even drew pentagrams on the bodies of some of his victims.

Ramirez's murder spree actually began in June 1984, when a 79-year-old woman was viciously murdered in her Glassell Park suburban home. Her throat was slashed, and she was stabbed to death. Accustomed to responding to such homicides in the Los Angeles area, the police regarded the crime as a routine case. Then, on March 17, 1985, a 30-year-old woman was dragged from her car in Monterey Park and shot to death by a total stranger. On the same day, a 43-year-old woman was killed and her roommate wounded in their Rosemead condominium. The survivor remembered the intruder for his long face, curly dark hair, protruding eyes, and discolored teeth.

What nobody suspected at the time was that Richard Ramirez had committed all three attacks. By the end of August 1985, his death toll had climbed to 13. In addition, the 25-year-old drifter from Texas had injured or raped a number of other victims. But the absence of a discernable pattern in his modus operandi and choice of victims contributed to "linkage blindness" and confused police investigators. Ramirez raped, sodomized, stabbed, slashed, shot, and bludgeoned. His victims were young and old, married and single, men, women, and children, and from all races.

On August 25, the Night Stalker escaped in a stolen car

after shooting a 29-year-old man in the head and raping his fiancée. Three days later, the police recovered the stolen vehicle complete with a set of fingerprints, which they traced to Richard Ramirez. They immediately issued an all-points bulletin and gave the suspect's mug shot to the media. Ramirez's photo was widely publicized, appearing on the front page of every major newspaper in southern California as well as on all local television newscasts. At a press conference, the serial killer's name was announced for the first time.

The next day was the last day of freedom for the Night Stalker. It seemed as if every citizen in east Los Angeles recognized his face. Showing himself in public, Ramirez was vigorously chased on foot by angry residents who were eager to put him in the hospital, or maybe in his grave. Indeed, the police arrived just in time to save his life. The apparently fearless and diabolical Night Stalker who for many months had terrified the people of southern California had overnight been turned into a cowering and frightened victim. As an officer prepared to handcuff him, the serial killer raised his hands over his head and begged: "Save me. Please. Thank God you're here. It's me. I'm the one you want. Save me before they kill me."[9]

When arrested for the string of murders, Ramirez claimed satanic inspiration. His palm bore the tattooed image of a pentagram. In court, Ramirez loudly proclaimed his allegiance to Satan and blamed his murder spree on the allegedly satanic lyrics in the record "Highway to Hell" by the heavy-metal group AC/DC.

Ramirez could hardly be described as the "boy next door." Yet even when seemingly normal people commit atrocious acts, friends and neighbors often search for extraordinary circumstances that might have driven them to behave in such an uncharacteristic way. The specter of satanic worship is frequently invoked to try to explain otherwise inexplicable behavior.

For example, the residents of the sleepy town of West Memphis, Arkansas, were at a loss to understand the arrest of three local teenagers on suspicion of savagely murdering three 8-year-old boys who had been out for a bike ride. It wasn't just the act of multiple murder that shocked the townsfolk, but the grotesque nature of the crimes themselves. The three slain youngsters had been found hog-tied with shoelaces, and with their skulls fractured. One victim's genitals had been entirely carved out, and another had suffered stab wounds to his penis. Two of the boys had been drowned, and the boy whose genitals had been excised bled to death. According to the medical examiner, all three victims appeared to have been raped; the third boy had been raped and sexually mutilated while still alive.[10]

On June 9, 1993, days after the arrest of the three suspects, the *Memphis Commercial Appeal* published portions of a 27-page statement from one of the teenagers in which he described bizarre, cultlike rituals that he and his friends had performed. "We go out and kill dogs and stuff," said 17-year-old Jessie Lloyd Misskelley, Jr., "and then we carry girls there [to the woods] . . . and we have an orgee [*sic*]."[11] According to Misskelley, in order to be accepted by his buddies, each had to barbecue a freshly slain canine and then eat its back leg. Rumors spread through West Memphis that one of the three suspects was a devil worshiper who frequently dressed in black and was known to carry a cat's skull.

News references to cult activity and satanic symbolism gave the incredulous public a focal point for speculation. Perhaps the murders involved the activities of a satanic cult in their midst. Maybe that could account for the gruesome and macabre nature of the crimes. It is doubtful we will ever know the full extent to which satanism influenced the West Memphis slayings. Were the killers local teenagers whose youthful experiments with the mysteries of the occult got out of hand? Or were they truly on the road to becoming committed disciples of Satan who would kill in their hero's name?

Satanism may have been a critical motivating factor in cult murders like the Matamoros slayings or for serial killers like Ramirez. We should be careful, however, not to exaggerate the influence of satanism on multiple murder. Satan is only one of many external forces that killers have been known to use in order to excuse their murderous behavior. Members of the Manson family blamed LSD, and Ted Bundy blamed pornography. For some killers, devil worship may be merely a convenient excuse and incidental to their tendency to be violent. Their murderous impulses likely existed long before they found Satan. We should therefore be more than a bit skeptical when killers invoke comedian Flip Wilson's famous line, "The devil made me do it."

9

For Love, Money, or Revenge

During the early morning hours of March 26, 1990, New York's Happy Land Social Club was swinging, packed from wall to wall with Spanish-speaking immigrants who, after escaping political or economic repression, had settled in the Bronx. It was three o'clock, but drinking, music, merriment, and laughter filled the small club—so much so that no one paid much attention to the two people quarreling loudly in a corner.

Thirty-six-year-old Julio Gonzalez, a Cuban refugee who came to the United States in 1980 on the Mariel boatlift, was furious with his girlfriend, Lydia, who worked at Happy Land. The coat-check girl and part-time bartender wanted nothing more to do with her old boyfriend; their seven-year relationship was over, and she told him so in no uncertain terms. But Julio wouldn't accept the rejection. If he couldn't have Lydia, nobody would. He ran from Happy Land to an all-night service station, where he bought $1 worth of gasoline. He then rushed back to the club to set it ablaze.

The 92 unsuspecting people inside the building were

still having a good time when the unemployed Cuban refugee returned to get even. Without warning, flames began to envelop the small building, and smoke billowed through the crowded rooms. Panic-stricken customers tried in vain to exit through the narrow front door, but most of them were overcome by smoke or trampled to death. Ironically, Julio's girlfriend, the inspiration for this vengeful act, was one of only five survivors. After confessing to the mass murder, Julio Gonzalez tried to explain his motivation. "I got angry," he said. "The devil got into me and I set the place on fire."[1]

Julio Gonzalez killed 87 innocent victims, yet he would hardly make most people's list of notorious mass murderers. Part of the reason for Gonzalez's obscurity probably stems from the fact that he and his victims were impoverished Hispanics, many of whom were new to the country. Minority crime generally does not receive the same level of attention or interest as that affecting white, middle-class Americans. To some extent, the lack of publicity given nationally to the Happy Land murders derives also from Gonzalez's use of fire as opposed to firearms. In the minds of many Americans, arson is not associated with mass murder the way that guns are. Much more important, though, is that the Happy Land case was a mass killing or massacre rather than serial murder. Had Gonzalez killed 87 people over a period of several years rather than all at once, he would likely have been as notorious as Ted Bundy. It's not just the body count that counts, it's the style of killing.

Unlike serial killings, massacres do not pose much of a challenge to law enforcement authorities. Whereas serial killers are often difficult to identify and apprehend, a person who massacres is typically found at the crime scene—slain by his own hand, shot by police, or alive and ready to surrender. Furthermore, because of the presence of eyewitnesses and the abundance of physical evidence, even those murderers who manage to flee the scene generally get caught quickly. Julio Gonzalez, for example, confessed to his crime after he was identified by his girlfriend.

Also in contrast to serial murders, massacres generally do not tend to generate a significant level of public fear and anxiety. Before a serial killer is caught, he may be on the loose for weeks, months, or years. Citizens are terrified; they want to protect themselves from becoming the next victim. Each newly discovered murder reenergizes the community's fears. In contrast, a massacre like Happy Land is a single event, though catastrophic. By the time the public is informed, the episode is over. There may be widespread horror because of the large number of people who die all at once, but relatively little anxiety.

Perhaps the most prominent reason for the comparative neglect of mass murder, however, is that it does not have the sensationalism of serial murder. The public, the press, and even professors seem to be drawn more to the sexual and sadistic proclivities of such predators as Ted Bundy or Jeffrey Dahmer. As further evidence that sensationalism is critical, serial murderers who do not engage in sexual sadism (e.g., those who slay in hospitals and nursing homes, or commit serial killing for profit) also remain relatively obscure.

Most people, when asked to imagine a mass murderer, think of killers who suddenly "go berserk" or "run amok." They may recall James Huberty, the unemployed security guard who strolled into a McDonald's Restaurant in 1984 and fatally gunned down 21 victims (most of whom were children) at random. Those old enough to remember may think of Charles Whitman, the ex-Marine who in 1966 opened fire from atop a tower on the campus at the University of Texas, killing 13 and wounding 31 others. Or they may think of Howard Unruh, a former World War II hero who in 1949 wandered down a street in Camden, New Jersey, killing 13 people in 13 minutes.

Fortunately these sudden, seemingly episodic and random incidents of violence are as unusual as they are extreme. Actually, though, most mass killers are quite deliberate, not spontaneous. They do not just suddenly explode. It is highly unlikely that a guy who gets fired by his boss and "snaps" would just happen to have two AK-47s and 1,200 rounds of ammunition in the trunk of his car for just such an occasion. More likely, he would have made arrangements long beforehand to commit mass murder.

A majority of mass killers target victims who are specially chosen, not just in the wrong place at the wrong time. The indiscriminate slaughter of strangers by a "crazed" killer is the exception to the rule. Instead, mass murderers typically slaughter people they know—family members, neighbors, and coworkers—based on a clear-cut and calculated motivation.

Twenty-eight-year-old Lawrence John DeLisle of Lincoln Park, Michigan, was just such a killer. He was undoubtedly a family man, but in a family plagued by misfortune and tragedy. Drowning was a DeLisle family tradition, and so was suicide.

Larry was named after his deceased uncle, who had drowned in 1957 while swimming with Larry's father-to-be, Richard, in Wampler's Lake. Despite Richard's frantic efforts to save his brother, Larry sank in 13 feet of water. Richard never forgave himself. From then on, he couldn't get close to anybody. In February 1988, Richard DeLisle, now 48 years old, was so depressed that he drove his brown

1977 Ford station wagon into the woods and shot himself with a .38-caliber pistol. He had failed not only at saving his brother's life but in his marriage and his business. His suicide note explained that his entire life had been a disaster.

The younger Larry was painfully aware of his uncle's tragic drowning and his father's suicide. He never knew the uncle for whom he was named, and for that matter he hardly knew his own father. Almost from birth, he was raised by his grandparents. His mother left when he was 1, and from then on, his father had very little to do with him. The only "gift" he ever got from his dad was the Ford station wagon in which he had taken his own life.

According to a relative, Larry "felt a closeness with his father when he was in that car that he never felt when he was growing up"; he "felt at peace . . . behind the wheel of this car."[2] But Larry didn't always see his father's car in such an affectionate light. He actually hated the car, and only took it because it was free. It needed frequent repairs and even carried bloodstains from his father's suicide that had never quite washed out.

Larry's bitterness toward the car was actually more a reflection of his feelings toward its previous owner. "He was a son-of-a-bitch, an asshole," DeLisle said as he tearfully recalled the memory of his dad. "He blew his fucking brains out and didn't say goodbye."[3] But Larry's anger toward his dad long predated the suicide. From Larry's point of view, his father was unfairly critical of him. "I could never measure up to him. You know what he called me? Pussy. I couldn't hit him back. I wanted to. I should have."[4] On August 3, 1989, though, Larry must have felt especially close to his father when he drove his Ford through two wooden posts at the end of Eureka Road in Wyandotte, Michigan, and sank it to the bottom of the Detroit River.

It was a particularly hot and humid Thursday evening, even for August. To escape the heat, Larry took his wife Suzanne and their four kids—8-year-old Brian, 4-year-old Melissa, 18-month-old Kadie, and 10-month-old Emily—out for a drive and some shopping. Larry also wanted to escape, at least for a short time, the burdens of his financial problems. DeLisle owed $18,000 in charge accounts, medical bills, and loans. Things were so bad for him that he couldn't make the payments on his life insurance policy and was forced to move his family into his brother's home, where they lived rent free. He also had to sell his new Aerostar wagon and instead drove his late father's car.

Notwithstanding his financial problems, or perhaps because of them, DeLisle was a hard worker, frequently putting in more than 50 hours a week on the job. He often came home late from work, tired and depressed, yet his face would light up in a big smile when he was greeted at the front door by his wife and kids. As a service manager for a tire store, he earned a $33,000 annual salary. But he spent every penny that he made, and much more, trying to make his family happy. He never drank or smoked; whenever he wasn't working, DeLisle was with Suzanne and the children. He loved to take them on day trips to the zoo in Toledo or in Detroit, or simply going out for ice cream together. He loved his family so much that he couldn't bear to see them suffer the hardship and embarrassment of debt or of having to freeload off his brother.

On this sultry summer evening, the family would be together for the last time. DeLisle stopped at a drugstore and waited in the hot car with the screaming baby while his wife took the other kids inside to buy a treat. At the checkout counter, Suzanne rummaged through her pocketbook for enough loose change to pay for a few cookies. Meanwhile,

Larry turned the car around on Eureka Road so it pointed in the direction of the river.

As soon as his family returned to the car and the kids were safely strapped into their seats in the back, DeLisle put his foot down. He was tired, hot, annoyed with his screaming baby, and generally fed up with his life. He wanted some peace and quiet, and he thought to himself, "I just want it to be over. There has got to be an afterlife that's better than this hellhole."[5] He contemplated the idea of mercifully putting his wife, his children, and himself out of their misery.

Without thinking twice, Lawrence DeLisle pushed as hard as he could on the gas pedal, held both hands firmly on the wheel, and aimed the wagon down Eureka Road straight for the river. "I can't get my foot off; I can't get my foot off!" he screamed, pretending that he had no control. Suzanne, realizing that they were doomed, tried to grab the wheel. She then reached over to shift the car into neutral and turn off the ignition, but she was too late. Racing at 45 miles an hour, the car plunged headfirst through the wooden barricade and into the drink. Because of the river's strong current, the car flipped over onto its roof before settling on the bottom.

Submerged in 30 feet of water, Larry responded instinctively to save his life. Asked why he changed his mind about committing suicide, DeLisle later explained, "Your pilot mechanism says, 'You can't breathe. You are sucking water. Float, fucker!'"[6]

Larry and Suzanne both managed to extricate themselves through open windows in the front seat. According to a witness, Larry surfaced just a few moments after the car hit the water; "He was just sitting, treading water." Meanwhile Suzanne was screaming, "My babies! Get my babies!"[7] The younger DeLisles were not so fortunate, however. All four children drowned while still strapped securely in their seats.

Larry DeLisle's suicide plot had instead become a mission of murder. During his trial for the deaths of his four children, DeLisle claimed that it had been an accident, retracting his earlier confession to the police. He maintained that leg cramps had prevented him from lifting his foot from the accelerator pedal and that he had struggled in vain to swerve away from the water.

Witnesses to the "accident" saw it quite differently. They reported that the car drove straight as an arrow toward the river. Further contradicting DeLisle's defense, the police observed that there were no skid marks left on the pavement. One expert testified in court that the six-foot-wide vehicle only barely swiped one of the wooden posts, spaced six and one-half feet apart. Given the high rate of speed at which he was moving, DeLisle would appear to have intended to direct his car into the river.

The public was decidedly unsympathetic. The police received many angry phone calls disputing DeLisle's side of the story. One caller warned the police that he would bring hundreds of people to protest if justice wasn't served. Outside the courthouse, spectators screamed, "Fry the bastard, kill him!" as DeLisle was being escorted away from his arraignment. The police "should take a big brick, tie it around his neck, and drown him down there four times," exhorted one irate onlooker. "He don't need no day in court."[8]

Despite the tragic death of her four children and the incriminating evidence that implicated her husband, Suzanne DeLisle stood by her man. "Even though the police feel that they know exactly what happened, they were not present—I was," she testified. "I remember the few seconds

1. Florida's wailing wall. Students at the University of Florida painted a special tribute to the memories of five murdered college students amidst the grafitti along a concrete wall on Gainesville's 34th Street. While in town for Danny Rolling's trial, George and Ricky Paules, parents of Tracy Paules, visited the site, leaving flowers at the base of the wall (Oscar Sosa, *Gainesville Sun*).

2. Death train. On December 7, 1993, an enraged mass killer turned the 5:33 commuter train to Hicksville into a slaughterhouse. Thirty-five-year-old Colin Ferguson, a native of Jamaica, was arrested at the scene and later charged with six counts of murder (*Newsday*, Los Angeles Times Syndicate).

3. The strong silent type. Without uttering a word of explanation, Ronald Gene Simmons was executed by the state of Arkansas for murdering his entire family (Dan Pierce, *Russellville Courier-Democrat*).

4. A caged animal. Russian serial killer Andrei Chikatilo watched his trial from a special cell designed to restrain the unruly defendant. Following his conviction for murdering as many as 53 boys, girls, and women, Chikatilo was executed by firing squad (AP/Wide World Photos).

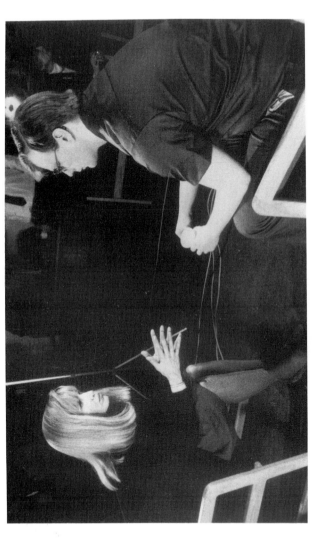

5. Nancy Glass with Dahmer. Serial killer Jeffrey Dahmer became a national celebrity after the grisly discovery of his den of destruction in Milwaukee. Television journalist Nancy Glass talked with Dahmer on January 12, 1992, in an exclusive interview for "Inside Edition" (AP/Wide World Photos).

6. Take back the streets. Following the arrest of confessed serial killer Joel Rifkin, women's groups staged a rally at the Jack the Ripper Pub in New York's Greenwich Village to protest the slow police response to prostitute slayings (AP/Wide World Photos).

7. Cafeteria killing. Some of the survivors of the October 16, 1991, massacre in Killeen, Texas, were able to escape through a broken window. Twenty-three of George Hennard's victims were not so lucky, however, and perished from gunfire (*Houston Chronicle*).

8. Live from Waco. On April 19, 1993, the world watched on television as more than 80 members of the Branch Davidian cult (including 24 children), perished in flames at their Waco, Texas, compound. Among the dead was cult leader and self-styled messiah David Koresh (AP/Wide World Photos).

9. Murder weapon recovered. The Ford station wagon driven by Lawrence John DeLisle of Lincoln Park, Michigan, was pulled from the Detroit River to be used as evidence in his murder trial for the drownings of his three children (*Detroit Free Press*).

before impact, and I know what happened. I believe in his innocence. The police . . . chose to overlook the obvious and look for something else: murder."[9]

The jury was unconvinced by Larry DeLisle's account, and it convicted him on four counts of murder and one count of attempted murder. Prior to sentencing, DeLisle made a last-ditch effort to convince the judge of his innocence. "My children were the greatest gifts my wife and I have ever shared," he maintained. "I could never hurt them, never. I loved them with every fiber of my being; they were my life."[10] Despite his sorrowful denial of responsibility, the judge gave DeLisle the mandatory sentence—life without the possibility of parole. Detective Sergeant Daniel Galeski reflected on DeLisle's motivation for killing his four children and attempting to take his own life and that of his wife: "He thought they'd all be together in the afterlife. It just didn't work out that way."[11]

Detective Galeski pinpointed one of the motivations underlying a number of family massacres: More than a few mass killers feel so desperate and unhappy that they see death as the only salvation. Life on earth is so horrible, they reason, that their loved ones also will be better off dead. Mass murder thus can be a perverted act of love. In what psychiatrist Shervert Frazier calls "suicide by proxy," the killer sees his loved ones as an extension of himself. He feels personal responsibility for the well-being of his wife and children and sees no other way out of his predicament. He may be depressed or despondent, but he is not necessarily deranged.

Lawrence DeLisle's instinct to survive overpowered his planned murder-suicide. Most who attempt to commit suicide by proxy are, like 37-year-old Hermino Elizalde of Chicago, better on the follow-through. By May 1990, Elizalde, described by friends as a devoted father, had become hopelessly despondent over his recent firing from his job as a welder's helper. Even more, he was deeply concerned that his estranged wife might take custody of his four daughters and one son, whom she accused him of mistreating. According to police, Hermino Elizalde had told friends that he would rather kill his children than "let them go."

The devoted father purchased a gallon of gasoline from a filling station some three blocks from his apartment. Returning home, Elizalde doused his sleeping children with gasoline and set them afire one at a time. When he was sure they were dead, he set himself on fire. By killing them all, Elizalde felt assured that they would be reunited in a better life after death.

A twisted sense of love and responsibility, however, clearly cannot explain many cases of mass murder. Why would a 31-year-old former postal worker, Thomas McIlvane, go on a rampage in Royal Oak, Michigan, killing four supervisors before shooting himself in the head? And what would provoke a 28-year-old graduate student, Gang Lu, to execute five others at the University of Iowa before taking his own life? Finally, why would 35-year-old Colin Ferguson open fire on a crowded Long Island train, killing six commuters? The common denominator in these three cases is the killer's desire to execute his enemies, real or imagined, for the sake of sweet revenge. Revenge—the desire to get even for perceived mistreatment by family members, a company, or a whole category of people—is by far the most frequent motivation for mass murder. In all forms of revenge-motivated mass murder, the perpetrator's objective is to punish all those whom he holds responsible, directly or indirectly, for his failures and disappointments.

On August 20, 1986, the morning after being reprimanded for poor job performance, 44-year-old Patrick Henry Sherrill "gave notice" in a most unconventional way. Arriving at the post office in Edmond, Oklahoma, at 6:45 a.m., the part-time letter carrier was dressed in his blue postal uniform and lugged his leather mail bag over his shoulder. The pouch was full, but not with letters. It contained an arsenal of weapons and ammunition with which Sherrill intended to even the score.

Sherrill's first victim was a supervisor who had threatened his job. He then opened fire on his coworkers as they sorted the day's mail. Stunned postal workers dove for cover behind bags of mail and sorting cases as the gunman maneuvered his way through the building in search of additional victims. There was little except their prayers to protect those trapped inside as they listened from their hiding places (in broom closets and under tables) for approaching gunfire. The barrage of bullets finally ended—in the nick of time for some, but too late for others—when Sherrill fired a fatal shot to his own head. By then, he had already killed fourteen and wounded another six.

Like many other mass killers, Sherrill's assault was more selective than random. He made sure ahead of time that the one coworker whom he liked would not be at work during his rampage. He deliberately started shooting long before the post office opened for business so that he only killed "the enemy"; no innocent customers would be injured. Sherrill's motive, in effect, was to kill the post office.

A third type of mass murder is motivated not by a passion like love or hate, but purely by greed. This form of mass killing is more expedient than expressive. The profit-motivated killer may or may not know his victims, and he doesn't necessarily bear a grudge against them. He commits

the murders in order to eliminate witnesses to a crime, usually robbery.

Even though the January 8, 1993, massacre in Palatine,
Illinois, remains unsolved, it has become increasingly clear
that it was motivated by profit. Anxious phone calls to the
local police reported that several of the employees at the
Brown's Chicken and Pasta restaurant in the normally quiet
suburb of Chicago had inexplicably failed to return home
after closing time. Just before midnight, a patrol car was
dispatched to Brown's, where two officers shined their
flashlights into the darkened building and rattled the windows but failed to locate any irregularities. Shortly afterward Emmanuel Castro, the father of a 16-year-old boy who
worked at the restaurant, officially notified the police that
his son was missing. A police patrol returned to Brown's at
2:30 a.m., but this time the officers entered the building
through an unlocked side door. They found seven murder
victims: the two owners of the restaurant and five workers,
all of whom had died of gunshots from a .38-caliber firearm.
One of the owners had also had her neck slashed. The safe,
containing $1,200 in cash, had been cleaned out.

Police investigators worked with few good leads. At
first, suspecting that the massacre had been motivated by
revenge, they questioned a 23-year-old man who had been
recently fired from the restaurant. After his 2-day interrogation and subsequent release, however, Cook County state's
attorney Jack O'Malley considered the massacre a likely case
of armed robbery. He told the press that the police had no
suspects, that "there is a murderer or murderers on the
loose," and that "businesses ought to take extra precautions."[12] A year after the murders, Palatine police chief Jerry
Bratcher, frustrated over the failure of his task force to crack
the case, reflected, "We had seven people murdered. All of

them were shot execution-style. Our assumption is it was a robbery that went bad."[13]

Because most mass killings are inspired by revenge, it is easy to overlook other motivations, even when they are obvious. Like the Palatine case, the August 1991 massacre of nine Buddhist monks in Maricopa County, Arizona, was initially thought to be motivated by hate—in this instance, a desecration of the group's temple. As additional evidence surfaced, however, it became clear that the nine victims were murdered to cover up a robbery of $2,650 in cash plus cameras, stereos, and other items. According to Alessandro "Alex" Garcia, age 16 at the time of the murders, he and his 17-year-old accomplice, Jonathan Andrew Doody, ransacked the temple to rob it of its contents. The two teens then ordered the victims to lie on the floor in a circular pattern, like the spokes of a wheel. Doody said to Garcia, "No witnesses," and they executed the victims.

Profit-motivated mass killings, like robbery-murder generally, are typically committed by teenagers and young men, often minorities. Revenge-motivated mass killings, by contrast, are committed by older (often middle-aged) white men who have had enough years of disappointment at home or on the job to evoke extreme feelings of vengeance. In fact, 40% of mass killers are in their thirties or forties, compared to a third of offenders who commit single-victim homicide.

Based on our analysis of mass killings from 1976 to 1991, the demographic profile of the mass killer reveals notable differences from that of the single-victim killer in terms of race and sex. Whereas single-victim killers are evenly split between blacks and whites, more than 70% of mass murderers are white. Though men predominate among both groups, the sex differences are more pronounced in mass murder. Nearly 95% of mass killers, versus 86% of single-victim slayers, are men.

The overabundance of men among mass killers (even more than among murderers generally) may stem in part from the fact that men are more likely to suffer the kind of catastrophic losses in self-esteem and social support associated with mass murder. Following a separation or divorce, it is generally the husband/father who is ousted from the family home and, therefore, is the one who is left alone. Job loss also affects men and women differently. Despite advances in the status of women in America, males more than females continue to define themselves in terms of their occupational role (i.e., what they do defines who they are) and therefore tend more to suffer psychologically from unemployment. Finally, men do not tend to maintain close relationships away from the family and the workplace. Thus they are less likely to have the benefit of support and encouragement when losing a relationship or a job.

Men also have unequal access to and training in the use of handguns and rifles. Three-quarters of mass murderers kill with a firearm. Indeed, it is difficult to kill a large number of people at one time using, for example, a knife or club as a weapon. Typically mass killers are fascinated with guns, own large collections of rifles that include military-style assault weapons, and have the shooting skills to use them effectively.

Twenty-five-year-old Charles Whitman, for example had grown up around firearms. His father, himself a gun aficionado, had taught Chuck to hunt when he was a young boy, and Whitman later fine-tuned his marksmanship skills while serving in the marines. The only combat Whitman ever saw, however, was his one-man attack at the University of Texas in Austin. On August 1, 1966, he climbed high atop the tower on the campus and began indiscriminately spraying the students below with gunfire. By the time he was gunned down by police sharpshooters, Whitman had killed 13 and wounded 31 more. The night before he had also killed his wife and his mother.

Whitman's autopsy revealed a walnut-sized malignant tumor of the brain, which was blamed for his "sudden episodic attack." Whitman's violent behavior, though, was anything but episodic or sudden. In fact, he had planned the massacre far in advance and had begun killing deliberately the night before the tower sniping. Moreover, no one can say with certainty what role the tumor may have played, because its location in the brain was obscured by the gunshots that ended his life. Although the debate over Whitman's behavior will never be settled, the assumption that the tumor was responsible is clearly not justified. Yet the same kind of reasoning was used to try to account for James Huberty's 1984 murder spree at a McDonald's restaurant. Hopeful that some neurological abnormality might be the cause, pathologists examined Huberty's brain tissue; they were disappointed when the autopsy failed to reveal a tumor or any other physical explanation for his rampage.

Charles Whitman's 1966 assault on the American psyche was widely termed the "crime of the century," reflecting the rarity of such mass murder at the time. Of course, those who saw Whitman's crime as history-making could not have imagined what new and much deadlier slaughters lay ahead in the next quarter century. From 1976 to 1991, for example, there have been some 350 mass murders of at least four people each, claiming nearly 2,000 innocent lives. Whitman's murder toll was surpassed by the murders of 16 in a small Arkansas town in 1987, 21 in a California McDonald's (mentioned above) in 1984, 23 in a Texas restaurant in 1991,

43 in a PSA aircraft over California in 1987, and 87 in a New York social club (see the beginning of this chapter) in 1990. These tragedies have pushed our anxiety to the breaking point. We have witnessed massacres in schoolyards and shopping malls, trains and planes, post offices, and fast food establishments. People everywhere wonder, is nowhere safe?

Several factors have recently coalesced to produce a deadly mix of resentment and despair. A growing number of middle-aged men are losing those aspects of their lives that give them meaning and support—particularly their families and their jobs. A shrinking and more competitive labor market has left thousands of men feeling hopeless and worthless. An increased rate of divorce, greater residential mobility, and a general lack of neighborliness have left many of them very much alone. Though the resulting acts are cowardly and reprehensible, a few of these desperate people feel they have no place to turn in order to resolve their problems except to their guns. The one problem they don't have, of course, is finding a high-powered weapon of mass destruction.

Mass murders frequently occur in bunches, prompting journalists to ponder whether the widespread publicity given to murder contributes to the epidemic of bloodshed. For example, during the fall of 1991, in little more than a month, the United States experienced a sudden outbreak of mass killings around the country. In Ridgewood, New Jersey, a postal worker shot and killed his boss, her boyfriend, and two coworkers after being fired. In Killeen, Texas, a 35-year-old unemployed man shot to death 23 people as they were leisurely eating lunch in a cafeteria. In Concord, New Hampshire, a man strangled and smothered to death his three young daughters to prevent his wife from having custody of them. On the campus of the University of Iowa, a 28-year-old Asian doctoral student gunned down five people after being denied a prestigious prize in physics. And in Royal Oak, Michigan, a 31-year-old postal worker killed four supervisors and then shot himself in the head.

Another rash of massacres occurred during a two-week interval just prior to Christmas 1993. An unemployed man shot and killed three workers at an Oxnard, California, unemployment office as well as a police officer during the getaway. Days later, a vengeful gunman murdered six commuters on a Long Island subway car. In an apparent act of revenge, a disgruntled ex-employee of a Chuck E. Cheese restaurant in Aurora, Colorado, allegedly killed four employees shortly after closing. And a middle-aged man shot up a parking lot at a Wal-Mart store in Hugo, Oklahoma, killing himself and two others.

It is truly more than coincidence that so many multiple murders cluster within a relatively short time frame. For a few disturbed individuals, well-publicized mass killings can provide a source of role models for their own behavior, even inspiring dreams of stardom. In September 1988, James Wilson of Greenwood, South Carolina, went on a shooting spree at a local elementary school. When the police searched his home, they discovered that Wilson had pinned to his wall a photo of his hero, Laurie Dann (who a few months earlier had committed a similar crime at a school in Winnetka, Illinois), taken from the cover of *People* magazine. Within days of the widely publicized shooting spree on a Long Island Rail Road (LIRR) train in December 1993, two men were arrested for making threats of violence against LIRR employees and passengers. Similarly, mass killer George Hennard had a documentary about James Huberty's 1984 rampage at a McDonald's restaurant in San Ysidro,

California, in his collection of videotapes. Hennard's 1991 attack at the Luby's Cafeteria in Killeen, Texas, resulted in the deaths of 23 customers, two more than his predecessor had killed in San Ysidro.

Some mass killers are quite explicit about the copycat influence of another case on their own behavior. Thirty-five-year-old Ridgewood, New Jersey, postal worker Joseph Harris, for example, was clearly inspired by the vengeful act of another postal worker several years earlier. On October 9, 1991, Harris dressed in black fatigues and armed himself with an Uzi assault rifle, a .22-caliber machine gun, and a variety of knives, swords, and explosives. His first stop was the home of his former supervisor, Carol Ott, where he slashed her to death and fatally shot her fiancé. Next on his list of wrongdoers was the post office itself: Arriving at two in the morning, he shot and killed two mail handlers who had just come to work for the night shift. After a $4\frac{1}{2}$-hour standoff with the SWAT team, Harris finally surrendered.

Following his arrest, the police searched Harris's residence, a cramped attic room that he rented in nearby Paterson. In addition to a variety of explosives, the police found a two-page "suicide" note that detailed the embittered man's plan. Harris described his grudge against the post office and specifically referred to Patrick Sherrill, who killed 14 employees in 1986 at the Edmond, Oklahoma, post office.

During the summer of 1990, New York City was terrorized by an unidentified masked man who copied one of the most intriguing serial killers in the annals of American crime—San Francisco's Zodiac Killer. New York's "Zodiac Shooter" shot individual pedestrians in the back on four separate occasions corresponding to an astrological schedule reminiscent of his role model in California. Also like the original, the Zodiac imitator sent taunting letters to the local press, giving them cryptic astrological clues indicating when he intended to strike next. Not so coincidentally, perhaps, the New York attacks closely followed the release of a paperback edition of Robert Graysmith's *Zodiac*, detailing the still-unsolved San Francisco killing spree.

In many ways, though, the New York copycat did not measure up to his idol. He lacked any sophistication or depth in his understanding of astrology. Not only were his astrological references inaccurate, but his writing was illiterate. More importantly, unlike the San Francisco killer, who in all likelihood enjoyed slaying dozens of people, the New Yorker may have only sought the notoriety. Although he shot his victims at close range, the New York gunman apparently never aimed to kill, nor did he fire more than once. Murder did not appear to be his motive. When one victim died as a result of medical complications, the Zodiac Shooter was never heard from again.

In the case of the Zodiac Shooter, a serious journalistic account of a real case of multiple murder inadvertently became his manual. This, of course, was not author Graysmith's intent, nor could he possibly have anticipated that an unstable New Yorker would find his words inspirational. Some killers may even have been encouraged by the Bible. For example, according to neighbors, accused mass murderer Colin Ferguson ranted and raved about racial discrimination as he read loudly from the Scriptures. It would, of course, be nonsensical to blame the Bible for promoting the crime that Ferguson allegedly committed on the Long Island Rail Road.

In contrast, a recent satire by Lonnie Kidd might recklessly, albeit unwittingly, put a stamp of approval on murder. His 1992 book entitled *Becoming a Successful Mass Murderer or Serial Killer: The Complete Handbook* might be easily misunderstood as a how-to book by people who are looking for an excuse to kill. In a section called "To Get Rid of Your Children, Your Spouse's Children, Other's Children," for example, Kidd suggests the following:

> You will have no problem finding lots of brat children to kill. They are also easily convinced to go off alone with you. You could easily beat them to death. Kick and stomp their little faces and heads into the ground! Hear them promise to be good little boys and girls; but, you know better! They will continue to be little brats if you do not do away with them.[14]

In a disclaimer, the author suggests that his book is "a way of calling attention to very serious phenomenon [*sic*] in a satirical manner." Notwithstanding the legitimacy of his avowed objective, not all of Kidd's readers will possess the sophistication needed to get the joke. Those who are already predisposed to mayhem and murder might instead find plenty of encouragement in the pages of Kidd's troubling manual.

10

Till Death Do Us Part

Christmas Day, 1987, was wet and cold for rural Pope County, Arkansas. It had rained off and on for most of the week, and the Arkansas River was unusually high. Forty-seven-year-old Ronald Gene Simmons spent the holiday alone, puttering around his run-down four-bedroom mobile home, which was anchored at the top of a hill 7 miles north of the tiny town of Dover. His 13 acres of land were situated well off the beaten path in a densely wooded area, cut off from the view of any neighbors. An imposing cinder-block wall, 50 feet long and 4 feet high, insulated the house from the main road. The wall served as a symbolic barrier in case the "No Trespassing" signs and long muddy driveway failed to discourage visitors. Inside the Simmons home, the phone, heat, and toilet had not worked for months. Scores of plastic bottles filled with water, used in place of plumbing, were scattered along the baseboards of the kitchen. Dirty pots and pans remained on the stove, and rubbish and old toys littered the living room.[1]

In sharp contrast to the disarray, the house was meticulously decorated for Christmas. Ornaments of red, green, and white construction paper were taped to the mantle of the fireplace, on which a tiny creche was displayed. Crepe paper stringers hung from the doorways. Capped with a five-pointed star, the family tree was encircled by silvery strands of tinsel and adorned with multicolored bulbs. Brightly wrapped Christmas gifts were neatly arranged under the tree. It was Christmas Day, but the presents remained unopened. The names on the gifts belonged to the dead.

Gene Simmons's macabre celebration had actually begun several days before Christmas, on December 22. Waking early, he helped his wife Becky get their children ready for school. This was the last day of classes before the holiday break, and the kids looked forward to Christmas parties with their classmates. Becky packed their lunches, and Gene supervised. When the children were dressed and ready to go, their father escorted them down the hill to the bus stop. He waved as the bus pulled away.

Carefully avoiding the ruts and the puddles, Simmons trudged back up the driveway toward the house. He quietly opened the sliding door to the living room and sneaked into the kitchen, where Becky was making another pot of coffee. He crept up behind his wife and, without hesitating, twice slammed a crowbar into her skull, knocking her unconscious. Simmons then entered his wife's bedroom, where their 3-year-old granddaughter Barbara lay fast asleep. He wrapped a yellow- and white-striped fish stringer five times around her neck and pulled with all his might. The girl was much too young to put up a struggle.

Twenty-six-year-old Ronald Gene Jr., slumbered peacefully in the adjoining bedroom. Curled up in a ball, he had pulled the blanket to his chin to protect against the extreme cold. But there was no protection from his father. The elder

Simmons quietly entered the room and hovered over the bed, pausing a moment to contemplate his next victim. Without awakening him, Simmons raised the crowbar and brought it down forcefully against the back of his son's head. He then shot him five times with a .22-caliber revolver. Simmons then returned to the kitchen, where Becky's motionless body lay sprawled on the floor. He bent over and put two slugs in her face.

Simmons hurried to clean up before the other children returned home from school. He dragged the bodies of his three victims some 40 yards behind the house to a large dirt pit. Measuring 6 feet in length and 5 feet in depth, the hole had been dug by the Simmons children months earlier when the ground was soft, ostensibly as a pit for an outhouse. One at a time, Simmons lowered the bodies of his wife, son, and granddaughter into the grave. But he didn't cover it yet. There was more work to be done.

In the afternoon, Simmons greeted his children—Loretta, age 17, Eddy, age 14, Marianne, age 11, and Rebecca, age 8—as they got off the school bus. They hurried up the driveway with eager anticipation. School was out for vacation, and their dad had promised them a "special holiday gift."

Simmons instructed the children to wait in the car for their turn to receive the surprise. The youngest, Rebecca, was first. Innocently she trailed her father into his bedroom, where he handed her a package. As she began to tear open the paper, Simmons grabbed her from behind and viciously strangled her with a fishing cord until her small body went limp. He then carried Rebecca to the bathtub and held her under the water to ensure that she was dead.

The other three children met the same fate. Working from youngest to oldest, Simmons led each into his bedroom to be strangled. He then hauled their lifeless bodies to the "family plot" behind the house and laid them alongside their mother. Loretta was the last to be placed in the grave.

Simmons tried hard to cover up his crimes. First, he doused all seven bodies with kerosene—not to burn them, but to ward off hungry animals and to reduce the stench. Then he filled the grave with dirt, protected it with a grid of barbed wire, and concealed it with a sheet of corrugated tin. The next three days at the Simmons residence were uneventful. Gene stayed at home, talking to no one and patiently waiting to implement phase two of his plan.

On December 26, other members of the Simmons clan, unaware of the massacre of their loved ones, came from out of town for their annual holiday visit. The first to arrive at the family home were Simmons's 23-year-old son, William, William's wife Renata, age 21, and their 20-month-old infant, William, Jr. Although tired from their trip, they hurried through the living room and into the dining room, expecting to greet "Mother Becky." Finding neither food on the table nor children playing with new toys by the tree, they suspected that something was wrong. But before they could solve the mystery, William and his wife were shot several times in the head.

Once he was sure that William and Renata were dead, Gene turned his attention to their screaming baby. Grabbing his tiny grandson, he wrapped a cord tightly around his small neck. He repeatedly yanked on the ligature, long after the boy had taken his last breath. Just to be sure, Simmons then submerged William, Jr., in a tub of water, as he had done with his own children days earlier.

Later that afternoon, Gene Simmons's eldest daughter, Sheila, age 24, arrived with her husband, Dennis McNulty, age 33, and their children, Sylvia, age 6, and Michael, 21 months. While Dennis unpacked the car, Sheila and the kids entered the house, expecting to find a celebration well under way. Instead they witnessed the scene of a gruesome massacre and soon became the victims of another.

Sheila removed her overcoat and walked into the living room to enjoy the Christmas tree and holiday decorations. Turning around, she spotted her younger brother's lifeless body lying in a pool of blood on the floor of the dining room. Just as she yelled out, her father rushed into the room and shot her at close range six times in the head. Upon hearing the sound of gunshots, Dennis dropped the suitcases and raced into the house, only to become the next victim. Attempting to disarm his father-in-law, he struggled heroically but in vain. After a few moments, Simmons managed to place his .22-caliber gun to Dennis's temple and squeeze the trigger, blowing his brains out with a single bullet. Sylvia fled to a bedroom to hide, and little Michael, sensing that Mommy and Daddy were hurt, screamed and cried. The children's terror was short-lived; within minutes they were both strangled to death.

By nightfall tranquility had returned, but things were hardly back to normal. Corpses were scattered about the floor, and the walls were splattered with blood in the ghastly aftermath; the Simmons home resembled a darkened slaughterhouse. There were to be no more visitors and no more victims, at least for the day. Phase three would come next.

On Monday morning, December 28, it was business as usual in Russellville, the center of commerce and government for rural Pope County. Situated just south of the Ozark mountains, Russellville (population 17,000) was little-known outside of the state of Arkansas. But that was about to change.

At ten o'clock, Gene Simmons drove his son's brown Toyota Corolla the 17 miles south on Highway 7 from his Dover retreat toward Russellville. He was wearing a flannel shirt, a black leather jacket, and a black straw cowboy hat pulled down over his brow. Simmons wore a determined look on his face. He had several scores to settle.

Simmons's first stop was the law offices of Peel, Eddy, and Gibbons in downtown Russellville. He parked his car near the front door of the single-story brick office building and went inside. Attractive 24-year-old Kathy Kendrick was returning to her reception desk as Simmons barged in. She recognized him immediately and said coldly, "Can I help you?" Months earlier at her previous job, Kendrick had been forced to tell Gene off when his unwanted sexual advances became too uncomfortable. It got so bad that she had notified her supervisor that she was being harassed.

Simmons never hesitated or spoke a word. He stood in front of Kendrick's desk, pulled a gun from his pocket, and aimed. "He just kept shooting and kept shooting," recalled legal secretary Brenda Jones. "There was blood coming out of Kathy's head. It was real dark, red blood, not like you'd expect to get from a cut. It was coming out the back of her head. She was breathing. She had trouble breathing, but she was breathing."[2] Kendrick died a few minutes after being rushed to the emergency room of a local hospital.

In the law office, no one intervened. Some were confused about what was happening; others, fearing for their own lives, hid behind file cabinets. "I thought he was going to kill everybody in the room," said Jones. "We didn't know why he was here."[3] But Simmons left without attempting to harm anyone other than Kendrick.

Simmons then drove 20 blocks west on Main Street to his next destination, Taylor Oil Company. He was looking for his former employer, 38-year-old Rusty Taylor, and found him working in the office. Before a surprised Taylor could ask Simmons why he was there, Gene fired two bullets into his chest. The gunman then tried to escape through the loading dock, but 34-year-old J. D. (Jim) Chaffin, a part-time employee of Taylor Oil, inadvertently blocked his path. Simmons shot Chaffin in the right eye and the bullet passed through his brain, killing him instantly.

It was the first day on the job for 35-year-old Juli Money, a bookkeeper at Taylor Oil. Hearing gunfire, she inched opened the door to her office and saw Chaffin lying on the floor, bleeding from the head. Money also saw Simmons as he stepped over the body. She vividly recalled the "horrid grin" on his face. "He just had a look in his eye like a mad dog," said Money. "And when he looked at Jim on the floor and Jim was bleeding profusely, he showed no emotion or anything. He just turned around and pointed at me and shot."[4] Fortunately for Money the bullet sailed through her hair, missing her forehead by a fraction of an inch. Feeling the "heat from the bullet," she screamed and fell to the ground as though she had been hit. She hid behind a stack of boxes until her assailant was completely out of sight. Simmons fled as quickly as he had arrived: From start to finish, the whole incident took less than a minute.

Gene dashed to his car and sped off. By this time, the Russellville police and the local media had already been informed of the two shooting incidents in town. Hearing a news bulletin on the car radio describing a gunman wearing a black coat and cowboy hat, Simmons tried a quick change of appearance. He removed his hat and coat and slipped on a blue baseball cap and blue jacket. Simmons raced three miles across town to the Sinclair Mini-Mart, a convenience store on the east side of Russellville. Only a few weeks earlier, after complaining that he was being underpaid and overworked, he had quit his job there as a part-time cashier.

Simmons walked into the minimart and immediately blocked the door so that no one could enter or leave. He drew his revolver from under his jacket and aimed it at his former boss, 38-year-old David Salyer, who was enjoying a morning coffee break with customer Tony Carta at a table in the rear of the store. Seeing the gun, Salyer shouted, "If this is a robbery, take what you want!"[5] Money was the last thing on Gene Simmons's mind, however; he shot at Salyer but missed. Simmons then fired at the cashier, 46-year-old Roberta Woolery. She screamed, but he shot her again. Wounded in the cheek, Woolery collapsed behind the counter, knocking over a rack of chips and candy.

With Simmons's attention diverted to Woolery, Salyer tried a counterattack. Shielding himself with a chair, he made a desperate charge at the gunman. "That's when he shot me," remembered Salyer. "My feet fell from under me and I threw the chair as I fell toward him."[6] Meanwhile, Carta, who had ducked behind an aisle of groceries when the shooting began, started pelting Simmons with cans of soda to drive him off. Oblivious to the cans exploding at his feet, Simmons fled as quickly as he came.

Simmons jumped in his car and sped around the corner to Woodline Motor Freight. He walked through a side door and across the office looking for Joyce Butts, age 35, the former supervisor who had scolded him a year earlier about his romantic advances toward Kathy Kendrick. With the same single-minded purpose he had displayed all day, Simmons ignored other employees and headed straight to Butts's desk. He pulled his gun from his jacket and shot her in the heart and head. It all happened so fast that, as one witness recalled, "she didn't have time to scream."

Simmons then turned into a nearby computer room. In the room he found Vicky Jackson, a woman he had befriended while he worked at Woodline as an accounts receivable clerk. Jackson pleaded, "Gene, please don't shoot me. Gene, please don't shoot me." He grabbed her and put a gun to her head but assured her, "Don't worry, I'm not going to hurt you. . . . I just came to kill Joyce."[7] He then laid his gun on a nearby desk and asked her to call the police. "I've done what I wanted to do and now it's all over," Simmons explained. "I've gotten everybody who hurt me."[8]

The Russellville murder spree lasted 45 minutes. When it was over, Kathy Kendrick and James Chaffin were dead, and Rusty Taylor, Roberta Woolery, David Salyer, and Joyce Butts were wounded but would survive. To this day, Butts lives with a .22-caliber slug at the base of her skull, as well as with vivid memories of a tragedy that continue to haunt her. The police, meanwhile, had no clue as to the full extent of the crime until they routinely questioned their prisoner about his family. Simmons's reaction was far from routine: Tears welled up in his eyes, his lip quivered uncontrollably, and he refused to talk. Without even making an effort to secure a warrant, the police hurried to the Simmons home to conduct an emergency search.

The house was locked up tight, except for one living room window out of which Simmons had crawled earlier that morning for his commute to Russellville. Peering through the glass door, Chief Deputy Baker saw what he thought was a body lying on the floor. Sheriff Bolin climbed through the window and immediately discovered the bodies of Sheila and Dennis McNulty sprawled on the living room floor, she by the Christmas tree and he just inside the front door. Both corpses were completely covered with blankets. In the dining room, police found William and Renata

Simmons. Their bodies were also covered, but nothing could hide the obvious. There was blood everywhere, on the walls, on the carpet, and on the Christmas tree. The search team then found young Sylvia dead in the small bedroom of the house, lying face down on a cot. The bedspread, embroidered with large, bright yellow flowers, hardly softened the macabre scene of senseless murder.

Not finding Simmons's wife or the children who lived there, the police knew they had to expand the search to the entire property. Winter days are short, though, and it was already late in the afternoon and growing dark. The search of the grounds had to be suspended. That night, viewers across the country were horrified by television news reports about the crime: "Seven killed in Arkansas's largest mass murder." But that was only half the truth.

The next morning, December 29, the police combed the property for clues and for remains. Searchers soon stumbled on a suspicious-looking sheet of tin that appeared to be concealing something. Pulling it away, they encountered a grid of barbed wire that, for safety's sake, had to be towed away by truck. Then they started to dig. Their first view of carnage was Loretta's T-shirt bearing the words "Jesus Loves You." Digging deeper through the loose dirt, they unearthed the bodies of Becky and all six children. The scene sickened even the most seasoned cop. In what was unlikely a coincidence, the heads of all seven victims were facing in the same direction.

Fearing that more bodies remained elsewhere, the police continued their search of the premises. The outhouses were empty, but the trunks of a Chevy Nova and Chevy Caprice left to rot in a secluded area of the property held more bad news. Opening the trunks, the police found two infants whose tiny bodies had been encased in plastic garbage bags. Their corpses were bloated and waterlogged from drowning. The 14 bodies found in and around the Simmons home, added to the murders in Russellville the previous day, brought the death toll to 16, making the Simmons rampage the largest family massacre and one of the largest mass murders in U.S. history.

What are the conditions that might provoke a person like Gene Simmons to commit mass murder, especially against the very people whom he presumably loved and needed? Why would a family man massacre his wife of more than 20 years, his children, and his grandchildren, then go on a killing spree through the town of Russellville? He had no record of violence, had an unblemished military career of 21 years, was not known around town as a troublemaker, and raised studious, well-behaved children. Five feet ten inches tall, slightly overweight, and sporting a gray goatee and balding head, Simmons looked innocuous. Did he suddenly go berserk? But the crimes of Ronald Gene Simmons were highly selective, well planned, and purposeful. He methodically targeted particular victims, people he knew very well. Like most other mass murderers, he didn't just snap.

Typically the road to mass murder is long, lonely, and rocky; it takes years before the perpetrator sees mass murder as the only way out. The mass slayer suffers a long history of frustration and failure, through childhood and on into his adult life. He has tremendous difficulty both at home and at work in achieving happiness and success. Over time, repeated frustration erodes his ability to cope so that even modest disappointments seem catastrophic.

The lifelong accumulation of upheaval and defeat places the killer "on the edge," so that the occurrence of a triggering event becomes overwhelming. In most massacres, the precipitating incident is either a separation from a loved one, the loss of a job, or the prospect of either. A separation can leave the killer feeling alone, lost, and abandoned. The loss of a job causes him to feel hopeless and profoundly inadequate because he cannot fulfill his role as the breadwinner in the family.

As a child and young adult, R. Gene Simmons led a rather unremarkable life. He wasn't easy to get along with; he also tended to bully his classmates, but not to the point where it was considered a serious behavior problem. Following high school, Simmons spent an undistinguished 5-year tour of duty in the navy. After a failed attempt to make it in civilian life, he enlisted in the air force. He served there for 16 years, achieving the rank of master sergeant and being decorated with five medals for meritorious service, including the Bronze Star.

Simmons retired from the military in 1979, and from that point on, frustration was a central and recurrent theme in his life. He drifted through a string of menial, low-paying jobs. He worked for about 3 months as a records clerk, a year as a waivers clerk, 4 months in a pickle factory, and more than a year as a part-time grocery clerk. Things were getting worse—not better—all the time.

Lacking any authority on the job, Simmons tried to impose a military structure on his family life. In his way of thinking, he was the general, and his wife and children the foot soldiers. As a civilian, he was forced to accept low-status jobs—indeed, positions traditionally reserved for women. But at home, he was the man in charge: the wife did "woman's work," children did the dirty work, and the man of the house called the shots. Simmons ordered his children to carry out tasks of drudgery around the house as soon as they were old enough. For example, the children were forced to dig a deep hole for the outhouse and to haul off heavy buckets of dirt. As it turned out, they even dug their own grave.

Not only did Simmons treat his family as subordinates, he imposed a "fox hole mentality" on them. Friends of the family agreed that he was a strict patriarch who allowed family members little outside contact. According to Becky's brother, Manuel Uliberri, "Simmons fenced her in so nobody could look inside the house. He had her isolated so she could not go anywhere or do anything. The only time she could go out was to wash clothes."[9] He censored his wife's mail, and he did not allow her to use the telephone or to drive the family car. His children were not allowed to stay after school for any activity, to attend the senior prom, to go to church, or even to walk to the bus unescorted. On the rare occasion when a Simmons child was allowed to be with friends, it was almost always at the Simmons home so that Gene could keep an eye on things. Liesl Smith, a classmate of daughter Loretta, once described Simmons as "the keeper of his kingdom."[10]

Many Americans suffer the kinds of disappointments experienced by Simmons, yet they do not kill. But mass murderers are also intensely isolated, physically or psychologically, from sources of emotional support. In short, they are loners. Simmons cut off his family from outside contacts, but in the end he was even more isolated than they. Feeling like the commander-in-chief in the family, he simply could not share the burden of decision making or his problems with his perceived underlings.

Although physically surrounded by family members, Simmons was also very much alone. He often retreated from his wife and children. According to Summer Mooney, a school chum of Loretta's who occasionally spent the night at the Simmons home, "Simmons had one little room he would stay in all the time. It was dark and seemed spooky and it stunk. Nobody ever went in there but him."[11] This was "Gene's room"; he went to this room to hide. This was the place where he relaxed, and the place where he slept alone.

As Christmas 1987 approached, Gene Simmons's life was far from merry. He had reached the bottom of the barrel as far as employment was concerned and decided to quit his job as a part-time clerk at the Sinclair Mini-Mart. Gene phoned his boss, David Salyer, to break the news: "I'm tired of the worst hours and pay of anybody here." Another sore spot was Simmons's lack of success in attracting Kathy Kendrick. His renewed advances toward her had once again been angrily rejected. At first he had sent her cards, flowers, and small gifts. When that failed to get a response, he tried waiting on her front doorstep, which only made her angrier.

Simmons obsession with Kendrick was in part a consequence of his sexual rejection at home, where his wife had refused to sleep with him for the past 6 years. The problem was not so much the fact that she would not have sex with him as the reason why she refused. In August 1981, while living in Cloudcroft, New Mexico, Gene Simmons had been charged with incest after impregnating his 17-year-old daughter, Sheila. To avoid arrest, Simmons fled the state with his family and settled in Arkansas.

Simmons's incestuous relationship with his daughter played a critical role in his deteriorating family life and subsequent act of murder. A web of resentments arising from the incident permanently warped many of the family ties. Obviously, Sheila was bitter enough to have reported her father to the New Mexico authorities. In turn, Gene Simmons felt betrayed by her turning him in, and, later, by her turning to another man.

In the spring of 1987, just 6 months before the massacre, Gene Simmons made a futile attempt to patch things up at home. He convened a family meeting to explain his sexual indiscretions to his wife, his daughter Sheila, and her husband. Gene asked for reconciliation; not believing his sincerity, they mockingly applauded his speech and laughed in his face. It was painfully clear to Simmons that he would never regain the love and respect of his family.

The only thing Simmons felt that he had left was anger and unrequited passion for his daughter. Months after the fateful meeting he decided to telephone Sheila, and he carefully prepared a detailed script that expressed both his love and disappointment. Following some opening comments, he got to the point:

> I want to start by saying, honey, I love you. Please don't lie to me, you have lied to me too much already, I love you, and I will go to my grave loving you. You have destroyed me, and you have destroyed my trust in you.
>
> Like a fool, I had plans of dedicating my life to making things up to you (and I told you so), but you have now robbed me of that plan. It's too late for that to happen now. You have left me with no hope. You were my sunshine, now you've taken my sunshine away.
>
> Do you think it was easy, last spring, getting up in front of everybody and saying what I said, and I got no reaction from you. I sure do hope you think it was worth it being the way you have been.
>
> You have caused me a great deal of pain, suffering, sorrow, and loneliness. You claim D. [Dennis] won't let you talk to me alone, well he is going to regret that and so are you.
>
> In over 968 days, I have kissed you only once. I adored you SMS [Sheila's initials]. I cared for you so much, and it really hurts. I miss you so very much, too. SMS, you have turned your back on me, and pushed me out of your life.

Time has proven you don't care. You chose to work against me instead of with me. I told you—united we stand, divided we fall.

You forget about all the little things I have done for you, and with you. You were my best friend. You were my confidant. You have given me the best years of my life, but you have also given me the worst years of my life.

You are my biggest disappointment in life. If you are trying to hurt me, then you should be very proud of yourself, because you have done a very good job of it.

You have destroyed me. D. thought he was so smart clapping his hands last spring. Listen very carefully to what I am saying. I do not want D. to set foot on my property. He turned you against me. You want me out of your life, I will be out of your life. I will see you in Hell.

My little princess, I may never see you again, and it really hurts. I will end by saying, I love you very, very deeply. Goodbye my precious sweetheart, goodbye my love, goodbye, goodbye, goodbye.[12]

Simmons never placed the phone call to Sheila, but left the script in a safety deposit box at the Peoples Bank and Trust Company in Russellville, perhaps for others to find. Appended to the script was a brief and unexplained note: "Kathy Michelle Kendrick was a contributing factor." Simmons apparently felt a need to leave behind an explanation for a crime that others would surely consider irrational and hideous.

Simmons's family life seemed to be crumbling around him, he was losing control. Although his kids still obeyed him, they now did so without a shred of respect for their father. The children had grown rude and insulting toward him. To a military man like Simmons, this verbal abuse was sheer insubordination.

But insubordination is nothing compared to desertion. Simmons was aware that his wife was on the verge of leaving him and taking the kids with her. In an emotional and revealing letter to her eldest son, William, Becky discussed life with Gene and her plans to leave him:

> I've remembered a lot of what you said, Bill, I am a prisoner here and the kids too. I know when I get out, I might need help, Dad has had me like a prisoner, that the freedom might be hard for me to take, yet I know it would be great, having my children visit me anytime, having a telephone, going shopping if I want, going to church. Every time I think of freedom I want out as soon as possible.[13]

With frustration, isolation, rejection, plenty of scapegoats, and a means to kill, R. Gene Simmons had all the factors needed to precipitate a bloodbath. He was losing his family; his wife, his daughter Sheila, and Kathy Kendrick had rejected him sexually; and he couldn't even keep a part-time menial job. These domestic and work difficulties became the proverbial straw that broke Gene Simmons's back. He chose murder as his way to get even with unfair bosses, unwilling lovers, and unfaithful kin. Blaming others for all of his unhappiness, he thought they should pay with their lives.

In family massacres, the killer often feels some ambivalence about the victims. More than just revenge, Simmons wanted to maintain control of his family's destiny. He preferred to commit murder rather than to be rejected or abandoned by his loved ones. For Gene, their death was better than their desertion, because he alone determined when, where, and how the separation would occur. He decided to get rid of his loved ones before they got rid of him, reasoning, "If I can't have them, then nobody can."

Gene Simmons does not fit the popular image of a mad gunman who runs amok, randomly shooting strangers who just happen to be in the wrong place at the wrong time. It is quite clear that he planned the massacre well in advance, acted in a methodical (even meticulous) fashion, and was careful in his choice of times, places, and victims. Simmons began formulating his scheme in reaction to the spring meeting with his family and continued contemplating murder through the summer and fall. Also, he attacked only certain people in Russellville; others he purposely left unharmed. The massacre was anything but episodic or spontaneous; It occurred over a period of several days and in five separate locations. Simmons was angry enough to seek revenge, but you can be quite angry without being crazy. In fact, had Simmons suffered from extreme mental illness, he would have been too confused to carry out such a prolonged, well-planned, and selective series of executions.

Gene Simmons may have been "insanely" jealous in his relationship with Kathy Kendrick and his wife, Becky. He may have been deviant and depraved in his incestuous relationship with his daughter Sheila. He may have been "mad" about his perceived mistreatment in a variety of jobs. But you don't have to be crazy to be immoral and possessive with other people, and you certainly don't have to be crazy to commit mass murder. Like most family mass killers, Gene Simmons was sane—he knew exactly what he was doing, and he was able to control his impulse to kill until the time was right. He willingly chose the path to mass murder.

Simmons had his day in court—and it was almost literally one day. At their client's insistence, defense attorneys Robert "Doc" and John Harris did not call even a single witness on his behalf. Prosecutor John Bynum went for the most extreme penalty—death—and had no trouble getting it. Wishing to be put out of his misery, Simmons blocked attempts to appeal his death sentence. On June 25, 1990, he was executed by lethal injection.

11

Firing Back

Paul Calden said he would be back, and he was true to his word. On January 27, 1993, 8 months after being fired from his job at Fireman's Fund Insurance in Tampa, Florida, the 33-year-old former claims manager returned to get even. This time, he would be the one to do the firing.

Just before noontime, Calden returned to the Island Center office complex, where he once worked. He was dressed in a dark blue business suit and disguised himself by wearing glasses and greasing back his salt-and-pepper hair. Calden walked through the double glass doors into the ground-floor corporate cafeteria in search of his former supervisors—those whom he held responsible for his extended joblessness.

Most of the Fireman's Fund employees in the cafeteria were too busy munching on Tuesday's blue plate special of chicken noodle soup and taco salad to notice that Calden, known to them as a troublemaker, had returned. One man recognized him, however, and thought to himself, "I wonder what he's doing here. Maybe he got a job with somebody else in the building."[1] Without uttering a word to anyone, Calden strolled to the service counter, ordered lunch, and then sat by himself near the cashier. After finishing his meal, Calden went outside onto the patio adjacent to the cafeteria and made small talk with Denise Gonzalez, a temporary worker, at Fireman's, about his planned trip to Alaska. All the while, he contemplated his other plan and waited.

For more than an hour, Calden paced back and forth between the lunchroom and the patio, drinking a Diet Coke and impatiently watching for his victims to arrive. Constantly scanning the room, Calden finally saw his former supervisors arrive and sit down together at a table near the back wall. As a ploy, he walked over to a trash can next to the managers' table as though to discard his empty soda. He then removed a 9-millimeter semiautomatic handgun from a paper bag under his suit jacket. Taking aim, Calden announced, "This is what you get for firing me," and started shooting.

Calden's first victim was 46-year-old Ronald J. Ciarlone, a controller at Fireman's. Calden placed the barrel of the gun against the back of Ciarlone's head and squeezed the trigger, killing him instantly. Moving around the table, Calden fired ten more rounds within a 30-second period. He murdered 43-year-old operations manager Frank Ditullio with six bullets in the head, chest, and thigh and 46-year-old Donald Jerner, a vice president at Fireman's, with a shot to the head. Human resources manager Sheila Cascade, age 52, and senior underwriter Marie MacMillan, age 56, were shot but survived their wounds. According to Diane Reed, a company employee who was seated a few tables away, Calden "stood right above them and shot them all in the head—except missing one woman. He killed only those he wanted to kill."[2]

As the shots rang out, chaos erupted all around the lunchroom. A 12-foot plate glass window was shattered by the gunfire. Food was strewn over the bloodstained gray carpet as terrified employees scurried for cover. Some ducked behind overturned tables; others found refuge in the kitchen. Women ran right out of their shoes. Only Calden remained calm. Amidst the mass hysteria and confusion, he deposited his gun at the cash register—with four bullets remaining in the clip—and quietly left through the front door. He had successfully accomplished all but the last stage of his deadly mission.

Calden drove his red Dodge Shadow, rented just for the occasion, 15 miles west along the Courtney Campbell Parkway across Tampa Bay to Clearwater. Standing at the 13th hole of the disc golf course at Cliff Stephens Park, he pulled out a Ruger .357 revolver and shot himself in the head. "Nobody knows why he picked that hole," said C. R. Wiley, Jr., a golf pro at the course who knew Calden. "Obviously, he laid himself to rest where he felt most at peace."[3]

Calden's deadly rampage unnerved corporate executives from coast to coast. During the following 2-week period, four more disgruntled employees got similar revenge for alleged unfair treatment, making managers and workers in businesses large and small extremely concerned about their personal safety. These events highlight what would appear to be a growing and disturbing trend. According to the National Institute of Occupational Safety and Health (NIOSH), workplace homicide is the third leading cause of occupational injury death in the United States, claiming 750 lives every year. NIOSH concludes nonetheless that workplace murder is *not* on the rise.

How could this be so, in light of the large number of incidents that have made headlines during recent years?

Could it all be media hype? The NIOSH homicide reports consist predominantly of murders committed by intruders, such as the apparent robbery-massacre in Palatine, Illinois, the execution of four young employees at a yogurt shop in Austin, Texas, as well as hundreds of single-victim robbery-murders of clerks and taxi drivers around the country. These kinds of incidents have not increased, if the NIOSH data are accurate. But the NIOSH data do not specifically address the prevalence of murders committed by disgruntled current or former employees. Available FBI data show very clearly that incidents of employees killing their supervisors have doubled over the last decade, with an average of at least two cases occurring each month in the United States. This does not even include instances in which workers kill other coworkers, nor does it account for the fact that ex-workers often return to the worksite to exact revenge.

What kind of person contemplates solving his employment troubles through mass murder? What is the profile of the worker who decides to take out his frustrations on the boss, if not on the whole company? Like Paul Calden, the vengeful worker is typically a middle-aged white male who faces termination in a worsening economy. He sees little opportunity for finding another job, and he suspects that all the breaks are going to younger competitors—or even to blacks, women, and foreigners. Having grown up in the 1950s and 1960s, an era of unparalleled prosperity, he feels entitled to a well-paying, meaningful job. Rudely awakened from the American dream, he resents that his birthright has been snatched from him, and he looks for someone to blame.

Rarely will a younger worker respond so desperately to a termination. For him, it is the loss of a job, not a career—merely a temporary setback along the road to the success that he expects ultimately to achieve. A 20-year-old may respond to his firing by saying, "Take this job and shove it." He will then just walk down the street and get another job at the Burger King.

By contrast, a 40-year-old feels shoved out by his employer. At this juncture, the middle-aged man expects to be at the top of his career, not hitting rock bottom. He is more likely than his younger counterpart to have dependents who count on him for financial support. In fact, his entire self-concept may be defined by his ability to fulfill the role of breadwinner. This set of self-expectations is a result not just of his stage in the life cycle but also of the ideas with which he was socialized.

Like other kinds of multiple killers, the overwhelming majority of vengeful, murderous employees are men. Men brought up in the 1940s, 1950s, and 1960s were raised in a culture in which the man brings home the bacon and his wife cooks it. Despite changing gender roles, men—much more than women—still tend to judge their self-worth by what they do. If they aren't doing anything, then what good are they? Furthermore, men tend to regard violence as a means for establishing or maintaining control, whereas women generally see it as a breakdown of control. Thus men who suffer psychologically because of the loss of a job are more likely to respond violently in order to "show them who's boss."

The 76 million baby boomers are not babies anymore. For many of them, youthful enthusiasm has been shattered and replaced by anxiety concerning their financial well-being and a growing sense of resentment. More and more are losing their jobs and do not see fulfilling employment alternatives on the horizon. Even those who normally are immune from economic exigencies, college-educated men in their 40s and early 50s, have become financially at risk. For the first time since World War II, the median income of these white-collar workers has fallen, slipping 17% from 1986 to 1992.[4] For this generation, a "midlife crisis" would call for a career counselor rather than a psychiatrist.

These demographic changes are exacerbated by the effects of a postindustrial economy in which desirable middle-income jobs, particularly in manufacturing, are becoming increasingly scarce. For a variety of reasons, including foreign competition and computerization of the workplace, the job market has been worsening. Millions of workers are being displaced by plant closings or relocations and massive corporate downsizing. And those workers who are displaced are finding it more difficult to secure new full-time jobs at similar wages.[5]

In the context of these demographic and economic changes, an increasing number of workers are becoming frustrated in their career goals. There is considerable evidence from both psychology and criminology that frustration tends to increase aggressive behavior. In the work setting, there are actually two kinds of job frustration that engender enough resentment to be translated into extreme violence. First, some vengeful workers have endured long-term, cumulative frustration because of repeated failures in their careers, resulting in a diminished ability to cope with life's disappointments. Although they have likely contributed to their own demise, they feel that they have been treated unfairly by all of their bosses and coworkers. From their distorted point of view, they never get the right job, the deserved promotion, a decent raise. Their firing at a crucial time in their lives becomes the final straw.

For example, Paul Calden's employment problems at Fireman's were nothing new for him. Despite having done well in school, finishing college, and showing considerable promise, he never really made it. Instead he moved from job to job, causing trouble wherever he worked. Just prior to his employment at Fireman's, Calden had been with Allstate Insurance, where he threatened his supervisor by deliberately displaying the butt of a gun inside of his briefcase. This manager was so frightened by Calden that he offered him an enormous severance package.

Other vengeful employees come to feel invulnerable to job loss because of their long-term employment with the same company. From their perspective, they have given their best years to the boss, have unselfishly dedicated their careers to the firm, have helped build the business—and what do they get in return? Fired!

Forty-seven-year-old Joseph Wesbecker was proud of his decades of dedicated service to Standard Gravure of Louisville, Kentucky. The plump and balding man had the reputation as a top-notch pressman, one of the best the company had. He put in so many hours of overtime that he earned the nickname "overtime hog." For all that he had done for the plant, Wesbecker couldn't believe that he was being treated with so little respect. Even worse, he felt that management was destroying him, and so he would have to get them first.

Wesbecker had tried a nonviolent solution to his grievances. In 1987, he lodged a complaint against Standard Gravure with the Jefferson County Human Relations Commission, claiming that the company had harassed him. At the threat of being fired, they had forced him to operate one of the noisy and difficult high-speed presses, even though they knew he couldn't psychologically tolerate the extraordinary stresses of this assignment. In settlement, Standard Gravure agreed to put Wesbecker on long-term disability, then rehire him if and when he recovered enough to go back to work.

Bad luck was nothing new to Joseph Wesbecker. It had plagued him throughout his life, beginning with the death of his father when Joseph was only a year old and of his grandfather 3 years later. While growing up, Wesbecker was moved from house to house; for an 8-month period, he was placed in an orphanage. He was a terrible student who finally dropped out of school in the ninth grade. As an adult, he seemed to slide deeper and deeper into a black hole of depression and paranoia. After two divorces, he had lost close connections with family members, coworkers, and friends. Only his job had remained as a constant source of self-esteem. For years, he had worked overtime on a regular basis for extra income and invested his money in the stock market. But now even his job was gone, and he was idle and felt alone.

Out of work on a long-term disability, Wesbecker had plenty of time to follow events in the news. He was particularly intrigued by Patrick Purdy's January 1989 rampage at the Cleveland Elementary School in Stockton, California, which claimed the lives of five Asian-American children. Days later, the middle-aged Kentuckian walked into a local gun store and paid $349 for an AK-47 very much like Purdy's.

Joseph Wesbecker was every bit as angry as the drifter in Stockton, but his "enemy" was closer to home. Rather than pin all of his problems on Southeast Asians, Wesbecker blamed his bosses at Standard Gravure. They knew that he was a manic-depressive who couldn't take stress, but *they* had turned the stress level up so they'd have an excuse to fire him. Wesbecker was depressed and irritable, experiencing severe bouts of tremors and insomnia. He was so confused that he couldn't even remember his own address. Compulsively he devoured ice cream by the gallon, a dozen Diet Pepsis daily, and box after box of cookies. To counteract his moodiness, a psychiatrist had prescribed both lithium and an antidepressant.

But medication wasn't enough to prevent Wesbecker from making threats (which were not taken seriously) to kill the bosses he hated so much. He admitted to his ex-wife before their divorce that he felt like taking a gun to work and killing "a bunch of people." He had shown one coworker a gun and indicated that he intended to use it. He had also told an old friend from Standard Gravure about his bizarre plan to blow up the company with plastic explosives on a large model airplane that he intended to detonate by radar. He had considered hiring a hit man to murder three company officials, but refused to pay the $30,000 fee. Why should he depend on a professional to do his dirty work? Wesbecker would get even on his own.

On the evening of September 13, 1989, Wesbecker cleaned his firearms. The next morning he awakened early, spread his keys, wallet, and insurance papers on a kitchen table, and set out $1,720 in cash and his last will and testament where his ex-wife would be sure to find them. He then loaded his AK-47, slipped on a tan zippered jacket, grabbed a canvas bag crammed with guns and bullets, and made an unscheduled visit to work. Left behind on the washing machine in the kitchen was an issue of *Time* magazine whose cover story, "Armed in America," described Patrick Purdy's shooting spree at the Stockton elementary school. Wesbecker had folded back the pages so that a photograph of Purdy's AK-47 was open and facing up.

Wesbecker's rampage at Standard Gravure lasted no more than 20 minutes. He parked his Chevy in the lot and, holding his assault rifle to his hip, took the elevator to the third floor. Without saying a word to anyone, he shot his way through the business office and bindery and then moved down the stairs to a basement tunnel, where he opened fire on more coworkers. Walking toward the reel room, Wesbecker encountered John Tingle, a friend of many years, and urged him, "Get back, get away, I don't want to hurt you."[6] His next victim was Richard Barger, a coworker who came down the stairs as Wesbecker moved through the hall. Wesbecker shot Barger five times and then, stepping over the body, took the stairs to the first-floor pressroom, where he opened fire again. As he pumped at least 40 rounds of bullets into his victims, Wesbecker laughed out loud. He then pulled out a 9-millimeter semiautomatic pistol and shot himself in the head.

Many of those shot by Wesbecker actually had very little to do with him or his employment problems; some hardly even knew him. If he was so methodical and selective, even bypassing an old friend, then why were so many innocent coworkers targeted? In a domestic "murder by proxy," a man might slaughter all of his children because he sees them as an extension of his wife, against whom his anger is actually directed. Similarly, in Wesbecker's case, his boss may have been out of town on the day of the shooting, but there were still plenty of the boss's employees around. Seeing these employees as an extension of management, Wesbecker murdered them as revenge against Standard Gravure. In a sense, Wesbecker was trying "to kill the company" in the same way that an estranged husband/father may kill his family.

Perhaps the most diffuse case of murder by proxy occurred on December 7, 1987, aboard PSA Flight 1771, en route from San Francisco to Los Angeles. When the BAE 146 four-engine jetliner took a sudden nosedive into the mountains north of San Luis Obispo, 43 passengers and crew members lost their lives. The death toll included 35-year-old David Burke, who had a few weeks earlier been fired from his job as a ticket agent for the airline; 48-year-old Ray Thomson, the supervisor who had fired him; and 41 others who were merely along for the ride.

During his 15 years with USAir (which owned PSA), Burke had a spotty employment record. Though suspected of a variety of indiscretions both on and off the job, it wasn't until a security camera captured him stealing $68 in beverage receipts that he was terminated. On the day of the airline disaster, Burke boarded the plane for Los Angeles with the clear intention of getting even with his former boss—who regularly took that flight—as well as with the company as a whole. Burke, recognized by airport security as a "familiar airline employee," was able to smuggle his Smith and Wesson .44 Magnum without being checked. He also carried a note in his pocket addressed to his former supervisor:

> Hi Ray. I think it's sort of ironical that we ended up like this. I asked for some leniency for my family, remember? Well, I got none. And you'll get none.[7]

Shortly after takeoff, the pilot radioed to the control tower that there was gunfire in the cabin. Moments later, a flight attendant rushed into the cockpit and reported, "We have a problem here." Burke then barged through the door and confirmed it, announcing, "I am the problem." Following a brief scuffle in the cockpit, the plane accelerated wildly and plunged 22,000 feet to the ground below.

Employment troubles frequently combine with other

significant difficulties—such as family, romance, or health problems—to produce the level of despair and anger required to drive someone to kill. Thirty-nine-year-old Richard Farley, for example, was so obsessed with a coworker, 25-year-old Laura Black, that he would do almost anything to get her.

For almost 4 years, Farley, a pudgy software engineer with Electromagnetic Systems Labs (ESL) in Sunnyvale, California, pestered, threatened, intimidated, and stalked the target of his desires. He found her smile irresistible; but the slim, brown-eyed young woman—herself an electrical engineer in the same firm—never returned his affection. She only wanted her pursuer to leave her alone so that she could get on with her life. Instead Richard sent hundreds of letters, called her at work, bought her gifts, observed her daily activities from a convenience store across from her apartment, joined clubs she belonged to, followed her on the campus where she was taking courses, and threatened to do her harm if she didn't go out with him.

Laura Black held her ground as long as possible without resorting to legal or official recourse. In 1986 she finally charged her stalker with sexual harassment on the job, and he was fired by ESL from his $36,000-a-year position. Not only was it now harder to keep an eye on his loved one, but Richard was also running out of money. Before finding a comparable job in another company, he lost his house, car, and computer and owed $20,000 in taxes. Farley moved from the affluent suburbs into a dilapidated single-story cottage in a low-rent district near downtown San Jose.

Despite these financial setbacks, Farley's fixation on Black continued in full force. When the frightened young woman discovered that Farley had somehow gotten hold of the key to her apartment, she felt that she had no choice but to file suit against him. In early February of 1987, a temporary restraining order was issued by the Santa Clara County Superior Court. Farley was forbidden to come within 300 yards of Black and was ordered not to threaten, follow, or phone her. The hearing to make the restraining order permanent was then scheduled for the morning of February 17. But what Richard Farley did on the afternoon of February 16 made the court hearing an unnecessary footnote to his one-sided love affair.

Farley loaded up with two shotguns, an assault rifle, and four handguns, as well as 1,100 rounds of ammunition, and drove his motor home to ESL. He parked in a lot adjacent to the building in which Laura Black's second-floor office was located. After sitting for awhile to consider what he was about to do, Farley climbed out of the motor home with his arsenal of weapons and walked toward Laura's building. He was about to get even by committing suicide in front of his precious Laura and make her feel guilty. He would get revenge against the company that protected Black and fired him.

In both economic and human terms, the damage Farley actually did was much greater. First, he fired his 12-gauge repeating shotgun at a man who just happened to be coming out of the building. Farley then blasted his way through the glass security door, dropping another man whose desk stood between the gunman and the stairs. A third victim was felled as he stood helplessly in the stairwell, attempting to get to the first floor. Upon reaching the second floor, Farley aimed his shotgun at anything that moved. Horrified workers scattered in all directions, trying to avoid the gunman's bullets. Four more employees—two men and two women—failed to get out of the way in time and were killed in the corridor.

Meanwhile, Laura Black was in her office and heard the commotion outside. Hearing the gunman approach, she slammed shut the door to her office and locked it. Farley raised his shotgun and fired through the door, hitting his beloved in the shoulder and causing her lung to collapse. He then moved on. After a 5-hour standoff, Richard Farley gave himself up to the police after negotiating for a turkey sandwich and a Diet Pepsi. In all, Farley had killed five and injured another four at the Sunnyvale plant where he had once worked.

Most disgruntled employees and ex-employees don't take out their anger on the company. Some may blame themselves, become depressed, and consider suicide as their only option. Others may take out their frustrations on their family or loved ones. But for the one who typically externalizes blame, responsibility always lies elsewhere. "It's not my fault," he reasons. "The boss doesn't give me good assignments, my supervisor doesn't appreciate my work, and the guy at the next desk keeps taking credit for my accomplishments." When cited for poor work performance, he lashes out at those he holds accountable for his failures.

Valery I. Fabrikant was a brilliant engineer and researcher who had come to Canada as a refugee in 1979. His heavy Russian accent was a challenge to his students at Concordia University in Montreal, but not enough to prevent his advancement in the academy. After he spent years as a researcher, the university promoted Fabrikant to the rank of associate professor in 1991. But the 51-year-old educator became increasingly embroiled in a series of heated exchanges with Concordia's professors and administrators. In the fall of 1991, Fabrikant's department recommended that he be fired rather than renewed for another 2-year period.

Although a faculty committee reversed the original ruling and instead offered him a one-year extension, Fabrikant was not appeased. Beginning in the spring of 1992, he sent electronic mail via computer to hundreds of faculty members at universities throughout Canada and the United States, accusing Concordia engineering professors of engaging in fraud. He suggested that his department wanted to get rid of him before he was able to expose their criminal behavior. The following excerpt from Fabrikant's August 20 e-mail message clearly expressed his view of academic injustice:

> I raise question of "scientific prostitution." The main difference between scientific prostitution and "honorary authorship" is that in the first case a completely bogus scientist, not capable of doing any research, hires somebody from developing countries or USSR by using governmental grant. This someone does research in which the parasite supervisor is included as author. The more publications this parasite accumulates, the greater grant he gets, the more people he can hire, the more publications he gets, etc.

In the same e-mail message, Fabrikant proceeded to name names—those of the two "parasites" in his department who had taken credit for work that was not theirs. He then filed a civil suit, claiming that these two colleagues had forced him to list them as the coauthors of his journal articles, even though they had not contributed at all to his research. He also alleged that it was routine among the professors in his department to claim responsibility for the research that they had not done. In Fabrikant's view, all of the tenured faculty and the dean were corrupt and to blame for his academic problems.

Fabrikant was fired by Concordia University in September 1992, but he didn't come back to get his revenge for months. On a muggy August afternoon in 1993, the former professor walked into the Henry Hall building on Concordia's campus in downtown Montreal wearing a dark suit, a white shirt, and sunglasses. He carried three pistols: a semi-automatic Meb, a snub-nosed Smith and Wesson .38 caliber, and a Bersa with an eight-round clip.

Fabrikant took escalators to the ninth floor, where his own office had been located, and wandered slowly down a short corridor looking for his former colleagues. His first victim was associate professor Michael Hogden. Entering his office, Fabrikant fired three bullets from his Smith and Wesson point-blank into the skull of the 53-year-old biochemist. He then turned back into the hallway to an adjoining office, where he calmly pumped two slugs (one from each of his semiautomatics) into Aaron Saber, a 46-year-old professor of mechanical engineering. As his second victim fell to the floor mortally wounded, the gunman moved to the door, shooting Elizabeth Horwood, a 66-year-old secretary in the department.

Fabrikant then moved purposefully past frightened students running for cover or ducking out of the way. Down the hall, he quickly entered the office of 48-year-old Phoivos Ziogas, chairman of the electrical and computer engineering department, and shot him in the abdomen. His final victim was professor Matthew Douglass, 65, whom he blasted twice in the head. When the police finally subdued Fabrikant and took him into custody, the body count was five killed and one wounded.[8] Ironically he failed to include the two "parasites" among his victims, because they were not around during the shooting.

Even disgruntled employees who hold their bosses and colleagues responsible for their misfortunes may not resort to mass murder, especially if they enjoy strong support systems—such as family and friends—to help get them through the tough times. Those who do become violent tend to be loners. They may live by themselves, have recently separated or divorced, or have moved thousands of miles from home. Socially isolated, they regard work as the only meaningful part of their lives. When they lose their job, they lose everything.

By all accounts, Paul Calden had little going for him outside of his job at Fireman's Fund Insurance. He was single, lived alone in a large apartment complex, and seldom had much to do with anyone else. One neighbor recalled, "I've never seen him with another human being, man or woman."[9] Instead, Calden spent his spare time watching television reruns of "Star Trek," playing a game of computer golf, and polishing his cherished white Acura Integra.

Joseph Wesbecker, while on long-term disability from Standard Gravure in Louisville, was similarly cut off from those who may have been able to ease his pain. He was twice divorced and had very tenuous relations with his two sons. Furthermore, while out on disability, he was separated from the few friends that he had at work. For Wesbecker, being out on disability was a triple threat: loss of income, loss of self-esteem, and loss of companionship.

Valery Fabrikant was cut off from his sources of encouragement and support by land and sea. Coming to North America for the sake of a job, he left behind in Russia those who might have been able to help him through his professional disappointments.

On the basis of the profile that has emerged (a middle-aged, isolated man who blames others, particularly his boss, for his failures), can we screen prospective, current, and former employees for violence proneness and act preventively before they take matters—and guns—into their own hands? This is precisely the approach that many companies are taking to try to deal with the growing problem of workplace murder. But although many companies undoubtedly could do a better job of screening applicants, it is questionable that any prediction strategy, no matter how thorough, will pay off. For several reasons, prediction is far more complex than simply following a checklist of warning signs.

In terms of preemployment screening, it may not be feasible or even legal (for reasons of privacy) to assemble as complete a background investigation as would be needed to "weed out" undesirable recruits. In Calden's case, for example, his previous employer would have been reluctant to give him a bad reference for fear of being sued. "I had mixed feelings about it," admitted John Dufel, Calden's former supervisor at Allstate. "I was thrilled that he left on good terms, and I was scared to death I was handing him off to someone else who might have to deal with Paul Calden down the road ... just like I'm sure that the people who gave us Paul Calden probably thought the same thing."[10]

Except for verifying dates of employment, many companies therefore follow the rule that if you can't say something nice, say nothing at all. In addition, the Americans with Disabilities Act of 1990 may even restrict screening on the basis of clinical depression unless it is clear that the job recruit is prone to become violent. Thus if a person like Wesbecker, with a history of depression, decided to seek a new job, his disability could not legally be used to reject him.

Even with a current employee who has been on the job for some time, it is often difficult to determine whether an

abrasive disposition is truly reason for alarm. To his colleagues at Concordia, Valery Fabrikant was a tremendous
nuisance, to say the least, and his collection of e-mail was
an embarrassment to the university. But nothing that he
said or did could clearly have foreshadowed his violent
rampage.

Profiles designed to predict rare events, such as workplace mass murder, tend to overpredict, producing a large
percentage of "false positives." Regardless of the specific
profile characteristics, many more employees will likely fit
the profile than will in fact seek revenge at work. There is a
very large haystack of angry, frustrated employees who
never smile and are always ready to blame others for their
shortcomings and make threatening statements, but very
few needles who will in fact commit mass murder. Moreover, an effort to identify problem workers may actually
create a self-fulfilling prophecy when a combative employee
becomes enraged by being singled out in a negative way. ("I
don't need counseling. You're the one who needs counseling. Actually, all you have to do is to start treating me fairly
and everything will be just fine.")

In the aftermath of a violent incident, of course, survivors tend to question why certain warning signs were ignored. Employees at Fireman's Fund were stunned but not
completely surprised by Paul Calden's vengeful rampage.
During his 2-year stint at Fireman's, Calden had a reputation for being a belligerent hothead. He constantly challenged his supervisors' authority, at one point nearly coming to blows because of a reprimand. He threatened to sue
the company for denying him a raise that he felt he deserved, and he shouted obscenities at a female coworker
who had taken his favorite parking place. He even filed a

harassment complaint because a fellow employee displayed a bumper sticker that offended him—not because it insulted his race or religion, but merely because it poked fun at the mascot of his alma mater, the University of Florida. But these "warning signs" only came into focus with hindsight. Prediction is quite another matter altogether.

12

The Postman Always Shoots Twice

It was August 20, 1986, when 44-year-old part-time letter carrier Patrick Henry Sherrill opened fire on his supervisors and coworkers at the Edmond, Oklahoma, post office, killing 14. His rampage signaled not only a new concern in workplaces everywhere, but a problem that the U.S. Postal Service in particular would be forced to confront on many occasions in the years ahead.

It is difficult to discuss workplace homicide without some reference to the U.S. Postal Service where violence is fast becoming as much a tradition as Bermuda shorts and special delivery. Since 1983, 11 separate violent incidents have occurred in postal facilities around the country, claiming a total of 34 lives. Even so, Postmaster General Marvin Runyon, speaking at a 1993 conference on workplace violence, claimed the United States Postal Service actually has a *lower* rate of workplace homicide than the national average.[1] But a closer examination exposes the fatal error in Mr. Runyon's reasoning. It is quite true that postal clerks are rarely held up for the contents of the cash drawer or even for the latest and hottest stamp issue ("Your Elvis stamps or your life, buster!"). It is also quite true that letter carriers are hardly ever at risk of being fired upon while delivering a satchel of Christmas cards; dog bites maybe, gunshots rarely. But the U.S. Postal Service has clearly had far more than its share of disgruntled employees who attempt to get even with their supervisors. The most striking example was "Black Thursday," May 6, 1993, when unhappy postal workers in both Michigan and California went on deadly rampages.

These attacks gave the American Postal Workers' Union an opportunity to take aim at management in a different way. According to union president Moe Biller, the fundamental problem behind these episodes is the "quasi-military structure and culture" of the Postal Service. Even Postmaster General Runyon seems to agree, having vowed to change the "authoritarian management style" that currently exists. Postal workers around the country have protested bitterly about capricious managers who treat them like children. Some letter carriers have complained that their bathroom breaks are monitored by managers wishing to make certain that time is not being wasted. Other workers have allegedly been suspended or sent home for minor rule infractions, such as whistling on the job. Still other postal employees have reported being spied on by supervisors with an overly aggressive concern for productivity.

Added to this is the daily stress associated with getting the mail delivered on time (through snow, rain, heat, and gloom of night), as well as the little respect postal workers get from the American public, which blames them whenever the mail is late or damaged. Postal workers are often stereotyped as lazy and portrayed in the media in a most unflattering way (as with television characters Cliff Clavin of "Cheers" and, more recently, Newman of "Seinfeld").

More important than the issues of management style and job stress, however, is the concern for job security that is especially prevalent at the post office. Despite civil service protections, many postal workers perceive—rightly or wrongly—that their jobs are on the line because of automation and reorganization, and worry about the implications for their careers. Indeed, what opportunities are there for a fired, middle-aged letter carrier, with his or her skills in sorting mail, toting a leather bag, and driving a low-speed jeep with the steering wheel on the curb side? He or she faces the prospect of going from a relatively well-paying job with the Postal Service to taking a minimum-wage job selling cigarettes at a local convenience store or maybe sorting mail in a company mailroom. On top of this, some postal workers feel a particularly strong sense of entitlement because of their long-term employment, civil service status, and "veterans preference." From their perspective, they have dedicated themselves to the Postal Service, and that loyalty is not being given back in return.

The widespread sense of abandonment has been exacerbated by the current efforts to downsize and streamline the Postal Service. The pressure to turn a profit stems from the Postal Reorganization Act of 1970, which made the Postal Service more independent and forced it to become financially self-sufficient. No longer able to rely on taxpayer subsidies, the Postal Service had to respond to the difficult economic conditions of the 1980s by reducing its work force substantially. Postal workers everywhere felt completely vulnerable. As one angry postal worker recently wrote, "My job is my life. Thus, the U.S. Postal Service is making an attempt on my life."[2]

Thomas Paul McIlvane couldn't have made his intentions any clearer had he mailed a registered letter to the Postmaster General. The 31-year-old letter carrier had been a problem employee for most of his six years working for the post office in Royal Oak, Michigan. He had been given repeated warnings for everything from taking an unauthorized lunch break to deviating from his postal route, from fighting with a customer to cursing at his supervisor. On no less than four separate occasions, McIlvane was suspended from work for periods of one to two weeks at a time. He had a bad reputation for combativeness and belligerence.

McIlvane's difficulties in dealing with persons in charge actually started long before taking a job with the Postal Service. As a marine, he was demoted in rank several times because of unwillingness to carry out the orders of his superior officers. Eventually he was discharged on conditions that were less than honorable, which barred him from joining the reserves as he had desired. Regardless of his spotty military record, however, he was still assured of veterans preference points in civil service hiring by the post office.

The situation at the Royal Oak post office took a sharp turn for the worse in 1990 when a new management team was brought in from Indianapolis. Four supervisors were transferred to Royal Oak following a U.S. General Accounting Office audit that found employee–management relations in Indianapolis to be severely strained.

It was almost inevitable that a person like McIlvane would clash with his new supervisor, Christopher Carlisle. Carlisle was a non-nonsense, "in your face" administrator who, by many accounts, seemed to manage through fear and intimidation. According to the findings of a congressional investigation prompted by the Royal Oak shooting,

"It is reported that Chris Carlisle would stand behind an employee and berate him or her hoping to provoke a response from the employee. If the employee then accosted Carlisle, he would discipline the employee."[3] It was also reported in the congressional hearings that Carlisle was not at all reluctant to suspend or remove an employee even if the action were later overturned on appeal; at least the employee would suffer financially while awaiting reinstatement.

The working relationship between McIlvane and management at Royal Oak went downhill fast. Finally, on September 10, 1990, McIlvane was given a formal notice of removal from his job. Although he was afforded the right to arbitration for possible reinstatement, it took more than 12 months for the appeal to be heard. In the meantime, McIlvane, now on unpaid leave, made frequent and wide-ranging threats of violence against Carlisle and other managers. According to William Kinsley, director of field operations at Royal Oak, McIlvane directed several threats at him, including a phone call in which he said, "Fuck you, faggot postmaster. I'm going to be watching you, and I'm going to get you."[4]

Many postal employees claim to have reported McIlvane's threatening manner to the Postal Inspection Service. Receiving hundreds of threat reports annually, the inspectors have discretion whether to investigate such situations; apparently, McIlvane's verbal threats were never probed. The union representatives who worked with McIlvane on his appeal were also well aware of his threats to retaliate should he lose his arbitration. McIlvane told the local union head, "If I lose the arbitration, it will make Edmond, Oklahoma, look like a tea party," referring to Pat Sherrill's massacre of 1986. Under the erroneous assumption that McIlvane's threats were covered by the attorney–client privilege, the union representatives failed to take action on McIlvane's threats.

On November 12, 1991, the arbitrator upheld McIlvane's removal. McIlvane was informed through a message on his answering machine telling him that he had lost. Two days later, armed with a Ruger .22-caliber semiautomatic rifle and hundreds of rounds of ammunition, he arrived at the Royal Oak facility at 8:45 a.m. During the next 10 minutes, he killed four employees—including his nemesis, Chris Carlisle—and wounded four others. McIlvane then pointed his weapon at his own head and pulled the trigger.

Following its deliberations, the congressional committee investigating the matter recommended a number of changes involving preemployment screening of job applicants, improved labor–management relations, tightened security at postal facilities, and aggressive procedures for handling threats made by embittered postal workers. The only recommendation that focused directly on the issue of job security in the Postal Service, however, was to guarantee speedy resolution of job-removal grievances. Because even the most enlightened and humane management may be forced to terminate postal employees either because of financial exigencies or worker incompetence, much more is needed to stem the rising tide of bloodshed by job-insecure postal workers.

Similarly, although enhanced screening of postal recruits may weed out a person like McIlvane (who had a history of insubordination during military service), it would not reject a person like Patrick Sherrill, whose only "crime" was to be a loner who enjoyed competing in sharpshooting competitions. Nor would tightened security measures, which might have deterred McIlvane from returning to the postal facility after losing his arbitration, have made a difference in the Edmond, Oklahoma massacre; as an employee of the post office, Sherrill was entitled to be there.

Postal officials must do more than pay lip service to humanitarian ideals. Perhaps management should take its lead from the private sector, where responsible companies honor their obligations to people who once worked for them. Outplacement services are critical, especially retraining programs for postal employees whose current skills are not competitive in the outside job market. Indeed, it will take much more than a kinder, gentler workplace to avert future post office massacres.

13

Fighting City Hall

John T. Miller, a 50-year-old "deadbeat dad," murdered four county workers in Watkins Glen, New York, who were responsible for collecting child support money. Having been arrested several times over a span of 20 years for nonpayment of child support, Miller was on the run from a system that he felt was stacked against men like himself. He felt victimized for being compelled to pay $6,780 in arrearages to support a daughter who had matured into her late 20s and was now on her own. Moreover, he had never married the woman who had filed the claim against him, and he even denied that the girl he was to support was his daughter. Still, he refused to consent to a blood test that might have proven his lack of paternity and absolved him of legal responsibility.

After years in hiding, the system caught up with Miller while he worked as a driver for New Era Trucking of North Ridgeville, Ohio. Upset to discover that his paycheck had suddenly been reduced, Miller learned from his supervisor that the court in Schuyler County, New York, had begun to garnish his wages. Frustrated and angry, Miller drove nonstop to Watkins Glen to try to resolve the dispute, which he had thought was behind him. Speaking with supervisor Florence Pike at the Schuyler County courthouse, he was told that "it was no mistake, and there is nothing that we can do."

The next day, October 15, 1992, Miller closed his account for good. At 10:00 a.m. he returned to the courthouse, carrying a briefcase and a duffle bag filled with ammunition. He walked up the stairs and into the child support office on the second floor. It was payback time. Removing a 9-millimeter semiautomatic pistol from his briefcase, he immediately shot 48-year-old Nancy Wheeler, a senior account clerk in the child support unit. Walking across the hall to another office, Miller in quick succession shot Florence Pike, age 50, investigator Phyllis Caslin, age 54, and part-time account clerk Denise Van Amburg, age 28.

Deputy Sheriff Alfred Foote was quick to arrive on the scene from his office on the first floor, but not quick enough to save the lives of Miller's four female victims. After ordering the building to be evacuated, Foote and other officers cornered the gunman in the second-floor hallway, where the latter stood poised with his pistol pointed at his head. Foote tried to defuse the situation by asking the gunman if he needed any assistance. But Miller was already calm, notwithstanding his suicidal pose, and assured the deputy that no one else was in danger. "He told us that people didn't have to hurry," recalled Foote. "They could take their time, that he had done what he had come there to do."[1]

Miller then started talking about the child support payments, and he became agitated. "The people here have ruined my life," he yelled. "I can't get a job or a wife because I owe so much child support."[2] Miller then walked in a small circle as though to find enough courage and pulled the trigger, ending his own life.

Multiple murders aimed at "the system" often appear indiscriminate or random, but even these acts are more selective than they look. Miller chose his victims not because they were directly responsible for his financial plight, but because they represented the system that he thought was unfair and that he blamed for his problems. In today's modern, complex world, more and more people are forced to deal on a daily basis with large, impersonal bureaucratic organizations. When things go wrong, and a client or customer has a complaint, who in the megasystem should be held accountable? In Miller's case, where did the buck stop? The boss who deducted money from his paycheck was only obeying the law. The clerks in the child support office were only carrying out a court order issued elsewhere. And the judge who issued the order had an obligation to impose the law. To get reparations, Miller targeted not any one of these participants in particular, but the entire system.

Mass murder in the workplace therefore is not limited to just embittered employees or ex-employees. Miller's four victims were murdered at their worksite, not his. Disgruntled customers and clients sometimes seek to avenge perceived mistreatment by banks, loan offices, law firms, and courthouses—in short, the system—through mass murder. For this reason, many people on the losing end of a legal battle do not necessarily go after the adversaries who beat them. Instead, they go after the legal system, the unlevel playing field on which they were forced to compete and lose.

For example, 45-year-old George Lott opened fire with a concealed 9-millimeter handgun during an appellate court proceeding in Forth Worth, Texas, on the morning of July 1, 1992. It appeared to those present in the crowded fourth-floor courtroom that Lott was shooting wildly at anything that moved. It appeared that two attorneys who were slain and a third attorney and two judges who were wounded just happened to be at the wrong place at the wrong time.

Lott escaped through the mass confusion only to show up 6 hours later at television station WFAA in Dallas. He wanted to tell his side of the story. Speaking with anchorman Tracey Rowlett, Lott outlined his deep-seated grudge against the judicial system that he believed had been unfair to him. "I sat and I listened awhile," explained Lott in a taped interview. "I got up and I shot several of them. I was shooting at the bench—at the judges. You have to do a very horrible, horrible thing to catch people's attention."[3]

Lott was outraged by the way his divorce had been handled. Two and a half years earlier, a jury had awarded custody of his son, Neal, to his ex-wife. The judgment was later upheld by the Second Court of Appeals in the same courtroom in which Lott had committed the shootings. And Lott's legal problems were not just domestic. He himself was a lawyer, but hardly a successful one by any standard. After graduating from the University of Texas Law School in 1981, he opened his own law office in South Fort Worth, hoping to build a viable practice. Four months later he was out of clients and out of business. For the next few years he didn't work, and he rarely left his apartment except to tend to his fishing boat. By 1988, things had gotten so bad that he allowed his state license to practice expire.

Lott's long-standing frustration with the judicial system came to a head when he lost his visitation rights after his ex-wife accused him of having sexually molested their son on several occasions. A hearing on the sexual abuse charges was scheduled for the end of July. But Lott never faced these charges in court. Instead, he faced charges of first degree murder, was convicted, and was sentenced to die. "This is a horrible thing I've done," Lott admitted on the day of the shooting. "I do expect to be killed for it. I believe in capital punishment. And if anything deserves capital punishment, this does."[4]

While John Miller and George Lott sought revenge against public institutions, other mass killers perceive that money-grubbing, heartless private corporations deserve to "die" for all their wrongs. At one time, the only option available to an irate customer was to file a complaint with the company or with the Better Business Bureau. Increasingly, however, it has become "appropriate" to file a grievance with a semiautomatic weapon.

On June 18, 1990, for example, 44-year-old laborer James Edward Pough called his boss to say that he had some things he had to do that day and wouldn't be in to work. His important errand was to pay a visit to the General Motors Acceptance Corporation (GMAC) office in Jacksonville, Florida. Six months earlier, Pough's 1988 Pontiac Grand Am had been repossessed after he had been unable to manage the monthly payments on his $9.95 hourly wage as a laborer. Even after he gave up the car voluntarily, GMAC had informed him in March that he still owed $6,394. During the month of January, Pough's wife Theresa had walked out on him, and by March she had succeeded in obtaining a restraining order that barred him from having contact with her. With all that had gone wrong up to that point, Pough was left to contemplate his loneliness and total despair.

Pough's despair turned to anger. At 10:45 a.m., he burst through the main entrance at the GMAC facility and immediately opened fire on two customers waiting at the service counter in front. He then went behind the counter and, for a full 2 minutes, blasted away at frightened employees as they scrambled under desks and out of back exits in an effort to flee. Pough was relentless in his pursuit of victims, following them from desk to desk and shooting many of them a number of times. He shot until he thought he had gotten everyone inside. He then fired a single round from his .38-caliber revolver into his head. Pough's final homicide toll at the GMAC office reached eight (seven women and one man); five more victims were wounded from the gunfire. It was later discovered that Pough had actually begun his killing spree on the day before, when he had fatally shot two pedestrians.

It is not just laborers like Pough who are motivated to commit mass murder as payback for economic hardship. In fact, white-collar wheelers and dealers can respond violently if they feel cheated. Lawyers are particularly vulnerable to clients who suffer financial catastrophe. At the August 1993 convention of the American Bar Association, in fact, one of the main topics of discussion was the rise of antilawyer sentiment in America. Participants expressed their outrage over jokes that ridicule attorneys, fearing that the tarnished image might provoke unhappy clients to commit violence against them. At the core of the discomfort and concern felt by the ABA members was a horrible mass killing that had occurred at a prestigious West Coast law firm barely a month earlier.

It happened on a sunny summer afternoon, July 1, 1993, in downtown San Francisco. A stocky 55-year-old man wearing a dark suit and carrying an oversized, lawyer-style briefcase rode the elevator of a glass and granite high rise in the financial district to the offices of the law firm of Pettit and Martin on the 34th floor. The smiling workers he passed in the corridor couldn't have known what Gian Luigi Ferri carried in his briefcase or in his heart.

Ferri walked briskly toward the law firm's conference room and pulled one of his three semiautomatic pistols from the case. He immediately sprayed the room with bullets as terrified lawyers and clients headed for cover. He then turned into an attorney's office down the hall and once more opened fire. Three people were killed on the spot; three more were wounded.

Ferri took the fire stairs to the 33rd and 32nd floors, where he found even more targets for his rampage. Never stopping to reload, he shot to death five more people and wounded another three. As he attempted to escape back down the stairway, two of his pistols jammed, and he was trapped between police coming in both directions. He took the third firearm from his briefcase and fired a final fatal shot under his chin into his brain.

Ferri was an Italian immigrant with a bachelor's degree in psychology who had divorced his wife in 1977. He tried his hand as a mortgage broker, but was plagued by a series of bad financial deals as well as bad luck and a bad temper. His situation had deteriorated so much recently that he had approached a law firm in Los Angeles to declare personal bankruptcy. A note that police found on Ferri's body blamed his problems on "criminals, rapists, racketeers, lobbyists," and on the FDA because it refused to regulate the food additive monosodium glutamate, which he believed had almost killed him on three occasions. But most of all, his note blamed people associated with a failed trailer-park business venture in the early 1980s—and especially his counsel in that deal, the law firm of Pettit and Martin.

Pough, Miller, and Ferri were all middle-aged men who saw financial ruin ahead of them not because an employer had fired them, but because of what they perceived to be an unjust and deceitful company, agency, or firm. For Pough and Miller, the sum of $6,000 was enough to break them psychologically, if not financially. Ferri's loss was more substantial, taking him from financial success to bankruptcy.

For 28-year-old Gang Lu, a graduate physics student from Beijing, China, the loss of a cherished academic award (the D. C. Spriestersbach Prize) for his University of Iowa doctoral dissertation on space-plasma physics demanded that justice be done. And Lu appointed himself judge, jury and executioner. Consisting of a plaque and $2,500 in cash, the award was "no big deal," according to professor emeritus James Van Allen.[5] But to Gang Lu, it was as catastrophic as was Ferri's bankruptcy. Not only was it a matter of shame to lose, but winning the prize would have virtually assured Lu of success in the tight academic job market.

On November 1, 1991, after months of anguish and detailed planning, Lu launched his all-out assault. He knew that his adversaries would be gathered at a regular Friday afternoon physics department seminar held in Room 309 of Van Allen Hall. Shortly after 3:30, Lu removed from his briefcase a .38-caliber revolver that he had purchased in July. Without saying a word—everyone was already painfully aware of his grudge—Lu started blasting away. He killed professors Christoph Goertz and Robert Alan Smith, both members of his dissertation committee, and shot Linhua Shan, his successful rival for the prize.

Lu then traveled down the hall and killed the department chairman, Dwight Nicholson. Next he went across campus to the office of T. Anne Cleary, the associate vice president for academic affairs, with whom he had filed an appeal. Lu killed Cleary and wounded her receptionist. He then returned to the physics department to finish off Shan, who had briefly survived his injuries. Lu then committed suicide.

Lu had worked out every detail of his rampage, and he was chillingly methodical in his implementation. In 12 short minutes of terror on campus, he killed five members of the university community and wounded one. In advance of the massacre, Lu had written to his sister in China, outlining his funeral wishes and sending her the contents of the bank account he shortly wouldn't need. Lu also wrote a letter to the media explaining his grievance against the physics department and describing how his gun, the "great equalizer," would help to right the terrible wrong. "Private guns make every person equal, no matter what/who he/she is," he wrote. "They also make it possible for an individual to fight against a conspired/incorporated organization such as Mafia or dirty university officials."[6]

It is difficult for many people outside of the academic world to appreciate the concepts of academic life and academic death. The phrases *publish or perish* and *curriculum vitae* both reflect the virtual life-and-death significance to academic achievement and failure. Gang Lu understood this, and felt that his career was doomed before it had begun. Economic resentment can be felt not only by vengeful employees but also by disgruntled clients and customers who seek to get even with the system—to win one for "the little guy." In a complex, bureaucratic society, more and more citizens are feeling powerless against the red tape and unresponsiveness of the system. Most, of course, will do little more than complain loudly about the injustice of government and big business. Only a few will literally fight city hall.

14

I Hate You to Death

Lodged on the northern face of Mount Royal overlooking the distinguished homes in one of Montreal's more affluent suburbs, the site of the École Polytechnique is as charming as the sound of its name. The University of Montreal School of Engineering, as it is known to English-speaking Canadians, is also known throughout North America as the site of one of the most devastating mass murders of all time.

On the rainy and cool afternoon of December 6, 1989, just after 5:00 p.m., 25-year-old Marc Lépine exploded into the six-story, yellow-brick engineering building, ready for battle and bent on revenge. Lépine was armed with a .223-caliber Ruger Mini-14, a semiautomatic hunting rifle that weighed a mere $6\frac{1}{2}$ pounds, but was capable of propelling cartridges at a velocity of more than 3,000 feet per second. The standard Mini-14 model ordinarily holds only five rounds in its magazine, but Lépine had equipped the rifle with a 30-round "banana clip" extension. He also brought with him more than 100 rounds of ammunition.

During the preceding week, Lépine had visited the building on several occasions, designing his route as carefully as would any self-respecting engineer. With his weapon concealed within a green plastic garbage bag, Lépine walked slowly and quietly through the doors of classroom C-230. Inside, he interrupted 60 undergraduates—nine of them women—who were listening to an end-of-semester presentation by one of their classmates. Dressed in a blue sweater and blue jeans, Lépine looked like a student who had mistakenly entered the wrong class. Even the emblem on his back—a skull adorned with glasses—was not all that unusual for a college student to wear. But when he removed his weapon from the plastic bag and started shouting orders, it was clear that Lépine had not just taken a wrong turn.

In a calm but forceful voice, the intruder instructed everyone immediately to stop what they were doing. Wearing a menacing grin on his face, he then directed the women to move off to one side of the classroom and commanded the men, including professor Yvon Bouchard, to leave. Some students were too frightened to move. Others were slow to respond, thinking that it was all just a bad joke. But Lépine showed them he wasn't kidding by firing a shot into the ceiling to hurry the students along, "I want the women," Lépine began to yell. "You're all a bunch of fucking feminists. I hate feminists."

Having gotten their undivided attention, Lépine started firing at the nine terrified women, hitting all of them and killing six. But he wasn't through. Leaving room C-230, Lépine moved methodically through corridors and between floors, shooting any woman who crossed his path. He maneuvered his way into the cafeteria on the bottom floor (which was cheerfully decorated with red and white balloons and various holiday decorations) and once again opened fire on frightened students.

The once-festive atmosphere in the lunchroom was decimated, with blood on the tables, chairs, and floor and the bodies of the dead and wounded strewn about. The gunman returned upstairs to look for more victims. By the time the police had arrived—delayed by a miscommunication that had initially dispatched them to the women's dorm—Lépine was ready to end the assault on his own. Pressing the gun against his forehead, he muttered, "Ah, shit," then squeezed the trigger.

When the police tactical squad entered the building, they discovered the bodies of 14 women, ages 21 to 31. The police also found Lépine's lifeless body at the front of a third-floor classroom, his head shattered from a bullet fired at close range. A revealing three-page handwritten suicide note in his pocket explained his hideous outburst. "I have been unhappy for the past seven years," Lépine lamented. "And, I will die on December 6, 1989. . . . Feminists have always ruined my life." An addendum contained a list of the names of 19 "opportunistic" Canadian women, including a sportscaster, several policewomen, and other public figures. "The lack of time," wrote Lépine, "has allowed these radical feminists to survive."[1]

It appeared as though Lépine had carefully and thoughtfully assembled his "who's who" of women doing what he saw as men's work, going as far as to research the phone numbers of many of them. But if Lépine had in mind a "hit list" of women whom he detested, why did he not target them specifically for his attack on feminism? Although his anger and resentment may have been irrational, he was well aware that such a battle plan was strategically impossible. It surely would have been difficult for him to avenge his troubled life by executing one victim at a time. Rather, he needed to kill a lot of women in a short period of time, and just about any "feminists" would do.

But if his desire was to achieve large-scale revenge, then why did Lépine not attack the nursing school, where far more women would be under his gun? Lépine's grudge was not so much directed toward womankind in general or against women who were performing traditional female roles, such as nursing. His resentment was focused on ambitious "feminists" who were pursuing careers within male domains such as engineering. Not only were the female student engineers symbolic of feminism, but in a sense they were literally taking his seat in the class. Because of his poor academic skills, Lépine had been denied admission to the very same school of engineering where he exacted his revenge.

Those who are psychoanalytically inclined might speculate that Lépine's contempt for women was a generalized form of his hatred for his mother. Perhaps she abandoned him at an early age, or perhaps he believed he was a victim of child abuse. Lépine's violent rampage at the University of Montreal could then be interpreted as a desperate final attempt to get even with his mother; his poor victims were only surrogates to act out his pent-up rage.

But actually Lépine seemed to have positive feelings about his mother, Monique Lépine, even though as a teenager he was not happy that she spent so much time at her nursing career and thus too little time with him and his younger sister, Nadia. Lépine instead seemed to have detested his father, a man who had brutally assaulted both his wife and his children and who showed very little interest in his family. At their divorce proceedings in 1970, Monique testified that her husband was abusive and that he showed little control of his emotions. He had beaten her in front of the children; struck her in the face; and hit Marc so hard that the young boy bled from his nose and his ears. When Marc was only 7, his father threw him, his sister, and his mother out of their apartment.

By the time he was 14 years old, the boy's resentment was so intense that he decided to take his mother's name of Lépine. It was at that time that Gamil Gharbi—son of Rachid Liass Gharbi, an Algerian-born Muslim—became known as Marc Lépine. Perhaps it would not be too farfetched to suggest that Marc Lépine's final assault was an extreme version of his father's behavior toward his mother. Lépine may have hated his father, but ultimately he identified with the aggressor. Changing his name may also have been more than a repudiation of his father's lineage. It also represented his desire to fit in, to be like everyone else, by being French Canadian.

Life was not easy for Marc Lépine. He was *not* like everyone else, or even close to it. He was the quintessential loser. He attempted to join the army but, for reasons that were never completely clear, was rejected. And he resented how women of the military were given equal recognition; after all, they were barred from the front lines. Lépine felt that they had no place in the military aside from their role as secretaries and nurses.

Marc Lépine's rampage was a violent act of bias against an entire group of people—in this case, women. As such, it was unquestionably a hate crime, as hateful and as criminal as one can imagine. His suicide note and his remarks to his surviving victims made it abundantly clear that Lépine blamed all women for his personal failures. He looked for "feminists" behind every negative experience that he had.

Mass killer George "Jo Jo" Hennard was similar to Lépine in his intense hatred of women. Hennard's crime itself would not necessarily have suggested a vendetta against any group in particular, but testimonials from his neighbors and his own written words clearly revealed that he blamed women, above all others, for everything that went wrong. He wanted to get even with them.

It was Wednesday, October 16, 1991, the day after Hennard had turned 35, and the long-haired, good-looking man from Belton, Texas, celebrated his birthday with a bang. Hennard loaded up his two semiautomatic pistols—a 9-millimeter Glock 17 and a Ruger P-89—put on his shades, and jumped into his 1987 Ford Ranger pickup truck for the 19-mile trip west to Killeen.

Lunchtime at Luby's Cafeteria was particularly crowded that day. Some 200 diners, many of them treating their supervisors for National Bosses' Day, were squeezed into the popular red-brick restaurant. Only some saw what happened, but all heard the crash as a light blue pickup truck—Hennard's Ford—came smashing through a 5-foot-high plate glass window next to the front entrance and crushed a table full of customers.

Surprised but concerned, diners dropped their drinks and sandwiches and rushed to help the driver, whom they imagined had been in a traffic accident. But this was no accident. With a cigarette dangling from his lips, Hennard stepped from his vehicle, aimed his gun directly at one of the customers he had hit in the crash, and fired. Next he gunned down a group of people as they stood motionless clutching their trays in the serving line. Moving through the eatery, the gunman coolly and methodically targeted his victims. "Wait till those fuckin' women in Belton, Texas, see this!" Hennard shouted with a smirk. "I wonder if they think it was worth it!"

By this time, everyone in the restaurant had been stunned into silence. They now understood exactly what was going on: There was a mass killer among them, and he was determined to shoot at anyone in his path. Some tipped over tables for cover; others played dead on the floor. A few escaped by hurling a chair at a window pane and crawling out through the broken glass. Twenty-eight-year-old Tommy Vaughn threw his own body (at 6 feet 6 inches and 300 pounds) through a glass window. One employee, 19-year-old Mark Mathews, crawled inside the kitchen's oversized dishwasher until he was rescued the next day.

Suzanne Gratia, who had taken her parents out for lunch, saw both of them die. She and her mother had ducked behind a table when Hennard shot her father, Al, point-blank in the chest from just a few feet away. Suzanne spied an escape route through a broken window, but her mother, Ursula, instead chose to creep out from behind the table to protect her critically wounded husband. She draped her body over his, and stared directly into Hennard's face, inviting him to shoot her too. He obliged.

The police arrived just a few minutes later, although it must have seemed to the survivors more like a lifetime. After several volleys of gunfire, during which he was wounded twice, George Hennard retreated to the restroom. He realized that his killing spree was over, and he ended it by shooting himself in the head. Including one victim who died a few days later, Hennard's murder toll at Luby's totaled 23. Twenty-two others were wounded in the attack, some seriously.

Days before the Killeen massacre, Hennard was one of millions of Americans who were glued to the TV set watching the highly-rated broadcast on nearly every network of Senate confirmation hearings for Supreme Court nominee Clarence Thomas. These particular hearings turned on the issue of whether Mr. Thomas had sexually harassed Anita Hill when she worked for him at the Equal Employment Opportunity Commission.

To some American men, the irony of seeing the man whose position it was to develop and enforce policy on harassment in the workplace himself be "hung out to dry" was an outrage. But to Hennard, it was worse than an outrage. He complained loudly and publicly that Anita Hill's allegations were ludicrous, and that it signaled how women were being allowed to take over the territory that rightfully belonged to men. Watching the Senate hearings as he ate dinner at a small neighborhood grill, Hennard started screaming at the TV, "You dumb bitch! You bastards opened the door for all the women!"[2]

Hennard blamed females, not just Anita Hill, for causing what he saw as the decline of American civilization. In June 1991, Hennard had walked into a local FBI office and attempted unsuccessfully to file a civil rights complaint against the women of the world. "He said women were snakes,"[3] recalled Jamie Dunlop, a former roommate of Hennard. Even more revealing of his deep-seated resentment, Hennard sent an angry letter to two young women, neighbors he hardly knew, complaining about the female vipers who were destroying his life:

> Do you think the three of us can get together someday? Please give me the satisfaction of someday laughing in the face of all those mostly white treacherous female vipers from those two towns who tried to destroy me and my family.
>
> It is very ironic about Belton, Texas.
>
> I found the best and worst in women there. You and your sister are on the one side. Then the abundance of evil women that make up the worst on the other side.
>
> I would like to personally remind all those vipers that I

have civil rights too. Just because I did not hire an attorney they do not have carte blanche to do what they want in violation of these rights.

I will no matter what prevail over the female vipers in those two rinky-dink towns in Texas.

I will prevail in the bitter end. In conclusion, I ask you do not disclose the contents of this letter to anyone other than immediate family members. It is no one else's business but ours anyway.[4]

Hennard's mass shooting was in large part motivated by hate, especially his hatred for women. In the heat of the moment, however, a spillover effect took hold, and his anger and resentment became generalized to include just about everyone in Belton County.

Mass murder inspired by hate, such as Hennard's assault on the Luby's Cafeteria, derives from generalized resentment aimed not at a few individuals but at an entire *group* of people who are seen as responsible for the perpetrator's problems. He is convinced that the country has changed for the worse, that politicians are leading us down the garden path to total ruination, and that people like himself—the "little guys"—have lost all control of their destiny. From his point of view he is being victimized, he resents it, and he is looking for someone to blame.

A growing number of observers have applied the term *downward mobility* to characterize the economic plight of an entire generation of Americans who are slipping down the socioeconomic ladder. For the first time in this century, many Americans believe that their children will *not* enjoy a better standard of living than they presently have. Instead of believing that they should help those who are less fortunate, many Americans feel personally threatened by the growing presence of women, newcomers, and minorities competing for diminishing amounts of wealth, status, and power. In fact, they feel as if they are being challenged to an increasing extent by a broad range of "outsiders." The economic pie is shrinking and there simply aren't enough slices to go around.

Cultural diversity and increasing economic competition have together produced a pervasive sense of resentment and closed-minded, twisted logic in the hearts and heads of many Americans. They find many convenient scapegoats to lay blame for their own personal failures and disenchantment: "Jews have too much power; they are responsible for our recession and therefore my unemployment." "Blacks unfairly benefit from reverse discrimination; because of affirmative action, I can't get a promotion." "Feminists are taking more than their share of jobs and they're not even qualified; I've busted my butt for years, and just because of these bitches I can't even feed my family." "Asians are grabbing all the college scholarship money paid for by my tax dollars; because of them, my son might not be able to attend college." "Immigrants coming to this country in unprecedented numbers are grabbing up all the jobs that should be going to hard-working American citizens; because of them, I can't find a decent job . . . and *I* was born here."

What are disgruntled and resentful Americans, fed up with "unfair competition" and sick and tired of feeling disadvantaged, to do? Ten or fifteen years ago, they might have grabbed a cold beer from the refrigerator, turned on a rerun of "All in the Family," and let somebody else take care of the problem. But Americans are now much more likely to respond assertively or even violently—to translate their resentment into action. Some with an ax to grind may choose to use something more powerful than an ax.

On occasion, hate crimes go well beyond an assault on one or two individuals. A few individuals are ready to wage war against any and all members of a particular group of people. In the hatemonger's view, all out-group members are subhumans—either animals or demons—who are bent on destroying our culture, our economy, or the purity of our racial heritage. He is concerned, therefore, about much more than eliminating some blacks from his neighborhood or a handful of women from his place of work. Instead he believes that he has a higher purpose in carrying out his crime. The perpetrator is on a moral mission to make the world a better place to live, and rid the world of evil. He perversely believes that his aggressive act is, in actuality, one of self-defense: get them before they take over.

Not every hate crime is clearly marked as such. Even when the crime is perpetrated exclusively against the members of a particular group, we cannot always be sure that it was motivated by bigotry or bias. Like George Hennard, Patrick Purdy was a young man filled with resentment who went on a deadly rampage. But unlike Marc Lépine, Purdy never broadcast his intentions, nor did he leave a note explaining his murderous behavior. Although he told his half-brother that he would soon make the newspapers (only days before he did), Purdy gave no hints concerning how or why.

The 25-year-old Purdy was almost always alone, had no girlfriends, and seemed to dislike everyone. He was conspiratorial and paranoid in his thinking. In the end, he singled out a particular group—Southeast Asians—as being especially blameworthy. For some 5 years, Purdy drifted from place to place. Working as a laborer, a security guard, or a welder, he traveled to Connecticut, Nevada, Florida, Oregon, Tennessee, and Texas—to any state where his past might not come back to haunt him. But, wherever he went,

Purdy challenged his bosses and simply couldn't hold down a job for more than a few weeks at a time.

Along the way, Purdy repeatedly got into trouble with the law. In 1980 he was arrested in Los Angeles for soliciting a sex act from an undercover police officer. In 1982 he was arrested on charges of possession of hashish, and the next year he was convicted of possessing a dangerous weapon. A few months after that he was arrested on a charge of receiving stolen property. In October 1984 he did a 30-day stint in county jail in Woodland, California, for being an accomplice to a robbery.

Three years passed, and Purdy's behavior became increasingly outrageous. In 1987 he was arrested for indiscriminately firing a 9-millimeter pistol in the El Dorado National Forest. On top of this, he was charged with resisting arrest for kicking a deputy sheriff and shattering a window of the patrol car with his feet. While being held in advance of trial, Purdy attempted to commit suicide by hanging himself from his jail cell and slicing open his wrist with his sharpest fingernail. But as with everything else he tried, Purdy failed at taking his own life.

By January 1989 life had become completely hopeless for Purdy. By this time Purdy despised almost everyone, but especially people in positions of authority and his personal "enemies," the newcomers to America's shores. Purdy had a special hatred for Southeast Asians. He often bragged about his father's conquests in the Vietnam War slaughtering all those "gooks." Purdy fantasized about following in his dad's army boot-steps, but it would have to remain a fantasy, as Patrick was only 7 years old when the U.S. forces pulled out of the Vietnam conflict. Purdy, though, would fight his own war against Southeast Asians, and this time, he would not fail.

For weeks, Purdy had been living in room 104 of the El
Rancho Motel on the edge of Stockton, California, a river-
front agricultural city located some 80 miles east of San
Francisco. Purdy spent hour after hour and day after day in
his "war room," manipulating the hundreds of toy soldiers,
tanks, jeeps, and weapons he had collected in order to sim-
ulate an attack and to develop an effective military strategy.
There were toy soldiers on the shelves, on the heating grates,
and even in the refrigerator.

Purdy prepared himself for battle as well. Perceiving a
conspiracy involving people in charge, he displayed symbols of anti-Americanism boldly and loudly. He had carved
the words "freedom" and "victory" into the butt of his AK-
47 military assault rifle. And on the camouflage shirt that he
wore over his military jacket, he wrote "PLO," "Libya," and
"Death to the great Satin." As reflected by the mistaken
inscription for the name of the devil, spelling was never
Purdy's strong suit.

On Tuesday morning, January 17, Purdy donned his
military flak jacket, picked up a handgun and an AK-47
semiautomatic assault rifle, and drove his 1977 Chevrolet
station wagon a couple of miles to the Cleveland Elementary
School in Stockton—the same elementary school he had
attended from kindergarten to third grade. When he had
lived there as a child, the neighborhood was white; now it
was predominantly Asian.

Arriving at the school just before noon, Purdy could see
hundreds of young children—most of them refugees from
Cambodia, Vietnam, China, and Mexico. Purdy preferred
the term "boat people" when he spoke disparagingly of
Asian refugees. Despite the chill in the air, the children
played joyfully at recess on the blacktop in front of the
brown stucco building, unaware of the war that would soon

be declared. As a diversionary tactic, Purdy parked his car and then set it ablaze with a Molotov cocktail in a Budweiser bottle. Then Purdy eased through a gap in the fence surrounding the school building and walked onto the crowded school grounds, where he opened fire.

Over a period of several minutes, Purdy sprayed 60 rounds of bullets from his AK-47 at screaming children in a sweeping motion across the blacktop. He showed no emotion, leaning back and calmly firing as automatically as his weapon. These romping, playful children, who had their whole lives ahead of them, seemed to him little more than objects, things, or targets.

Purdy didn't stop until he heard the sirens of approaching police cars. He then removed the handgun, which he had saved for this purpose, from his belt. Purdy died instantly from a single shot from the gun, on which he had written the word "Victory." Purdy's victory toll was high: Five children, ages 6 through 9, all from Southeast Asia, were dead, and 29 more (in addition to one teacher) were wounded.

Purdy's murderous rampage against innocent children was based, at least in part, on racial hatred. He had frequently made hostile racial comments to coworkers about the influx of Southeast Asians into the United States and had protested bitterly about the large number of Southeast Asian classmates in industrial arts courses he was taking at the local community college. He complained that the newcomers were taking up all of the jobs, and he resented having to compete with them. Just prior to his murder spree, Purdy told another resident of El Rancho Motel, "The damn Hindus and boat people own everything."[5]

While his sense of losing ground to immigrants may have been delusional, Purdy couldn't compete with anyone.

The demographics in his community had changed dramatically. In less than 8 years, the population of Southeast Asian refugees in Stockton had gone from fewer than 1,000 to more than 30,000. Thus, in his manner of blaming others for his failures, he prepared himself to fight back the influx of "yellow people" in his own way. But Purdy did not choose to attack some workplace that he felt was infested with immigrants, nor did he set his sight on a restaurant or shopping mall populated by newcomers. Why did he choose children as targets to carry out his mission?

Purdy did not apparently feel the need to leave behind a note explaining his actions. Thus, we can only speculate about his exact reason—if indeed he had one—for targeting a schoolyard, of all places, in which to carry out his plan of attack. He may have wanted to avenge the difficulties he had experienced with boyhood classmates at the Cleveland Elementary School almost 20 years earlier. Perhaps he was angry that the poor education he felt he had received there had left him ill-prepared for life; he had written in private notes to himself how dumb he felt. Or, if his design was to get back at society for his own misfortunes, he may have targeted its most cherished members. Perhaps Purdy's thinking was more tactical in deciding that a schoolyard was a fairly confined and well-populated area in which he could easily gun down dozens of victims without risk of being overtaken. Certainly, he wasn't about to pick on someone his own size and not anyone equally armed. Whatever the contributing factors, Purdy definitely hated the newcomers from Vietnam and Cambodia who had taken over his old elementary school, if not the entire community. Most likely he deliberately set his sights on a school that had a majority (over 70%) Asian-American population.

Patrick Purdy was a rebel with a cause—actually, in his

paranoia, he had plenty of them. Of course, Purdy's victims were total strangers to him and were not responsible for his disappointing existence. To him, they may have seemed no different from the toy soldiers, the plastic Viet Cong, he had maneuvered back in room 104 of El Rancho Motel. Yet at the same time they were symbols of everything in his life that had gone wrong.

White males cannot, of course, claim sole ownership of resentful attitudes. Many minority Americans are angry as well, seeing a racist behind every possibility for advancement. Some even envisage a large-scale conspiracy on the part of white-supremacy groups, corporations, and government to deprive them of success, if not their lives. Thus whereas Lépine, Hennard, and Purdy were all members of the dominant group beating back the threat of a minority, mass murder can also serve as the weapon of a minority to retaliate for its perceived oppression. This grim lesson was tragically learned in a big way in New York City.

On any other day, it was the 5:33 local to Hicksville. But on December 7, 1993, it was the 5:33 express to hell. Hundreds of commuters, exhausted from a long work day in Manhattan, boarded the Long Island Rail Road commuter train at Penn Station, unaware and unprepared for the horror that would soon erupt in car number three. Just about 6:10 p.m., as the train raced toward Garden City in suburban Nassau County, a heavy-set but gentle-looking man rose quietly from his seat at the rear of the car and turned the weary scene into instant chaos.

Without warning, the gunman pulled from his canvas bag a Ruger P89 9-millimeter semiautomatic pistol, a lightweight handgun known for its high velocity and accuracy, and started filling the air with gunfire. Stunned riders struggled to find cover in a train that offered very little. The gunman slowly walked backward down the aisle, row by row, shooting alternately to his left and then his right.

Midway through the car, the assailant paused to reload with a second 15-round clip, then promptly resumed his attack. He moved to the front of the car and disappeared momentarily into the vestibule connecting to the forward car, but he soon returned. Fifteen rounds later, when again he stopped to reload, three heroic commuters rushed at the gunman and pinned him against a seat. Moments later, the train pulled into the Merillon Avenue station. As terrified commuters bolted from the train, an off-duty transit police officer (who was on the platform to pick up his wife) boarded car number three and handcuffed the restrained gunman.

By the time the 3-minute barrage had ended, four victims—three men and one woman—lay dead, and another 19 were wounded. The death toll rose to six as two young women later succumbed to their severe bullet wounds. As bad as it was, the carnage could have been worse: The gunman came prepared with a bag filled with more than 100 rounds of Black Talons, deadly hollow-nosed bullets that penetrate the body and then ricochet within.

The scene of the massacre was beyond anyone's worst nightmare. "There was blood on the train, on the platform, down the steps," reported one member of the rescue team, "40 to 50 feet of blood."[6] Surviving witnesses, the luckier ones, spoke frantically of a madman who went berserk and shot randomly. To them, the attack appeared totally indiscriminate. After all, no one on the train had provoked this man physically or verbally, he seemed to have just suddenly snapped.

Notwithstanding the impressions of witnesses to the horror, there was a method to this man's madness. A handwritten note found in the assailant's pocket—perhaps intended as a suicide script—later revealed that the crime was a planned act of vengeance against races and institutions that he despised with a passion. He saw racism everywhere: in the worker-compensation system that failed to assist him sufficiently after his work-related injury, and at Adelphi University, which had suspended him in June 1991 for belligerence and contentiousness. He espoused hatred of whites, Asians, and conservative "Uncle Tom" blacks—people who possessed the very things he did not, especially money and a job. These were his oppressors, and they would have to pay for his misery.

The gunman may not have known his victims, but he was nonetheless selective in determining when, where, how, and against what kinds of people he would avenge his deep disappointments and dark despair. With deliberation and planning, he sought out a place and time (a commuter train at the evening rush hour) that would guarantee he could target "rich folk" who were gainfully employed. The gunman was so in control of his actions that he purposely postponed the slaughter until the train had passed the city limits of New York. According to his murder plan, he wished not to embarrass David Dinkins, who at the time was the mayor of New York City.

Perhaps on account of the racially charged nature of the incident, the police and the mass media withheld for a day—until the initial shock had passed—the fact that the gunman was black and that his motive involved racial hatred. But as more of the details surfaced about the man arrested at the scene, it appeared that 35-year-old Colin Ferguson was a mass murder waiting to happen. Ferguson was himself the product of affluence. Born January 14, 1958, the son of a successful pharmacist and executive, Ferguson

St. Louis Community College

Current Check-Outs summary for MACK, KAT
Tue Aug 23 09:18:09 CDT 2005

BARCODE: 30008000503953
TITLE: Overkill : mass murder and serial
DUE DATE: Sep 13 2005
STATUS:

was raised in Havedale, a well-to-do suburb of Kingston, Jamaica. As a youth, the intelligent and intense boy benefited from the very best education that money could buy at an elite prep school. He seemed to have a bright future ahead of him.

All of this privilege and potential would, however, start to unravel when Ferguson was 20. His father was killed in an automobile accident, and his mother died from cancer a year later. With much of the family fortune spent on medical bills, Ferguson moved to the United States, seeking out a new start. But it was just the beginning of the end; over the next decade, his expectations would be shattered. Beginning as a clerk for Eddie's Liquor and Junior Market Stores in Long Beach, California, Ferguson moved from job to job, chronically feeling that his employment was beneath him. His career troubles escalated after moving to Long Island. He fell from a stool while working as a clerk for the Ademco Security Group of Syosset, Long Island, forcing him to go on worker compensation.

Surviving on his small weekly checks was a struggle. Eventually Ferguson was awarded a lump-sum settlement of $26,250, but these funds didn't go very far. Soon thereafter Ferguson was once again hounding the worker compensation board, sometimes calling several times a day, to reopen his claim for increased support.

For a while Ferguson found some satisfaction by resuming his studies, but his academic success was short-lived. In the spring of 1990 he made the dean's list at Nassau County Community College. He then transferred to Adelphi University in the fall, but within a year was suspended for his repeated arguments with faculty over issues of racism. Even his hopes and dreams for marriage and family were frustrated. In 1986 he married Audrey M. Warren, but the relationship was brief and rocky, as the couple separated after a year and divorced shortly thereafter.

Having failed at work, school, and home, Ferguson was nearing the end of his ability to cope. One final indignity was to be told by his landlord, Patrick Denis, that at the end of the month he would be kicked out of his home, an undersized one-room refuge in Flatbush that he rented for $150 per month. Denis, himself a black American, had overheard his tenant ranting and raving on repeated occasions about the need for blacks to kill whites. He became increasingly alarmed about Ferguson's mental instability and wanted nothing more to do with him. For all of Ferguson's misfortunes, disappointments, and frustrations, there would be hell to pay. Ferguson was there to collect in full on the ill-fated 5:33 train to Long Island.

Just like murder in general, the overwhelming majority of mass killings are intraracial. For those instances, however, in which a mass killer specifically targets members of another group—people who are different in terms of race, sex, national origin, or sexual orientation—the underlying motivation tends to involve intense hatred and bigotry. In the killer's delusional thinking, he is a victim who has every right, if not a duty, to avenge his unfair treatment by eliminating as many of the "offending" group members as possible. The murderer is not out to get any particular enemy: he'd like to get them all. In his hate-filled and bigoted mind, mass murder is not criminal; it is pure justice.

15

Going Berserk

Most mass killers target people they know—family members, friends, or coworkers—in order to settle a score, to get even with the particular individuals whom they hold accountable for their problems. Others seek revenge against a certain class or category of people who are suspected of receiving an unfair advantage. But a few revenge-motivated mass murders stem from the killers' paranoid view of society at large. They imagine a wide-ranging conspiracy in which large numbers of people, friends and strangers alike, are out to do them harm.

As we have seen, family and workplace mass murder is typically committed by a perpetrator who is clearheaded and rational, though resentful and depressed. By contrast, a random mass murder often reflects the distorted thinking of a psychotic on a suicidal mission. This kind of mass killer blames the world for his problems and decides to get even. The more people he kills, no matter who they are, the sweeter the revenge. To some extent this psychotic reasoning may also be found in such hate-motivated mass killers as Patrick Purdy, who targeted absolute strangers just because they were Southeast Asians. But those who carry out a random massacre believe that almost everyone is their enemy; they hate virtually all of humanity.

Mass murderer William Cruse, for example, suspected that nearly everyone was against him. He focused his anger on his noisy neighbors, gossipy grocery clerks, and the children who played on his block; but he really hated all of the residents of the Palm Bay, Florida, community in which he lived. On Thursday evening, April 23, 1987, the 59-year-old retired librarian went on a bloody rampage in a local shopping center, killing six people and injuring another 12. At his trial, several psychiatrists testified that William Cruse suffered from a severe mental illness known as paranoid schizophrenia. He believed that he was the target of a wide-ranging conspiracy to destroy his life, and he often imagined seeing acts of disrespect and indignity that were designed to anger him.

As a young man, Cruse seemed happy and healthy enough. He graduated from the University of Kentucky in 1951 with a B.A. in history and in 1954 with a master's degree in library science. From 1955 to 1967, he worked as a librarian at the Cincinnati public library. But Cruse had long-standing psychological problems that became more severe with advancing age. As a middle-aged adult, he was described by neighbors in his home state of Kentucky as a weird and strangely cantankerous man who despised children. In 1980, he was charged in Lexington with public intoxication.

After Cruse moved to Palm Bay, his already considerable paranoia deepened. He was convinced that the people on his block were spreading false rumors that he was a homosexual. The clerks at the local Winn-Dixie and Publix supermarkets must have heard the gossip somehow, Cruse imagined, because they appeared to stare at his crotch whenever he went shopping. He even thought he saw one grocery store clerk stick out his tongue at him for no reason.

From Cruse's paranoid perspective, the neighborhood children repeatedly harassed him and trespassed on his property. He interpreted normal juvenile behavior as a personal assault on his privacy. If a child attempted to retrieve a wayward ball, Cruse saw it as trespassing. If the kids on the block made noise, he took it as harassment. In response, he shouted obscenities and made sexually suggestive gestures. After a while, Cruse felt so beleaguered that even a child innocently strolling past his house was enough to send him into a frenzy; he would rush out and shoot his rifle into the air.

At six o'clock on the fatal evening in April, Cruse heard a noise outside his house. He peeked through the blinds to find two young boys walking back and forth past his bungalow. Cruse confronted them outside, screaming vulgarities at them, but they only laughed in his face. Enraged even more, he then rushed back into his house to get his three guns—a Ruger .223-caliber semiautomatic rifle, a .357-caliber Ruger revolver, and a Winchester 20-gauge shotgun—and a bagful of bullets.

By the time he came back out front, the boys were nowhere to be found. Having nobody else to victimize, Cruse aimed his rifle at a 14-year-old boy who was shooting baskets in his driveway across the street, striking him in the buttocks. He then jumped into his white Toyota and drove to the nearby shopping mall in which the Publix supermarket was located. First he opened fire at point-blank range on two college students as they strolled nonchalantly in the parking lot. Then he walked over to a woman who was sitting in her car and shot her in the head.

Cruse tried in vain to get into the Publix market through an automatic exit-only door, but he was so confused that he couldn't find the entrance. Giving up in frustration, he then drove his Toyota to the Winn-Dixie supermarket in a shopping center across the road. Rushing to the grocery store, he confronted two policemen who had been dispatched in response to the shooting. Cruse quickly gunned them down as they attempted to block the entrance to the store. He then shot his way through the Winn-Dixie, firing at frightened customers and employees as they fought to get out of his way.

Cruse followed a 21-year-old woman into the ladies' restroom and, for 6 hours, kept her hostage. In the meantime, the police formed a human barricade surrounding the store. Cruse talked to his captive about killing both of them, but he released her shortly after midnight. The police apprehended him as he attempted to escape.

Cruse plead not guilty by reason of insanity. He claimed no memory of the tragic massacre, and defense psychiatrists confirmed that he was a paranoid schizophrenic. But despite Cruse's history of bizarre behavior and delusional thinking, the jury wouldn't buy the defense. Perhaps fearing that he might escape too easily if it were to return an insanity verdict, the jury found Cruse guilty on six counts of first-degree murder and recommended the death penalty.

Unlike mass killings in which specific victims are targeted because of a grudge, random massacres are not necessarily preceded by a clear-cut precipitant such as the loss of a job or a relationship. The psychotic killer can create his own catalyst in his mind, even if no major external event occurred. Thus, for example, a clerk who is perceived to stick out his tongue is enough to drive someone like William

Cruse over the edge. Also unlike family-related and work-place rampages, in which the perpetrators generally engage in long-term planning, random slaughters are occasionally a spontaneous response to objectively trivial or innocuous experiences. There is no evidence, for example, that William Cruse contemplated his attack in Palm Bay for any longer than a few moments.

Part of the reason why random massacres occur so infrequently is that their perpetrators are typically too out of touch with reality to carry out their plan of attack in an effective, methodical manner. They may attempt mass murder, but they generally fail to complete it—perhaps succeeding in killing one or two of their many "adversaries." Indeed, it may be difficult to concentrate on killing scores of people if the voices keep interrupting.

The deranged mind of 26-year-old Dion Terres of Kenosha, Wisconsin, apparently prevented him from exacting as much revenge on society as he had sought. He lived by himself, had no real friends, and hated the world and everybody in it except for Ted Bundy, Jeffrey Dahmer, Aileen Wuornos, and Hitler, whom he admired. More than just a serial killer groupie, Terres believed that his thought processes were just like those of serial killers, except that he was smarter. In addition to his odd fascination with the champions of murder, Terres suffered from numerous delusions. He claimed to have exhumed the corpse of Abraham Lincoln and to have placed it in his bathtub. He reported hearing voices, and he worshipped Satan.

For Dion Terres, 1993 was not a good year. In March, he was fired from his job assembling cellular phones at the Motorola plant in Arlington Heights, Illinois. Irate over being terminated, Terres went out and purchased an AR-15 assault rifle from a local gun dealer, though he stopped well short of using it on his former boss. Then in August his girlfriend, 16-year-old Kimberly Sinkler, said she wanted nothing more to do with him after he began making veiled threats about raping and poisoning her.

By August 10, Terres could take no more of life. Dressed for battle in his military fatigues, he tossed two guns (including the AR-15 that he had bought in March) onto the passenger seat of his blue sedan and drove 2 miles to the McDonald's on Pershing Boulevard in Kenosha. Parking in the lot next to the drive-through window, Terres grabbed his weapons and got out of the car. At this point, he realized that he had locked his keys and, even worse, his 30-round ammunition clip for the semiautomatic rifle inside the car. He was getting more and more confused and disoriented. Forgetting about the spare clip in his breast pocket, Terres threw the AR-15 onto the pavement and decided to forge ahead with just his .44-caliber revolver.

There were some 20 employees and customers inside the restaurant when Terres made his entrance. Standing over two young boys who were eating their lunch, he shouted, "I want everybody out of here!"[1] Before anyone could move, however, Terres fired away. Fifty-year-old Bruce Bojesen was shot in the head and died instantly. Sandra Kenaga, age 39, died the next morning from back wounds. One other person received a minor injury in the arm. Terres saved the last bullet for himself; he shoved the revolver under his chin and pulled the trigger.

Those who survived the attack were lucky because Terres had locked himself out of his car, had forgotten to take the clip from inside, and had forgotten about the spare clip he was carrying. They were lucky that Terres's state of mind got in his way. He had the frustration, catastrophic

loss, isolation, conspiratorial thinking, and access to firearms needed to become a mass killer—everything but the
ability to think clearly and act methodically.

Mass murderers such as an estranged father/husband
or an embittered employee who attempt to settle a grudge
against a particular list of victims tend to be middle-aged. It
is generally not until they reach their 30s or 40s that life's
frustrations accumulate to the point that they seem intol-
erable and insurmountable. But those who go berserk and
kill indiscriminately as a result of psychotic thinking can
come from any age group. Schizophrenia, for example, often
has its onset in late adolescence. Thus someone as young as
Terres, or even younger, can perceive that the whole world
is out to get him and decide to get them first. And any minor
incident could trigger off a rampage.

It is also not a strict requirement that a commando-style
killer be a man. It was in the late afternoon of October 30,
1985, that a young woman walked hurriedly from the parking lot into a shopping mall in Springfield, Pennsylvania.
Unlike other shoppers with their bags and packages in
hand, 25-year-old Sylvia Seegrist carried a .22-caliber semiautomatic rifle and was dressed in battle fatigues and black
boots.

Pausing briefly at the entrance to the mall, Seegrist eyed
her prospective victims and opened fire. Her first target was
a 2-year-old boy who couldn't escape fast enough. Seegrist
fired point-blank at the youngster; his body slumped to the
ground in a heap. She then rushed into the mall, firing
indiscriminately at least 15 times as she made her way along
the main walkway. One bullet hit a 64-year-old man as he
attempted to take refuge in a nearby shoe store. Seegrist
continued her shooting spree until a college student man-

aged to wrestle her to the ground and take her weapon. By that time she had hit ten people with gunfire, killing three of them.

At her arraignment, Seegrist told the judge, "Hurry up, man. You know I'm guilty. Kill me on the spot." She was charged with murder, attempted murder, aggravated assault, and possession of an unregistered firearm. Seegrist was found to be criminally insane and was committed indefinitely to a psychiatric hospital.[2]

Only the criminal aspects of the case had been resolved. What remained was a question of civil law: Was the shopping mall in some way responsible for Sylvia Seegrist's rampage and therefore liable to the victims for the damages? Was the mall negligent in failing to provide adequate security for its customers? Should the mall have initiated commitment proceedings against Seegrist who had been known to the security force for her belligerent and threatening manner?

In court, a security expert for the plaintiffs testified that a well-trained guard stationed in the main entrance to the mall could have stopped Seegrist from shooting customers. The plaintiffs' psychiatrist noted that she had visited the McDonald's restaurant in the mall shortly after a widely publicized rampage at the McDonald's in San Ysidro, California, in July 1984. At that time she had suggested—mainly to herself, but out loud nonetheless—that she might repeat the mass murder in Springfield and pointed her finger like a gun while saying "rat-tat-tat-tat." Several more times over the course of the next year she returned to the mall, acting in a bizarre manner and making threats or threatening gestures. The psychiatrist for the plaintiffs suggested that the mall management should have attempted to have Sylvia Seegrist committed to a mental hospital.

The defendant's psychiatrist testified it was extremely doubtful that Seegrist would have been committed for making threats. Pennsylvania laws had been tightened in recent years in order to prevent unjustified civil commitments; it was no longer possible to hospitalize a person against his or her will without clear-cut proof of dangerousness. Moreover, even if successfully committed, Seegrist could not have been held very long. A criminologist testifying for the defense emphasized that most people who make threats never follow through with them. He argued that a reasonable person could not have foreseen the occurrence of the crime because mass murder is extremely rare. And even if it had been foreseeable, Sylvia Seegrist's shooting spree was still unstoppable unless the entire mall had been turned into an armed camp.[3]

In February 1990, a Delaware County jury decided that the shopping mall was indeed liable for damages and awarded an undisclosed amount of money to Sylvia Seegrist's victims. Seegrist herself remains hospitalized in an institution for the criminally insane. Only after murdering three innocent strangers was there sufficient proof to ensure that Seegrist would receive the long-term psychiatric care that she had long needed.

It is not possible to trace how Sylvia Seegrist developed her unusual passion for military paraphernalia. But for 41-year-old James Oliver Huberty, fascination with firearms was somewhat of a family tradition, dating back at least to a great uncle who had invented a machine gun used during World War I. There were guns everywhere in the Huberty home—in the bedroom, in the kitchen, on the shelves in the parlor, and in the basement, where James maintained his own makeshift firing range. He spent hours practicing his shooting whenever he wasn't cleaning his guns or modifying a semiautomatic weapon into one that was fully automatic.

For most of his adult life, Huberty had been slipping down a deep hole of depression and paranoia. By the time he moved his family to California, and then lost his job as a security guard for a condominium complex in San Ysidro, he had reached rock bottom. On Wednesday, July 18, 1984, he went on an uncharacteristically relaxing family outing with his wife, Etna, and his two daughters, Zelia and Cassandra. Huberty then changed into his favorite, most comfortable clothes: military fatigues that he had purchased through an army surplus mail-order catalogue. He wrapped his favorite weapon, an Israeli-made Uzi assault rifle, in a blue-and-white checkered blanket and said goodbye to his wife and his daughter Zelia. "I'm going hunting," he told his wife of 19 years.

In the middle of San Ysidro, a working-class suburb of San Diego just north of Tijuana, Mexico, there are no hunting grounds. Etna knew that, but she also knew that her husband frequently babbled nonsense. Recently he had been experiencing hallucinations, including imagining a 3-foot Jesus conversing with him in the living room. She urged her husband to seek professional help, and he was beginning to realize that he needed it as well. In fact, on July 17, he placed a call to a local mental health clinic seeking an appointment. By the time someone from the clinic called back, however, it was too late.

Huberty drove the short distance to the McDonald's just a few blocks down San Ysidro Boulevard. He parked his beat-up Mercury sedan in the parking lot out front and strode through the door, armed to the teeth and hungry for revenge. Looking up from their Happy Meals, children sat frozen in disbelief as Huberty started shouting and shooting. "I've killed a thousand," screamed Huberty. "I'll kill a thousand more." People both inside and outside of the restaurant were in his line of fire. One young girl died from a bullet wound in the back of her neck despite her mother's attempt to shield her. Two teenage boys riding bicycles past the restaurant were struck down by stray bullets, as was a motorist on the freeway behind the McDonald's. When the police arrived, the area resembled a battlefield. By the time a sharpshooter from the SWAT team drew a bead on Huberty from a distance, 21 people had been killed and more than a dozen wounded in the 77-minute siege.

Huberty's trip to the San Ysidro McDonald's may have taken a matter of minutes, but his journey in effect began decades earlier back in Ohio. And it was a journey "low-lighted" by failure, withdrawal, and disappointment. Shortly after marrying Etna in 1965, James Huberty took a job working for a Canton funeral home. But his career as a mortician was short-lived; even though he did a fine job in the embalming room, his cold and unsympathetic demeanor with grieving mourners was a significant problem. Trying his hand next at welding, Huberty spent more than a decade working for Babcock and Wilcox, an engineering firm in nearby Massillon. With overtime James earned nearly $30,000 per year, but in 1982 hard times hit and the plant closed down, leaving Huberty nowhere to turn except to the West Coast.

Through his years in Ohio, Huberty became increasingly reclusive, cutting himself off from all friends. Even his relationship with Etna was one of dependency rather than companionship. She cooked, cleaned, and washed for him, managed the household expenses and other matters, and even chauffeured him back and forth to work. Besides his job, the only activity that he found satisfying was his gun collection. Being without friends was not a problem—he could always count on his guns.

If only we had gun laws as strict as those in England, some Americans lament, James Huberty might never have become such a prolific mass killer. Of course they likely have not heard of Michael Ryan, a resident of Hungerford, England, who killed 15 people and wounded just as many during a 4-hour rampage through town before taking his own life. His victims included his own mother, his neighbor, and his two dogs, but most of those gunned down were perfect strangers who just happened to get in the 27-year-old Ryan's way. Ryan was able to accomplish his tour of murder, which began at his home and ended at the school that he once attended, despite the country's rather restrictive gun laws.

Ryan had long had a bad reputation for belligerence. Despite his argumentative nature, however, he never had a brush with the law or involvement in the mental health system. Indeed, neither a criminal record nor a history of profound mental illness is a requirement for mass murder, even the indiscriminate type. Although he may have tended toward paranoia, he was far from psychotic in his thinking. Thus, each time Ryan applied to have his gun permit expanded, he was able to survive the screening process—which included an interview with local police to verify his sporting purpose. By 1987 Ryan was licensed legally to own semiautomatic rifles for the sake of sportsmanship, but he viewed it as a license to murder. In the process, he committed the crime of the century, at least by English standards; in America, it would have been the crime of the week.

It took more than a large arsenal of weapons for Ryan to carry out his assault on his hometown. He developed gun-handling skills through membership in a variety of gun clubs, the same memberships that earned him the legal right to own his weapons. But mass murderers don't have to join hunting clubs to become expert marksmen. Many of them are trained to handle high-powered firearms in preparation for military careers. The skills they acquire in the military for going to war prepare them in civilian life for going berserk.

When it comes to pseudo-commandos, Julian Knight of Melbourne, Australia, was as gung ho as they come. For as long as he could remember, the 19-year-old Aussie adopted into a military family had focused nearly all his energies and thoughts toward a career in the armed forces. Knight fashioned himself as a war hero, but the only war he ever was to fight was a civil war. On August 7, 1987, along Hoddle Street in Melbourne, the enemy consisted of innocent strangers, seven of whom were killed and 19 more of whom were wounded. And unlike fellow pseudo-commandos James Huberty and Patrick Purdy, Knight survived to become a hero in his own eyes. "I performed exactly as my Army superiors would have expected me to perform in a combat situation," reflected Knight from his jail cell. "In other circumstances I would have gotten a medal for what I did."[4]

Knight was indeed well trained to kill. He received his first gun, an air rifle, as a gift for his 12th birthday. Even with this relatively harmless initiation into weaponry, within 2 years Knight was being trained in the use of an M-16 rifle. Within 2 more years Knight was learning ambush tactics after joining the Melbourne High School cadet unit. By the time he reached the military academy, he was expert in the use of a variety of pistols, automatic rifles, submachine guns, grenade launchers, and hand grenades. His passion consumed all aspects of his life: For example, he sought to use his favorite periodical, *Soldier of Fortune* magazine, as reference material for his school papers.

Julian Knight may have had a clear vision of his career goals and ambitions, but his intensity likely led to his downfall. He was rejected on all fronts, beginning with his birth parents when he was a 10-month-old baby. His obsession with combat played a major role in his troubles with classmates, as well as in his rejection by his girlfriend just a few days before the shooting. His weird fascination with the military was disturbing, even scary, to those around him.

Most critical, however, was his failure at his lifelong ambition to graduate from the Duntroon Military College, an elite program for training military officers. Despite finishing high school with a C average, Knight was accepted into the prestigious military school in 1986; after all, he was bright, with an IQ as high as 132. But in the military academy, his personality got the better of him. Knight had difficulty accepting the rigid hierarchy of authority and frequently got embroiled in disputes with his superiors. His hopes for a military career all but ended in a Canberra nightclub when he pulled a pocket knife on a sergeant, leading to his expulsion from Duntroon.

During the 9 weeks after his arrest for assaulting his superior officer, Knight became increasingly depressed and desperate. Adding to his frustration over his failing military plans, the transmission in his car blew up, and his girlfriend left him. He was now ready to do what he had been trained to do. He would finally get even with the world that had for so long cruelly rejected him, and he would get a chance to demonstrate his incredible power.

Just after 9:30 on the evening of August 7, Knight left his apartment on Ramsen Street in the Clifton Hill area of Melbourne armed with a Ruger .22-caliber semiautomatic rifle, a .308-caliber M-14 rifle, and a 12-gauge Mossberg pump-action shotgun. He also packed 200 rounds of ammunition—enough for an army, in this case, an army of one. During the next 40 minutes, Knight exhausted his entire cache of ammunition as he walked north on Hoddle Street and doubled back along the railway tracks, shooting indiscriminately. Following a shootout in which a police helicopter was gunned down from the sky, Knight finally was captured. But he still took a parting verbal shot at the police, later charging in the press that they were "ill-equipped and ill-prepared."[5] As a self-styled authority on military tactics, Knight felt he knew better.

Whatever the source of his grudge against society, the mass killer must also have access to a means of mass destruction. The United States, in particular, makes it easy enough for a vengeful madman to purchase all the guns and ammunition needed to carry out his attack. Massacres can and do occasionally happen in countries like England, Australia, and Canada, but they are nothing to match the bloodshed in the United States. Though gun proponents are correct when they argue that firearms are not to blame per se for the behavior of mass killers, guns do make their attacks far bloodier. It is nearly impossible to slay quickly 21 people with a knife or with one's hands.

In addition to the greater lethality of the firearm, guns also distance the attacker psychologically from his victims. It is possible that James Huberty or Sylvia Seegrist might not have been emotionally able to kill young children had they had any physical contact with their victims. But with a rifle, they could dispassionately shoot down innocent strangers as if they were moving objects in a video game or even toy soldiers on an imaginary battlefield.

For mass murderers Huberty and Knight, the gun is

like an old friend. In times of stress, they might go target shooting to ease frustrations. Some mass killers have even measured their own self-worth in terms of their marksmanship abilities. It is easy to understand, therefore, why so many have seen the firearm as the way ultimately to resolve their grudge against society. The increased availability of high-powered, rapid-fire weapons like those used by James Huberty is also a large part of the reason why the death tolls in mass murders have climbed so dramatically in the recent past. Of the ten largest mass killings in United States history, seven have occurred since 1980.

Can any form of gun control stem the tide of mass murder? Unfortunately, waiting periods and background checks, as prescribed by the Brady Law of 1994, will not necessarily provide an effective preventive measure. Few mass killers have criminal or psychiatric records. Moreover, they would hardly be deterred by a short delay in their execution plans. Most massacres, including many random killings, are planned over a long period of time. In the face of a 5-day waiting period, the would-be mass killer reasons, "I've waited five weeks, what's another five days?" Furthermore, most mass murderers would not consider buying a weapon through illegal means; they see themselves as law-abiding citizens who are only looking for some justice.

When it comes to reducing the carnage from mass murder, the focus of gun control legislation should be on slowing down the killer—on reducing the body counts. Banning rapid-fire weaponry and oversized ammunition clips may not stop him from committing murder, but it very well might stop him from committing mass murder.

16

Remembering All the Victims

During the Christmas season of 1978, residents of West Summerdale Avenue in Des Plaines, Illinois, watched in horror as body after body was removed from the crawl space beneath the Gacy home at number 8213. In the days to follow, as news crews focused their cameras on John Wayne Gacy's burial ground, neighbors were repeatedly interviewed about what they knew, what they saw, and how they felt.

Even after all 29 bodies were excavated from the property, interest in the murder site persisted. A steady stream of tourists invaded the block, understandably upsetting neighbors, just in order to get a glimpse of the infamous house of horrors. Gacy's home was eventually razed, yet curiosity seekers still came by to stare at the empty lot that once entombed so many young victims. Anonymous visitors decorated the weed-filled yard with their macabre artistry, including a replica of an electric chair and fake tombstones. Some gawkers, too lazy or too embarrassed to get out of their cars, chose instead to drive in circles around the lot. "It got so you wouldn't know what you would see when you looked out the window," commented one neighbor.[1]

In 1988 the lot on which John Wayne Gacy's house once stood was finally sold, and a new building was constructed on the site. The new owners, eager to distance themselves from the tragedy of a decade earlier, were able to have their house number switched. Despite the change in appearance and address, however, the location still attracts occasional sightseers to Des Plaines.

In Killeen, Texas, souvenir hunters had a field day. By answering a "for sale" ad, they could snoop around the nearby home once occupied by mass killer George Hennard, Jr. Pretending to be serious house hunters, they walked through the house, and many took small mementos of their visit to the madman's mansion.

The Oxford Apartments in Milwaukee, site of Jeffrey Dahmer's grisly crimes, also became a tourist trap, attracting curious visitors from as far away as Japan. In November 1992, the 49-unit building was demolished. The owner had to place guards and barbed wire around the property to fend off arsonists and scavengers, some of whom offered the guards as much as $75 for a souvenir brick. In 1994, the refrigerator in which Dahmer kept human organs was auctioned off to the highest bidder.

Neighbors of Ronald Gene Simmons in Dover, Arkansas, didn't wait for the bulldozers to arrive. The ramshackle house in which 14 members of the Simmons clan were shot and strangled was burned to the ground late one night, a year after the murders. The motive of this arson was clear: to remove all tangible reminders of the mass killing.

Unlike the homes of Simmons, Dahmer, and Gacy, it has remained business as usual at the sites of many other mass killings. Luby's Cafeteria reopened for business weeks after the mass killing of 23 customers and employees, and the Edmond, Oklahoma, post office was closed for only one day for the purpose of cleaning up. Edmond letter carriers had to deliver the mail that was stained by the blood of their coworkers. The residents of the town received their blood-soaked letters in plastic bags bearing a printed apology: "The contents have been damaged in handling by the Postal Service. . . . We regret any inconvenience you have experienced."

Palatine, Killeen, Dover, San Ysidro, and Edmond have one notable trait in common: They were small towns with small reputations until they became host to mass murder. When mass murder strikes a small town, it becomes forever associated in the minds of millions of Americans with the heinous act that occurred there. The goodwill and charity of its citizens are quickly overshadowed by the act of a single gunman. Residents of Edmond, for example, would like their town to be remembered for popular Olympic gymnast Shannon Miller or for the 1988 PGA Championship; to their chagrin, however, it is in many circles far better known for the 1986 postal massacre. In addition, it is particularly difficult for members of a small town to move beyond the community stigma brought on by a mass murder. Towns-people tend to identify closely with the geographic unit in which they live. Everyone feels victimized, therefore, even if they were not directly hurt.

The impact of mass murder on the public image of big cities is minimal by comparison. New York may have had its "Son of Sam" murders, but people in Omaha or Santa Fe hardly think of this particular serial-killing spree when they consider visiting the Big Apple (although they may worry about street muggings and theft). Similarly, the Los Angeles area is more associated with Disneyland characters and

Hollywood stars than with Richard Ramirez or Charles Manson, and Montreal is better known for its hockey team and French food than for the 1989 massacre of 14 female engineering students.

In the aftermath of the Montreal shootings, members of the university community, the city, and the nation came together to memorialize the victims of the tragedy. Long after the slain students were eulogized and buried, their memories were sustained by a plaque—bearing the names of the dead—that was conspicuously placed on the building in which the murders had occurred. Years later, a second memorial was constructed out of stone and placed near the campus arts center. This project was initiated by a local women's group and sponsored by local businesses.

Attempts to pay tribute to the victims of a mass slaughter do not always come off as smoothly as in Montreal. In San Ysidro, California, for example, a controversy raged for years over how to commemorate the victims of the McDonald's massacre, most of whom were Hispanic. Immediately after the 1984 incident in which 21 victims were murdered, the McDonald's Corporation tore down the bullet-ridden restaurant and donated the property to the community.

Following the McDonald's gift, politicians debated what to do with the land. Some argued that a large-scale memorial was out of place in a congested commercial area, or that it would only bring back painful memories. Others contended that constructing a memorial of decent proportions—a park or a chapel—would make a fitting tribute; besides, it was simply the right thing to do. Hispanic residents were particularly outspoken as advocates for an official monument. According to an ancient custom observed in rural parts of Mexico, the site of a tragic death is sacred because the spirit of the deceased remains at that spot.

While the public debate dragged on, one concerned resident of San Ysidro took it upon himself to build his own handmade shrine: a blue wooden shed at the murder site containing religious paintings, candles, and figurines. On the side of the shrine were written the names and ages of all 21 people who had been slain at the McDonald's. In 1988 the acre of land was sold to Southwestern College for $40,000, a fraction of its original market value. Two years later the college constructed a building, only a small corner of which was devoted to a permanent memorial.

Over the past two decades criminologists, criminal justice officials, and the general public have become more sensitive to the needs, problems, and concerns of those left behind to grieve murdered loved ones—a victimization of another kind. Of particular importance and value have been strategies established to assist those who have lost a loved one to homicide. Victim/witness advocates have been assigned by the courts to help console and inform family members who suffer through testimony describing the hideous circumstances of their loved ones' deaths. At the same time, families of murder victims have found empathy and understanding from support groups like Parents of Murdered Children and private agencies such as the Adam Walsh Victim Resource Center.

The problems of surviving victims of multiple murder are intensified partly because of the peculiarities of multiple murder itself, but also because of the intrusion of the mass media. In high-profile cases, journalists often try to get close to surviving victims to obtain quotes and stories. The attention paid by reporters is often of great comfort and support to the family, particularly in vulnerable times when any willing listener is greatly appreciated. This can be a double-edged sword, however. Surviving victims can experience a tremendous sense of abandonment when their case is no longer newsworthy and their media sounding boards move on to report on newer crimes. "At first there was like a big rush," said Jill Paiva, whose mother, Nancy, was murdered years earlier by an unidentified serial killer in New Bedford, Massachusetts. "After that it was like everybody forgot about it and nobody cares."[2]

Surviving victims understandably tend to want to know everything regarding the death of their loved ones and the effort by the criminal justice system to bring the perpetrator to justice. Because of the newsworthiness of serial-murder investigations and prosecutions, however, police and prosecutors tend to be especially cautious about sharing information about the investigation with victims' families. Officials fear that confidential material will surface in the newspaper. As a consequence, law enforcement authorities become more guarded about discussing the case (even with surviving victims) out of concern that the family will succumb to pressure from the media for details.

In Gainesville, Florida, for example, the task force investigating the 1990 murders of five college students had to maintain tight control over what details of the crimes could be released to the families. Aware that reporters from around the country were constantly trying to interview the grieving parents, the police were cautious not to jeopardize the investigation. The families, in a sense, were seen as a liability.

Whether intentional or not, some information pertaining to a multiple murder and its investigation is bound to reach story-hungry reporters. When such information is released or leaked to the press, the relatives often learn about developments in the case from reading the newspaper. It is a major source of discomfort and aggravation to surviving victims that they are not the first to be told of whatever information is released to the public. For example, Judy DeSantos, whose sister was murdered by the New Bedford serial killer, was frequently caught off guard by new information printed in the local newspaper. Understanding that certain facts of the case had to remain confidential, she nonetheless felt that she and other family members had a right to know before the general public did.

Serial killers have a tendency to kill in particularly gruesome ways that often involve acts of torture prior to the murder and/or mutilation afterward. Surviving victims are therefore confronted with the knowledge that their loved one suffered a great deal before dying, or that the corpse was defiled and desecrated. Moreover, signs of mutilation may prevent a viewing at the funeral. For example, the parents of Gainesville victim Christa Hoyt had to endure the painful task of dealing with the fact that their daughter had been murdered, eviscerated, and decapitated. Because of the gruesome manner in which their daughter was slain, the Hoyts were not permitted to view the crime-scene photos. To do so might have provided them some degree of psychological closure, but it also would have been devastating.

Although probably intended merely as a defense mechanism against public anxiety, false rumors and insensitive jokes often spread through a community having an insatiable appetite for details in high-profile multiple-murder cases. These tend to add insult to injury for the surviving victims. Of greater insult to surviving victims, however, is the glorification surrounding the killer. The individual responsible for the crimes is too often celebrated and even admired because of his infamy, while the victims for whom the survivors mourn are quickly forgotten.

The families of Jeffrey Dahmer's victims suffered the

indignity of watching Chevy Chase make light of the case on "Saturday Night Live" while millions of viewers laughed, not to mention the hundreds of Jeffrey Dahmer jokes that circulated for years. Even worse, the families found nothing funny about seeing Jeffrey Dahmer's likeness on trading cards and in comic books. Some mothers of the victims were so incensed that they appeared as guests on nationally syndicated talk shows to express their outrage over the Dahmer craze.

Surviving victims of most homicides can at least make some sense of the underlying motivation for their tragedy, even if they cannot accept its legitimacy. For example, a mother whose daughter is slain by an ex-boyfriend can understand the motive of jealousy. Serial killers, however, tend to select strangers as victims and for no particular reason. As a result, surviving victims must not only deal with their loss, but also with more profound questions concerning why it happened to them.

In multiple-victim slayings, particularly serial killings, the state will often charge and prosecute the accused on fewer than all the crimes suspected. Frequently, only a few of the stronger cases are needed to guarantee a maximum penalty. For example, Atlanta child slayer Wayne Williams was charged and convicted on only two counts of murder, even though he was linked to as many as 28 deaths. Similarly, Ted Bundy was executed for three murders in Florida but was likely responsible for dozens of other murders around the country for which he was never prosecuted. As a consequence of partial prosecution, some surviving victims can feel that their loved one was neglected by the courts and did not receive justice. Furthermore, they lack closure to their tragedy. This is particularly true in killings that involve multiple states or provinces, in which many of the jurisdictions will never have the opportunity to try the case.

Because of the apparently motiveless nature of the crime, serial-murder cases sometimes remain unsolved. The notion that the killer literally got away with murder retards the healing process for the surviving victims. In massacres, conversely, the perpetrator frequently is killed either by suicide or in a police counterattack; the death of the offender robs the victims' families of the chance to seek retribution and full justice, as well as to vent their anger.

Frustrated families often seek alternative channels for expressing their unresolved pain. In a positive way, they may form support groups or political action groups. Following the law-firm massacre in San Francisco, for example, families of the victims joined together in advocacy against assault rifles. In a negative way, however, the families of other mass murder victims identify scapegoats for their rage. In the Palm Bay massacre, for example, local police were severely criticized following William Cruse's shooting spree for failing to respond sufficiently to complaints about his disturbing and bizarre behavior prior to the crime.

The families of the killers themselves are also scapegoated and victimized by negative public opinion. Not only is their child or loved one taken from them, but they are blamed—often without justification—for not intervening in time or for their role in "creating a monster." Haunted by self-doubt and wondering what they might have done differently, many suffer profound feelings of guilt and depression. Yet they typically receive more condemnation than compassion from former friends, neighbors, and even relatives; there are no support groups for these survivors.

Etna Huberty, for example, has been bitterly chastised

for not preventing her husband, James, from going "hunting" for humans at the San Ysidro McDonald's when he told her as much. In a poignant plea on behalf of her friend, Ann Ruiz of San Ysidro wrote in a letter to the *San Diego Union:* "Mrs. Huberty needs to conquer her guilt feelings. Her life has been destroyed and she has no idea what the future will bring. . . . Doesn't anyone have any feelings for this woman's grief? It is 22 times that of the rest of the people."[3] In recognition of her suffering, $1,000 was given to James Huberty's widow out of the San Ysidro Family Survivors Fund in order to help her move her children back to her hometown of Massillon, Ohio. This sum of money was earmarked for Huberty by former columnist Norman Cousins, who donated a total of $2,500 to the fund. When some of the other contributors learned of this, they demanded that their own donations be returned and organized a protest march.

Francis Piccione, mother of the Los Angeles Hillside Strangler, wasn't criticized for her failure to respond or for receiving victim compensation money, but she was held accountable in the court of public opinion for being a bad mother to Kenneth Bianchi. In addition to her villainous status, she has her own sense of grief. As she remarked tearfully, "My heart goes out to everyone of the families who lost a child. I have lost a son, too."

Thus there are numerous victims of multiple murder—those who are slain, their grieving families, the killers' relatives, and even the communities that are stigmatized as a result. One participant is, however, never a victim: the person who commits the murders.

In this book we have attempted to explain the motivation and circumstances that inspire the act of multiple murder. We have discussed the failures and frustrations that strain the coping mechanisms of the workplace killer. We have explored the loneliness and isolation of the mass murderer who lacks any form of support and encouragement. We have profiled the serial killer whose quest for power derives from an abuse-riddled childhood devoid of love and acceptance. We have examined the obedience of the cult killer to a charismatic father figure who exploits his follower's insecurities and need to feel special.

It is important, though, that explanation never be confused with excuse. Multiple killers have raised their own variety of excuses, but we have downplayed the causal connection between murder and such phenomena as pornography, child abuse, head trauma, neurological impairment, Satanism, drugs, and mental illness. Though each of these factors may contribute in some way to the making of a mass or serial murderer, none should be considered a determining factor, either by itself or in combination. Millions of people with similar biographies and disadvantages do not kill; many go on instead to lead productive lives. Regardless of the biological, psychological, social, and economic hardships they may suffer, multiple murderers generally are capable of making personal decisions as to how and how not to behave. They are therefore not victims, but are "guilty as charged" when they make the murderous choice.

Notes

Chapter 1

1. Michael Quintanilla, "Promises to Keep," *Los Angeles Times*, January 10, 1994, p. E1.

Chapter 2

1. Carey Goldberg, "I Was Like a Crazed Wolf," *Los Angeles Times*, April 28, 1992, p. 1.
2. Ibid.
3. Ronald M. Holmes and James De Burger, *Serial Murder*. Newbury Park, CA: Sage, 1988.
4. Eric W. Hickey, *Serial Murderers and Their Victims*. Pacific Grove, CA: Brooks/Cole, 1991, p. 124.
5. PBS, "Frontline: Monsters Among Us," November 2, 1993.
6. Ibid.
7. CNN Specials, "Murder by Number—Wesley Allen Dodd," January 3, 1993.
8. PBS, "Frontline: Monsters Among Us," November 2, 1993.
9. Robert K. Ressler, Ann W. Burgess and John E. Douglas, *Sexual Homicide: Patterns and Motives*. Lexington, MA: Lexington Books, 1988.
10. "Sheriff's Remark May Have Helped in Joubert Arrest," United Press International, October 14, 1984.
11. Ibid.

Chapter 3

1. Colin Wilson and Donald Seaman, *The Serial Killers.* New York: Carol Publishing Group, undated, p. 292.
2. Eric W. Hickey, *Serial Murderers and Their Victims.* Pacific Grove, CA: Brooks/Cole, 1991, p. 197.
3. H. Paul Jeffers, *Who Killed Precious.* New York: St. Martin's, 1991, p. 45.
4. Ibid., pp. 44–45.
5. N. Ansevics and H. Doweiko, "Serial Murderers: Early Proposed Development Typology," *Psychotherapy in Private Practice,* vol. 9, no. 2 (1991), pp. 107–122.
6. PBS, "Frontline: The Mind of a Murderer," no. 206, March 1984.
7. Robert Jay Lifton, *The Nazi Doctors.* New York: Basic Books, 1986.
8. Personal interview with Lawrence Bittaker, November 1991.
9. *Maclean's,* January 25, 1982, p. 20.
10. "Surprise Guilty Plea Entered in Florida College Killings," *Dallas Morning News,* February 16, 1994, p. 1A.
11. Personal interview with Clifford Olson, September 1991.
12. Associated Press, "Dahmer Tells Judge He Blames Nobody But Himself," February 17, 1992.

Chapter 4

1. "'The Exorcist' and the 'the Devil'," *Milwaukee Journal,* July 29, 1991, p. 1.
2. Associated Press, "Dahmer Tells Judge He Blames Nobody But Himself," February 17, 1992.
3. Eli Sagan, *Cannibalism.* New York: Harper Torchbooks, 1981.
4. Karen Blakeman, "Berdella's Motive: Total Control," *Kansas City Times,* December 30, 1989, p. A18.

Chapter 5

1. Robert K. Ressler, Ann W. Burgess and John E. Douglas, *Sexual Homicide: Patterns and Motives.* Lexington, MA: Lexington Books, 1988.

2. Leslie Allen Williams' letter, *Detroit News,* June 18, 1992.
3. Dobson interview with Bundy at Florida State Prison at Starke, February 1989.

Chapter 6

1. PBS, "Nova," October 18, 1992.
2. Daniel Goleman, "A Misfit Who Turns to Murder," *New York Times,* July 2, 1993. p. B6.
3. John Nordheimer, "Bundy Is Put to Death in Florida After Admitting Trail of Killings," *New York Times,* January 25, 1989, p. 1A.
4. PBS, "Frontline: The Mind of a Murderer," March 22 and 29, 1984.
5. Alison Bass, "A Touch for Evil," *Boston Globe Magazine,* July 7, 1991, p. 21.
6. PBS, "Frontline: The Mind of a Murderer," March 22 and 29, 1984.
7. From Kenneth A. Bianchi's medical file.
8. PBS, "Frontline: The Mind of a Murderer," March 22 and 29, 1984.
9. Personal interview with Frances Piccione, 1986.
10. Personal communication with Kenneth Bianchi, 1986.
11. PBS, "Nova," October 18, 1992.
12. Sam Meddis, "FBI: Possible to Spot, Help Serial Killers Early," *USA Today,* March 31, 1987, p. 5A.
13. Joel Norris, *Serial Killers: The Growing Menace.* New York: Doubleday, 1988, p. 244.
14. PBS, "Nova," October 18, 1992.

Chapter 7

1. Dirk Johnson, "Ex-Nurse's Aide Admits Murders of 24 in 4 Years," *New York Times,* August 19, 1987, p. A17.
2. Michele Chandler and Lori Mathews, "Families Doubt Nursing Home Murders," *Detroit Free Press,* December 5, 1988, p. 3A.
3. Joyce Eggington, "The Bad Mother," *Good Housekeeping,* April 1989, p. 247.
4. Joyce Eggington, *From Cradle to Grave.* New York: Jove Books, 1990.
5. Jerome Burne, "Health: Murder by Manipulation," *Indépendent,* June 8, 1993, p. 17.

6. Richard Pendlebury, "Allitt Is Locked Away Forever," *Daily Mail,* May 29, 1993, p. 9.
7. Peter Elkind, "The Death Shift," *Texas Monthly,* August 1983, p. 109.
8. Peter Elkind, *The Death Shift: The True Story of Nurse Genene Jones and the Texas Baby Murders.* New York: Viking, 1989, p. 108.
9. Ibid., pp. 154–155.

Chapter 8

1. James Alan Fox and Jack Levin, "Satanism and Mass Murder," *Celebrity Plus,* July 1989.
2. Ibid.
3. "Desire for a Family Draws Young People," *USA Today,* April 19, 1989, p. 7A.
4. Maury Terry, *The Ultimate Evil.* New York: Bantam, 1989.
5. Ibid., p. 144.
6. Rob Polner, "Son of Sam' Killer Says He Had Help," *Newsday,* November 8, 1993, p. 6.
7. James Alan Fox and Jack Levin, "Satanism and Mass Murder," *Celebrity Plus,* July 1989.
8. Personal communication with Steve Daniels, 1992.
9. Clifford L. Linedecker, *Night Stalker.* New York: St. Martin's, 1991, p. 158.
10. Steve Barnes, "Expert Gives Gruesome Testimony in Child Murder Case," Reuters, January 27, 1994.
11. Pam Lambert, "Police Arrest Local Teens in the Cultlike Killing of Three Arkansas Boys," *Time,* June 21, 1994, p. 43.

Chapter 9

1. Lucette Lagnado, "Fire Suspect's Startling Confession," *New York Post,* March 27, 1990, p. 5.
2. Joel Thurtell, "Tragedy Had Hit Family Before," *Detroit Free Press,* August 10, 1989, p. 19A.
3. Lawrence John DeLisle's interview with Detective Sergeant Daniel Galeski, August 10, 1989.

4. Ibid.

5. Ibid.

6. Ibid.

7. Joe Swickard, "Witnesses Say DeLisle Didn't Attempt Rescue," *Detroit Free Press*, June 12, 1990.

8. John Castine, "Many at Site Have Minds Made Up," *Detroit Free Press*, August 12, 1989.

9. Excerpt from Lawrence DeLisle's presentence statement, August 1, 1990.

10. Lawrence John DeLisle's interview with Detective Sergeant Daniel Galeski, August 10, 1989.

11. Joe Swickard, "Judge Questions DeLisle Verdict at Sentencing," *Detroit Free Press*, August 2, 1990.

12. "Michael A. Lev and Flynn McRoberts, "Massacre Stymies Police," *Chicago Tribune*, January 12, 1993.

13. David Silverman, "Mystery in Palatine; One Year Later, Seven Slayings Still Unsolved," *Chicago Tribune*, January 9, 1994.

14. Lonnie Kidd, *Becoming a Successful Mass Murderer or Serial Killer: The Complete Handbook.* Cleveland: Lonnie Kidd, 1992, p. 100.

Chapter 10

1. Material in this chapter was drawn from interviews with survivors and attorneys in the case.

2. Adam Petman, "Chronicling a Massacre," *Boston Globe*, January 3, 1988, p. 1A.

3. Ibid.

4. Ibid.

5. Stephen Steed, "Motive of Revenge Suspected," *Arkansas Gazette,* December 30, 1987, p. 12A.

6. Ibid.

7. Rodney Bowers, "Nightmares Her Memory, Victim Says," *Arkansas Gazette*, May 12, 1988, p. 1.

8. Bill Simmons, "Mass Murderer's Relationships with Wife, Children—Not Working," Associated Press, January 3, 1988.

9. Michael Haddigan, "Child Abused, Relative Says," *Arkansas Gazette,* December 30, 1987, p. 1.

10. Ron Davis, "A Daughter's Letters of Fear," *Newsday,* January 2, 1988, p. 4.
11. Michael Haddigan, "Child Abused, Relative Says," *Arkansas Gazette,* December 30, 1987, p. 1.
12. "Contents of Simmons Note Revealed," *Russellville Courier Democrat,* February 12, 1989, p. 11.
13. Bob Stover, "Letter by Simmons' Wife Tells of Life as 'Prisoner' at Home," *Arkansas Gazette,* January 3, 1988, p. 1.

Chapter 11

1. Bill Duryea, "He'd Done What He Came to Do," *St. Petersburg Times,* February 2, 1993, p. 1B.
2. ABC, "20/20: Workplace Violence," April 16, 1993.
3. Craig Pittman, "Laid to Rest Where He Was Most at Peace," *St. Petersburg Times,* February, 1993, p. 1B.
4. "Older, Well-Educated Men See Big Drop in Earning," *Sarasota Herald-Tribune,* February 13, 1994, p. 3A.
5. Joseph A. Kinney and Dennis L. Johnson, *Breaking Point: The Workplace Violence Epidemic and What to Do About It.* Chicago: National Safe Workplace Institute, 1993, p. 79.
6. Jim Adams, "Joseph T. Wesbecker: The Long Dark Slide 1942–1989," *Louisville Courier-Journal,* December 31, 1989, p. 1A.
7. Eric Malnic, "Note of Doom Written by Burke, FBI Says," *Los Angeles Times,* December 12, 1987, p. 28.
8. Paul Kaihla, "Concordia's Trials," *Maclean's,* November 9, 1992, pp. 52–55.
9. "Friends Say Tampa Killer Showed Signs of Cracking," *Orlando Sentinel,* January 29, 1993, p. B1.
10. ABC, "20/20: Workplace Violence," April 16, 1993.

Chapter 12

1. Loner in 30's Called Typical Workplace Killer," *New York Times,* December 19, 1993, p. 27.
2. Personal communication with postal worker, March 28, 1993.
3. United States House of Representatives Committee on Post Office

and Civil Service, *A Post Office Tragedy: The Shooting at Royal Oak.* Washington, DC: U.S. Government Printing Office, 1992, p. 55.
4. Ibid., p. 23.

Chapter 13

1. Alessandra Stanley, "Angry at Child-Support Demands, Gunman Kills 4 in County Office," *New York Times,* October 16, 1992, p. B4.
2. Ibid.
3. ABC, "20/20: Courtroom Security," November, 1992.
4. Ibid.
5. Steve Marshall and Charles Bullard, "Killer Coveted Award," *USA Today,* November 4, 1991, p. 2A.
6. Time-Life Books Editors, *Mass Murderers.* New York: Time Warner, 1992, p. 78.

Chapter 14

1. Time-Life Books Editors, *Mass Murderers.* New York: Time Warner, 1992, p. 144.
2. "A Texas Massacre," *People,* November 4, 1991, p. 67.
3. Ibid., p. 66.
4. "Mass Slayer's Letter to Two Young Women He Admired," *Houston Chronicle,* October 17, 1991, p. 17A.
5. Leonard Green, "Stockton Killer Hated Asians, Report Says," *San Francisco Chronicle,* October 7, 1989, p. C11.
6. "He Wouldn't Stop Shooting," *New York Daily News,* December 8, 1993, p. 3.

Chapter 15

1. Mark Lisheron and Edmund S. Tijerina, "Gun Rampage Could Have Been Worse," *Milwaukee Journal,* August 12, 1993, p. A10.
2. Associated Press, "Pennsylvania Woman Kills Two in Shooting Spree," *Boston Globe,* October 31, 1985, p. 3.

3. Lawrence W. Sherman, "Was a Mall to Blame for a Mass Murder?," *Wall Street Journal,* April 4, 1990, p. 24.
4. Time-Life Books Editors, *Mass Murderers.* New York: Time Warner, 1992, p. 70.
5. Paul Conroy and Lindsay Murdock, "Police Weren't Ready for Me, He Says," *Age,* November 11, 1988, p. 21.

Chapter 16

1. Louise Kiernan, "Buildings Easier to Escape Than the Memories," *Chicago Tribune,* January 17, 1993, Chicagoland section, p. 1.
2. Tom Coakley, "Unsolved and Unending: Slaying Victims' Kin Still Hurting in New Bedford," *Boston Globe,* January 24, 1994, p. 13.
3. Sandra Michioku, United Press International, July 25, 1984.

References

American Psychiatric Association. *Diagnostic and Statistical Manual of Mental Disorders (rev. 3rd ed.)*. Washington, DC: American Psychiatric Association, 1987.

Banay, R. S. "Psychology of a Mass Murderer." *Journal of Forensic Science* 1 (1956): 1.

Baron, S. A. *Violence in the Workplace: A Prevention and Management Guide for Businesses*. Ventura, CA: Pathfinding Publishing, 1993.

Berne, E. "Cultural Aspects of Multiple Murder." *Psychiatric Quarterly* 24 (1950): 250.

Bruch, H. "Mass Murder: The Wagner Case." *American Journal of Psychiatry* 124 (1967): 693–698.

Bush, K. A., and J. L. Cavanaugh. "A Study of Multiple Murder: Preliminary Examination of the Interface Between Epistemology and Methodology." *Journal of Interpersonal Violence* 1 (1986): 5–23.

Darrach, B., and J. Norris. "An American Tragedy." *Life* 7 (August 1984): 58–74.

Deitz, P. E. "Mass, Serial and Sensational Homicides." *Bulletin of the New York Academy of Medicine* 62 (1986): 477–491.

Earley, P. *Prophet of Death: The Mormon Blood-Atonement Killings*. New York: Avon Books, 1991.

Egger, S. A. "A Working Definition of Serial Murder and the Reduction of Linkage Blindness." *Journal of Police Science and Administration* 12 (1984): 348–357.

Egger, S. A. "Utility of the Case Study Approach to Serial Murder Research." Paper presented at the annual meeting of the American Society of Criminology, Atlanta, GA, 1986.

Egger, S. A. *Serial Murder: An Elusive Phenomenon.* New York: Praeger, 1990.

Eggington, J. *From Cradle to Grave.* New York: Jove Books, 1990.

Elkind, P. *The Death Shift: The True Story of Nurse Genene Jones and the Texas Baby Murders.* New York: Viking, 1989.

Ellroy, J. *Murder and Mayhem.* New York: Signet Books, 1991.

Evseeff, G. S., and E. M. Wisniewski. "A Psychiatric Study of a Violent Mass Murderer." *Journal of Forensic Science* 17 (1972): 371–376.

Fishbein, D. H. "Biological Perspectives in Criminology." *Criminology* 28 (1990): 27–72.

Fleming, T. O., and S. Egger, eds. *Serial and Mass Murder: Theory, Policy, and Research.* Toronto: University of Toronto Press, forthcoming.

Fox, J. A., and J. Levin. "Serial Killers: How Statistics Mislead Us." *Boston Herald* (December 1, 1985): 45.

Fox, J. A. "The Mind of a Murderer." *Palm Beach Post* (January 29, 1989).

Frazier, S. H. "Violence and Social Impact," in J. C. Schoolar and C. M. Gaitz (eds.), *Research and the Psychiatric Patient.* New York: Brunner/Mazel, 1975.

Galvin, A. V., and J. M. Macdonald. "Psychiatric Study of a Mass Murderer." *American Journal of Psychiatry* 115 (1959): 1057–1061.

Graysmith, R. *Zodiac.* New York: Berkley Books, 1976.

Harrington, A. *Psychopaths.* New York: Simon and Schuster, 1972.

Hazelwood, R. R., and J. E. Douglas. "The Lust Murder." *FBI Law Enforcement Bulletin* (April 1980): 1–5.

Hickey, E. W. *Serial Murderers and Their Victims.* Pacific Grove, CA: Brooks/Cole, 1991.

Holmes, R. M. *Profiling Violent Crimes.* Newbury Park, CA: Sage, 1989.

Holmes, R. M. *Sex Crimes.* Newbury Park, CA: Sage, 1991.

Holmes, R. M., and J. De Burger. *Serial Murder.* Newbury Park, CA: Sage, 1988.

Holmes, R. M., and S. T. Holmes. *Murder in America.* Newbury Park, CA: Sage, 1994.

Howlett, J. B., K. A. Haufland, and R. K. Ressler. "The Violent Criminal Apprehension Program—VICAP: A Progress Report." *FBI Law Enforcement Bulletin* 55 (December 1986): 14–22.

Jeffers, H. P. *Who Killed Precious?* New York: St. Martin's, 1991.

Jenkins, P. "Myth and Murder: The Serial Killer Panic of 1983–5." *Criminal Justice Research Bulletin* 3 (1988).

Kahn, M. W. "Psychological Test Study of a Mass Murderer." *Journal of Projective Techniques* 24 (1960): 148.

Keppel, R. D. *Serial Murder: Future Implications for Police Investigations.* Cincinnati: Anderson, 1989.

Levin, J., and J. A. Fox. *Mass Murder: America's Growing Menace.* New York: Plenum Press, 1985.

Levin, J., and J. McDevitt. *Hate Crimes: The Rising Tide of Bigotry and Bloodshed.* New York: Plenum Press, 1993.

Lewis, D. O., R. Lovely, C. Yeager, and D. D. Femina. "Toward a Theory of the Genesis of Violence: A Follow-Up Study of Delinquents." *Journal of the American Academy of Child and Adolescent Psychiatry* 28 (1989): 431–436.

Leyton, E. *Compulsive Killers: The Story of Modern Multiple Murderers.* New York: New York University Press, 1986.

Leyton, E. *Sole Survivor: Children Who Murder Their Families.* New York: Penguin Books, 1991.

Linedecker, C. L. *Night Stalker.* New York: St. Martin's, 1991.

Linedecker, C. L., and W. A. Burt. *Nurses Who Kill.* New York: Pinnacle Books, 1990.

Lunde, D. T. *Murder and Madness.* San Francisco: San Francisco Book Company, 1976.

Magid, K., and C. A. McKelvey. *High Risk: Children Without a Conscience.* New York: Bantam Books, 1988.

Marshall, B., and P. Williams. *Zero at the Bone.* New York: Pocket Star Books, 1991.

Masters, B. *Killing for Company.* London: Coronet Books, 1985.

McDougal, D. *Angel of Darkness.* New York: Warner Books, 1991.

Meddis, S. "FBI: Possible to Spot, Help Serial Killers Early." *USA Today* (March 31, 1987).

Newton, M. *Hunting Humans: The Encyclopedia of Serial Killers.* New York: Avon Books, 1990.

Norris, J. *Serial Killers: The Growing Menace.* New York: Doubleday, 1988.

Olsen, J. *The Misbegotten Son.* New York: Delacorte Press, 1993.

Pendlebury, R., "Allitt Is Locked Away Forever." (May 29, 1993).

Quinn, J. F., J. E. Holman, and P. M. Tobolowsky. "Case Study Method for Teaching Theoretical Criminology." *Journal of Criminal Justice Education* 3 (1992): 53–70.

Ressler, R. K., and A. W. Burgess. "Violent Crime." *FBI Law Enforcement Bulletin,* special issue, 54 (August 1985).

Ressler, R. K., A. W. Burgess, and J. E. Douglas. *Sexual Homicide: Patterns and Motives.* Lexington, MA: Lexington Books, 1988.

Ressler, R. K., and T. Shachtman. *Whoever Fights Monsters.* New York: St. Martin's, 1992.

Rule, A. *The Stranger Beside Me.* New York: Signet, 1980.

Schwartz, T. *The Hillside Strangler: A Murderer's Mind.* New York: Doubleday, 1981.

Sears, D. J. *To Kill Again: The Motivation and Development of Serial Murder.* Wilmington, DE: Scholarly Resources, 1991.

Spanos, N. P., and J. F. Chaves (eds.). *Hypnosis: The Cognitive-Behavioral Perspective.* Buffalo, NY: Prometheus Books, 1989.

Starr, M., et al. (1984). "The Random Killers." *Newsweek* (November 26, 1984): 100–106.

Terry, M. *The Ultimate Evil.* New York: Bantam Books, 1989.

Time-Life Books (Editors). *Mass Murderers.* New York: Time Warner, 1992.

Time-Life Books (Editors). *Serial Killers.* New York: Time Warner, 1992.

Valenstein, E. S. "Brain Stimulation and the Origin of Violent Behavior," in W. L. Smith and A. Kling (eds.), *Issues in Brain/Behavior Control.* New York: Spectrum, 1976, pp. 43–48.

Westermeyer, J. "Amok," in C. T. H. Friedmann and R. A. Faguet (eds.), *Extraordinary Disorders of Human Behavior.* New York: Plenum, 1982, 173–190.

Index